Pathways
of
Learning

Essays in American and

European History

by David B. Kier

For Irma Eichhorn:
    Professor, colleague, friend
    Half a century of thanks
        and gratitude

Books by David Kier:

Jody

Ravenscroft

The Door to the Shadows

Goblin Tales

Pathways of Learning

Trafford rev. 02/01/2011

 www.trafford.com

North America & international
toll-free: 1 888 232 4444 (USA & Canada)
phone: 250 383 6864 ♦ fax: 812 355 4082

Contents

II. Europe

Prologue

More than any other time, the 1950s and early 1960s was a Golden Age in American education. Tremendous national prosperity and a deep sense of purpose and pride created a learning environment that promoted excellence and produced the highest standards in history. There was an eagerness for achievement and a respect for educators that bordered on awe, and a commitment to diligence that future generations would barely understand. It was a special time for all who participated.

It was an electric time for the Social Sciences, and especially for the study of history. For those lucky enough to have been university students (junior colleges were a rarity), the experience was all-consuming. It was the heyday of the "scientific method." Students learned what was called the Rankean maxim: *"wie es eigentlich gewesen"* (the way it really happened): to put their prejudices on the back burner and strive for a rational, objective understanding of history.

These nineteen essays are from a student of those halcyon days, who went on to teach twenty-seven different classes and nearly fifteen thousand college and university students in a career that spanned six decades. Some of the essays were written for fellow academics; others were written exclusively for students. They have been rewritten for publication, with consistency of usage and style in mind.

The selection by no means covers everything of import. Some essays have disappeared with the passage of time. Others, that yet survive, do not easily fit the schema for this collection and have been omitted.

I. America

TJ and TR: A Tale of Two "Revolutionaries"

Looking for parallels in history is a fascinating undertaking. Though the subjects in this essay lived a hundred years apart, readers should find more similarities than differences.

The end of a century and the beginning of another is frequently a signal moment in history. Politically, socially, economically, and psychologically it is unique. It is a time for measuring and assessing what has gone before; for looking ahead, either hopefully or apprehensively, at a yet uncharted future. For not a few, that means dark foreboding: it is, after all, an *end*. Who can say that a "new beginning" will offer anything but grief and gloom?

In America, the end of the eighteenth and nineteenth centuries offers the student of history all of those quandaries. For good or for ill, two giants of American political life shepherded the nation at those junction

9

points: Thomas Jefferson and Theodore Roosevelt. What follows is a brief look at those two men and what they, and their times, did or did not have in common.

The nineteenth century began nervously, even ominously. John Adams was its first steward, but deep economic problems, a personal cantank-erousness that alienated friend and foe alike, and a pedantic foreign policy that resulted in a "Quasi-war" with France, all but guaranteed that he would not play a major role in the shaping of the new century. That task would fall to Thomas Jefferson (TJ), and the first few years of the 1800s would bear his imprint.

Fifty-seven years of age when elected to the presidency in 1800, TJ had already made his mark upon the fledgling Republic. Co-author of the Declaration of Independence, Governor of Virginia, Secretary of State under George Washington, and Vice-President in the Adams administra-tion, he had nothing left to prove. Years later, he would surprise many with the observation that he did not consider the job of President all that important. Why, then, did he *seek* that office?

Part of the answer can be found in his background. He was a studious, almost painfully shy individual, who felt comfortable only in small, intimate surroundings. He grew up without a father, and the relationship with his mother was lukewarm, at best. It hurt him deeply that she never acknowledged his talents and achievements.

Defensive, easily riled (he had an explosive temper), TJ married the perfect foil: Martha Skelton. To her he devoted an abundance of romantic and intellectual energies. Six children came from their union, and her death at thirty-three plunged him into a melancholy from which, his closest associates reported, he never fully recovered.

Such, then, was the complex individual who accepted his Party's call to the Presidency in 1800. And it literally was *his* party: during the Washington years he forged the creation of a group known as the Jeffersonian Democrats, also called the Democratic-Republicans. It urged rule by an educated majority, believed in minimum defense spending, and advocated responsible free speech.

The election of 1800 has been called (perhaps too romantically) the "Revolution of 1800," owing partly to the nation's repudiation of Adams and the charismatic appeal of the urbane, well-educated, and youthful-appearing TJ. It was not an easy victory: his high standards for culture, plus his appeal to more than the intellectual *élite,* frightened the *Brahmans* of New England. Many saw in him another Washington, whom they considered a tyrant. This sectionalism, coupled with TJ's admitted deism (an Enlightened French idea that all but took God out of the equation in day-to-day living) horrified the stronghold of Puritanism. New Englanders feared the new president would encourage the burning of Bibles and "speciously pollute" Christian girls and women.

At bottom, this was political mud-slinging. TJ made no bones about his dislike of New England, and its "favorite son," John Adams. His sharp criticisms of industry drew much ire: encouraging big business (especially in Boston) was a capstone of the Adams administration. The very idea of *educating* the urban masses ("to rake the geniuses from the rubbish") pushed Federalists almost to hysteria.

In reality, it is hard to make a strong case for TJ as a "revolutionary." Once his presidency began, compromise was necessary. A true realist, he simplified the Executive branch of government; he did not strip it of its constitutional identity. He chose to surround himself with the finest minds, North *and* South, and included a Swiss, Albert Gallatin, to show the "diversity" of his Cabinet. He *did* allow his predecessor's most controversial measures to lapse (such as the Alien and Sedition Acts), but without the fanfare and acrimony that New Englanders expected. He even struck a conciliatory pose on the potentially explosive subject of slavery, *agreeing* with Adams that the institution was evil, but urging a middle course. It would take another five decades to bring that institution to an end. To the surprise of most easterners, TJ bent the law in an effort to blunt the imperial aspirations of his own vice-president, Aaron Burr.

Much of this can be explained by a far-reaching world view. A globalist who had lived in France and studied its own quest for supremacy, TJ understood geopolitics. He knew that whatever "vision" might revolutionize America, first there had to be a solid foundation. That is one explanation for the purchase of the Louisiana Territory, and the hiring of Lewis and Clark to chart and propagandize it. The purchase trebled the size of America. More important, it was the first step toward getting the nation a window on the Pacific, and subsequently trade with China and the rest of the Far East. Meanwhile, people were encouraged to "fill up America with Americans," and make the United States a world power.

Revolutionary? Not from an all-inclusive point of view. In many ways, TJ was just a continuation of Adams (whom *no one* called revolutionary). Indeed, some of his policies may be seen as reactionary, even imperialistic. Sometimes there was a progressive bent and the display of an honest concern for the people. A realist, then; not an ideologue; a man who, because of the time in which he lived, maximized his opportunities to permit an impetus for those who would follow.

A hundred years later the scenario was not dissimilar. The United States had just emerged from a very stressful decade. The creation of a radical Populist Party prompted urban, middle- and upper-class Americans to worry about widespread civil strife. This was analogous, in many ways, to the disquietude that a century before had led to the Whiskey

Rebellion. In both cases, a focus on foreign affairs served to distract the populace: the XYZ Affair and the "Quasi-War" of 1797, and the Spanish-American War of 1898.

The twentieth century began with a president who would not stamp the new epoch with his imprint. William McKinley, like John Adams, was intensely conservative, with an economic agenda that favored big business. Unlike Adams, successful foreign policy escapades at the end of the century had elevated McKinley to a position of considerable popularity. An assassin's bullet, in 1901, thwarted whatever plans he may have had for anything else.

His successor was forty-three year-old Theodore Roosevelt (TR). Scion of a well-entrenched and prosperous Dutch-American family, his elevation to the presidency was not particularly well-received by the country's political *élite*. "That damned cowboy!" was the opinion of Mark Hanna, who had made McKinley president. TR was too much a maverick, too controversial, too "bull-headed." Many Republicans feared he would distance himself from McKinley's policies, and plunge the nation into social and economic chaos. It reminded not a few of the Federalists' almost hysterical reaction to TJ a century before.

These concerns reflected the realities of the new century. With peace assured by America's victory over Spain, optimism followed. With prosperity virtually assured, it was time to focus on the "other America:" the poor. Thus, the twentieth century began as "the age of Progressivism," and TR was its first presidential spokesman.

TR and Progressivism were hardly incompatible. In the 1880s he had made a reputation as a "gentleman reformer," and learned much about the urban poor through his association with sociologist Jacob Riis. One can even find a parallel in TJ's career, save that he was always urging people to get away from the cities and its squalor. On the other hand, TR counseled that the cities were here to stay, and that it was our task to make them more livable. He went a step further: as president he warned of widespread revolution if we did not achieve that goal.

Such bluntness upset the "Old Guard," but he stuck to his guns. His approach, which later would be identified as "the New Nationalism," recognized that big business was a fact of life, and must be checked by a corresponding big government. Like TJ, he was suspicious of "well-intentioned journalists," whom he frequently criticized for making his job harder than it already was. On that subject, he was bombastic: when Upton Sinclair (author of *The Jungle*) tried to tell him how to make the nation better, his response was swift and caustic. He branded Sinclair a "muckraker."

On the other hand, both TJ and TR had a love affair with natural splendor that needed no prompting from the fourth estate. TJ's pastoral Monticello was representative of that love; TR finalized his own passion into a massive conservation movement. A number of national parks and monuments were his proudest legacy.

15

On the subject of foreign policy both men were active, even devious. TR, for example, flagrantly bent international law (the 1904 Moroccan Crisis) in order to guarantee his election. Likewise, his Caribbean policies ("walk softly and carry a big stick") became the meat of revisionist criticism for the rest of the century, and beyond. The capstone was the building of the Panama Canal. Here, the parallel between TJ and TR was perhaps most striking: both men wanted "the China trade;" both were willing to push the power of the presidency as far as they could to get it.

Was TR a "revolutionary?" The answer, as it was with TJ, must be no. Time-honored business practices (economic nationalism, the gold standard) continued. Reforms, by and large, were modest (thus inspiring the Democrats, first under Woodrow Wilson, to devise a Progressive program of their own: "the New Freedom"). Much-ballyhooed "trust-busting" was egregiously misunderstood by the American people. TR did not set out to *destroy* big business; he wished to redirect the energies of the "Robber Barons" who controlled it, to make it more consistent with the realities of the new century.

Ultimately, both TJ and TR were striking individuals, who because of (or in spite of) their backgrounds and their times, steered the nation in intelligent, carefully-worked out courses of moderation. Each man was possessed of a colossal vanity; each was supremely confident of their ability to lead. Yet neither relished the office with which they are most frequently associated. Even TR, upon being elected for the first (and only) time in 1904, suggested as much to the voting public. He accepted the stewardship, but was smart enough to realize that it was not the most important thing in a long and crowded life.

Manifest Destiny:
Another Look

In our post-modernist Age, the story of America's westward expansion bristles with deep ethnic and sociopolitical controversies. This essay presents a less combative interpretation.

One of the most intriguing stories of American history concerns the trek westward, especially in the period after the War of 1812. It was a movement away from traditional Anglo-Saxon enclaves, and into a frontier that three quarters of a century later would be declared "closed" by historian Frederick Jackson Turner. Thereafter explanations would run the gamut: from pastoral, romantic showcases of rugged individualism and the taming of the wilderness, to post-modern treatises highlighting the rape of the land and the near-extermination of the people who lived there before the white man first appeared. Emotions on this subject run hotter than reason; consensus is unlikely.

The frontier (defined as an enormous parcel of land, west of the Mississippi River to the Pacific Ocean, and south from Canada to Mexico) had been eyed by people in and out of the American experience for years. The Spanish, English, French, Portuguese... even the Russians... made bold overtures into that mammoth arena. During his presidency Thomas Jefferson contemplated getting American commerce to and from China and the rest of the Orient. That lay at the heart of his acquisition of the Louisiana Purchase in 1803. The ploy worked, and the result was the beginning of a policy of continental expansion.

The trade that eastern Americans desired with countries on the other side of the Pacific required a good port, and most agreed that should be San Francisco. Early on, that port belonged to Spain (and then to Mexico, after a revolution in 1821). Numerous attempts by the American government to purchase it failed, and set back the timetable for what the United States considered important: exploitation of natural resources, the relocation of slaves to "solve" the North-South slave controversy, and the building of fortifications to protect Americans from the British, the French... and the Indians.

Thanks to generous federal land laws and well-financed advertising, the West by the 1830s was beginning to look "American." This was at the heart of the Turner thesis: what he called the democratization of the frontier. That civilizing trend, which emanated primarily from New England, brought churches, schools and other institutions that demonstrated the "worthiness" of easterners to Americanize the continent.

Missing, though, was the fact that simply *having* eastern institutions in the West did not guarantee civilization: the land was unruly, chaotic, dangerous, and filled with people who had neither the commitment to, nor an interest in, managing affairs as people did in Boston. Moreover, there were no blacks or Mexicans in Turner's picture of the frontier, and the Indians were just "noble savages." His was an idealized notion that failed almost every test. Law and order? Frontier justice frequently was the gun and the rope. Morality? Brothels and saloons far outnumbered churches and schools. Education? One room schoolhouses were hardly centers of intellectual ferment ... even in the few communities that had them, or even *wanted* them.

The opening (and then closing) of the frontier had more to do with politics and economics than anything else. Every president, from Jefferson forward, dedicated himself to success through control of the frontier. Deals of enterprise were constantly being presented to (and rejected by) Mexico. Britain, too, was pressured. It finally yielded in the 1830s, selling the Oregon Territory to the United States and retreating to sanctuary in British Columbia. Mexico lost its most cherished real estate, first in the comic opera affair known as the Texas Rebellion of the mid-1830s, and then in a short war against "the colossus of the north" in the 1840s.

Along the way problems grew and multiplied. Americans went west, but they did not go everywhere equally. They gravitated to California (for that was the "jumping off" place for the Orient). Many stopped half-way and settled in Texas. Settlement in New Mexico, Idaho, Arizona, and Wyoming never matched Texas and California, and presented an American government that pushed "Manifest Destiny" with a dilemma: those places were "on the way," too, so they had to be protected... and that cost a lot of money.

As well, there was a host of unanticipated problems. Many Mormons decided Utah was the promised land, and introduced polygamy. Children of the South chose to take their culture with them - and that frequently meant bringing slaves, which opened up other areas of concern. Indians east of the Mississippi River were forced west, where they clashed with people, red *and* white, who were already there. The chaos that followed made for a nightmare that lasted for decades.

Along the way, buffalo and other game animals disappeared. Forests, prairies, and large and seemingly inexhaustible supplies of natural mineral resources similarly paid the price for civilization.

In other words, the conquest of the frontier was not well thought out by the people who imagined it. The plan was to connect with China and beyond; everything else was haphazard, and frequently destructive. The proof of that can still be seen today, two centuries later. Most of the West is underpopulated. Its extant resources have been protected only by recent generations. Much of the area is so different from what the planners first saw as to resemble another world. As for the route that Lewis and Clark took to make it all happen? Staffers from **Readers Digest** replicated the journey in 1976 and found that much of the land was polluted, scarred, stripped and despoiled. Were the original trailblazers to see it today, it would be largely unrecognizable.

Populism as Parable

Fairy tales as social criticism is a familiar theme. *Cinderella, Sleeping Beauty, Alice in Wonderland...* the list is a long one. This essay offers a look at America's premier fairy tale.

In the modern Age, the plight of the farmer has been an easy subject for the current crop of historians. Frequently tying their subject to labor injustices, sexism, and oppression of farm workers, agriculture and animal husbandry are fair game for "progressive" thinkers.

Scholars have examined rural America in the nineteenth century, but mostly from the outside in, for that was the age of "Robber Barons:" unscrupulous tycoons in banking, steel, and railroads who dictated rates to America's rural workers... and sometimes used brute force if those rates were contested. All of this happened, despite a nagging fact: rural America comprised nearly 80% of the population. With numbers like that, they should have "run the tables," via the democratic process. But most farmers and ranchers chose *not* to vote. That has vexed and infuriated post-modernists, whose entire *modus operandi* has depended on getting "oppressed" Americans to vote... whether they want to or not.

A partial answer, and clearly a simple one, is that farmers and ranchers were (and still are) rugged individualists. Largely conservative and isolationist, they spurn large towns and cities, are intensely suspicious of government, and wish only to be left with their "forty acres and a mule," and provide a living for themselves and their families.

Some "city slickers" in the nineteenth century tried to change that, either by "consciousness-raising" (Karl Marx didn't have much luck in rural America), or by derring-do. "What you farmers need to do," wrote a newspaper reporter, "is raise less corn and more hell." The quote was wrongly attributed to Mary Elizabeth Lease, an early supporter of farmers' rights. For post-modernists, eager to find her niche in progressive circles, however, there is a caveat: Lease blamed the Jews for the world's problems, and in a book called *The Problem of Civilization Solved* (1895) she advocated world conquest by the white race, and the elimination of those Jews.

Farmers and ranchers *did* come together, but for reasons that had little to do with politics. The Grange ("Patrons of Husbandry") has been around since 1867, mostly as a stereotypical meeting place, where farmers and ranchers could square dance, ooze liquor out of a stone jug, and talk about the weather.

As it so often happens in history, the weather turned out to be one of the keys to rural activism. In particular, the 1890s was a dreadful time for agriculture, as plummeting temperatures meant reduced growing seasons and poor harvests. That, plus ever-present price-gouging by the railroads, compelled rural Americans to meet in Omaha, Nebraska, on July 4, 1892, and rally behind one of the most radical political parties in American history. Called the "Populists," they demanded inflation, free silver, an eight-hour work day (to get the support of city workers), tax reform (aimed at the urban rich), government regulation of the railroads, and the secret ballot. Half a century later rural Americans would distance themselves from such a Marxist plan, and it is inconceivable to think that *any* agri-businessman today would seriously consider such notions.

Not coincidentally, 1892 was a presidential election year. The Populist Party didn't win, but its bold play got the attention of the Democrats, who had been politically adrift since the Civil War. Four years later they incorporated a number of Populist ideas into their own platform, and though they again lost, the seeds were planted for their eventual return to power. In 1912 they won the White House, for only the second time in fifty years.

Interest in the Populist phenomenon has not faded with the passage of time. In a 1964 journal article, historian Henry Littlefield wrote that Populism could be explained by examining **The Wizard of Oz.** In the late

1970s I chanced upon his essay and felt compelled to make an investigation of my own. What I found both surprised and intrigued me - and my students in the decades that followed. Here was strident social criticism, offered up in a series of books that, for nearly seventy years, were thought to be "only" for children.

It is a simple story. When Dorothy lands in Oz, she is befriended by some little people, because her tornado-driven house from Kansas has killed a wicked witch (of the east), who had been terrorizing them. When a good witch named Glenda appears to confirm that fact, yet *another* wicked witch (of the west) appears, seeking vengeance for her dead sister. Ruby slippers magically disappear from the corpse and reappear on Dorothy's feet. Advised by Glenda to keep them on for protection, Dorothy wishes only to go home. To do so, she proceeds east (at Glenda's instruction), via a yellow brick road. Along the way she enlists the aid of three strangers, who have problems of their own.

At the end of the road (the Emerald City) a benevolent wizard offers to help, if Dorothy first brings him proof of the death of the remaining bad witch. She agrees. After battling flying monkeys and other denizens of their evil master she kills the witch... only to learn that the wizard was a charlatan, and that *she* had the power to go home all this time.

The parable? Dorothy of Kansas likely is William Jennings Bryan, a reform candidate from Nebraska, whose stand in defense of silver (the color of the slippers in the *Oz* books) enraged Wall Street (the wicked witch of the east) and the railroads (the wicked witch of the west). His supporters were the American farmers (Munchkins). Bryan treads upon the yellow brick road (the gold standard, a symbol of big business), and gets the support of Everyman: individuals lacking brains, heart, and courage - all of which are necessary in order to "fight city hall." Getting no help from the wizard (President McKinley), Bryan and his three companions go it alone, defeat the monkeys (the Plains Indians, hired by the railroads) and kill the witch with a bucket of water (the farmers most vital commodity), only to learn that... it was only a dream?

In real life, Bryan ran for the presidency three times... and lost. Big business and the gold standard continued to flourish. As for the farmers and ranchers? The weather in the first decade of the twentieth century improved, and rural Americans all but forgot about their problems with big business and government. They went back to their conservatism and their isolation.

There is another interpretation, devoid of politics, that was presented by NBC as a 1990 television movie called *The Dreamer of Oz*. Intended for general audiences, it showcased the acting talents of John Ritter and followed a plausible and enjoyable story line, but with different explanations.

What did the *author* have to say about the meaning of the *Oz* books?

We may never know, for L. Frank Baum left no memoirs or letters to indicate any political preferences or hidden meanings. We *do* know that he began writing his stories in the 1890s, lived in the Great Plains, traveled by rail, and doubtless saw much that begs for analysis. Beyond that, there is only opinion.

Regardless, the story of rural America in the late nineteenth century is a microcosm of a time in flux, and ultimately change, that continues to intrigue professional and amateur historians alike.

The Quest for Empire in Late 19th Century America

Foreign policy has fascinated me for more than half a century. Modernists tend to minimize its importance, preferring instead to channel their energies into domestic issues. Consequently, huge numbers of students leave school woefully ignorant of the rest of the world. This essay was first presented to my students in the 1990s.

The quest for empire - whether commercial, colonial, or territorial - has been a key issue in American history, from the founding of the Republic to the present day. During the early nineteenth century the primary motivation was the "China market," and was assisted by the acquisition of the Louisiana Territory, the Southwest, and the Oregon Territory. The Civil War interrupted this grand design, but by 1867 the quest was renewed, with the purchase of Alaska from Russia.

The modern Age began with that purchase. Along the way America acquired Hawaii and extended commercial feelers around the world. With the transformation of American business to a steel-based enterprise, the need for raw materials (rubber, tin, and oil) fueled a drive for further expansion. At the same time a change was taking place in the military. The United States had thought of the armed forces in small, mostly defensive terms. That changed with the spread of the Industrial Revolution. Captain Alfred Thayer Mahan provided the spark for that change when his book, *The Influence of Sea Power Upon History,* was published in 1890. It launched a debate that would not end until World War II. He argued the primacy of navies, not armies, and in greater numbers than ever before. The result was the first modern arms race.

Everywhere his book inspired the construction of large, steel-clad warships, even in Britain - which already had the grandest fleet in the world. It was the same story in France, recoiling from the doldrums of a post-Napoleonic decline, and in Germany, united in 1871 by Otto von Bismarck. Russia, long suffering from insecurity and inferiority complexes, added a unique touch: an experimental warship that was nearly round! By 1900 the United States had the third largest navy in the world; quite an extraordinary contrast to just twenty years before, when it ranked only ahead of Chile.

The challenges of that revolution changed and blurred America's purpose. No longer able - or even desirous - of remaining a pastoral, largely agrarian society, the United States embraced the new expansion with consummate zeal. Not surprisingly, this resulted in massive changes in society and touched off a number of fiery debates. Immigrants came in colossal numbers, mostly from Europe and the British Isles, where other revolutions had run their course, leaving behind gross social inequities. The majority of these immigrants clogged big eastern cities, setting the stage for sociological nightmares that would come to fruition in the twentieth century.

The appetite for expansion divided the nation as had nothing else since *antebellum* slavery. Some "rugged individualists" took full advantage of social Darwinism (which was said to have been created to fit the needs of the new age). Certainly Rockefeller, Carnegie, Vanderbilt, and Gould proved there were immense fortunes to be made, though, it was argued, very little of their fortunes went to the common weal. Who was to pay for "the great unwashed"? Equally posed was another question: should *anybody* pay for the masses? After all, the nation was founded on the principle of opportunity, not entitlement.

As the debate raged - and frequently erupted in violence in cities like Chicago, New York, and Philadelphia - another question was raised: in becoming expansionist, was the United States getting stronger, *vis-à-vis* the rest of the world? For decades, America had been everyone's whipping boy; a colossal joke in the eyes of "true" civilizations like Britain, Germany, and France. Even Russia - America's only historic friend - considered America no more its equal than Japan... that nation of "shirt-tailed monkeys" that would defeat them in the Russo-Japanese War of 1904-

1905.

The proof of America's "arrival" was the Spanish-American War of 1898. Employing modern armaments and strategies, the United States easily bested the one notable European power that had resisted the industrial revolution. Through a generous peace treaty, by which the U.S. paid Spain handsomely for the victory, America signaled to Europe its "right" to be a member of the concert of nations.

As the new century began, the quest after empire had made America an important player on the world stage. The problems that came from that did not go away; in fact, they only grew and multiplied. But it is difficult today to imagine the modern world without that late nineteenth century departure.

The Impact of "the Lost Generation"

One should study an era's writers at least as much as the politicians. They tend to be more honest in their assessment of society, whereas politicians tend to say and do almost anything in order to get votes. The lesson in this case is the 1920s.

In the popular imagination, post-World War I America has come to be known as "the Roaring Twenties," a time of bathtub gin, the glitter of jazz and baseball, and a raucous "anything-goes" lifestyle. It did not begin that way. Hanging over the nation was deep uncertainty, fueled by massive unemployment, strikes, a rise in the crime rate, the appearance of "hobo jungles," and a Red Scare.

This has prompted a search for "the real America," and the ones who made the biggest contribution toward finding it were the writers: an American intelligentsia that forever would be typed as detailing the pain and pleasure of the "lost generation."

It was not the first time writers had tried to explain America. After the

War for Independence, that generation's writers - led by Thomas Paine (*The Age of Reason*, 1796) - described the nation as he saw it. He did it so shockingly that many communities distanced themselves from him. Following the controversial War of 1812, James Fenimore Cooper (*Last of the Mohicans*), Washington Irving (*Rip Van Winkle*), and others, contributed their own, equally controversial analyses. Before and after the Civil War, a galaxy of *literati*, led by Ralph Waldo Emerson, Henry David Thoreau, Nathaniel Hawthorne, and Harriet Beecher Stowe, lent their talents to the task of defining "the real America."

In the 1920s the lead was taken by F. Scott Fitzgerald. Encouraged by Gertrude Stein in Paris (a popular haven for American writers), "Scotty" became the spokesman for "the lost generation" through the publication in 1920 of *This Side of Paradise*. The phrase itself is variously interpreted. One day in Paris, writer Gertrude Stein was having her car serviced, when a mechanic sallied forth a few pejorative remarks about women drivers being representative of "a lost generation." To most people, though, the phrase refers to the millions of young men sacrificed in the War: a lost generation of poets, philosophers, and the like.

In the 1920s Fitzgerald was "the best of the brightest," bemoaning the passage of America from innocence and the rampant immorality and reckless behavior witnessed by him and his fellow expatriates. *The Great*

Gatsby, published in 1925 - despite his belief that it was the worst book he had yet written - came to be identified with that flamboyant epoch more than any other book. In it, greed and a *sans souci* climb up the social ladder produced disaster and a reevaluation of the meaning of life.

Ernest Hemingway also surfaced in the Twenties, but in a much milder way than the crusty old warrior the world would come to know in the Thirties and Forties. Before his sorties into death in a bullring on a Sunday afternoon there was *The Sun Also Rises* (1926) and *A Farewell to Arms*, a 1929 bestseller that was one of the first noteworthy anti-war books of the twentieth century.

Puritanism conflicted with Gomorrah inspired D. H. Lawrence. *Lady Chatterly's Lover* (1928) was so scandalous in its treatment of bourgeois morality (even containing the seven "forbidden" words), that his native England did not permit its publication until 1953. It sold well in an America, though, whose favorite song was "anything goes."

Perhaps the best communicator of the Twenties was Sinclair Lewis. His *Main Street* (1920) captured the hypocrisy of small-town America. As the nation slipped into its happy-go-lucky mode, a 1922 sequel jolted everybody. *Babbitt* was about a banker who vicariously climbed the ladder of success, with disturbing consequences. Three years later Lewis produced *Elmer Gantry*. It poked fun darkly at those Americans gullible enough to believe the pitch of tent-revival shakedown artists. In 1930 he was rewarded for his labors with the Nobel Prize for Literature, the first

American to be so honored.

Other writers in the Twenties took their shots. John Dos Passos, a wealthy Portuguese-American, early on felt guilt about unearned wealth and compensated with the scathing left-wing trilogy, **USA**. In the Thirties, with the Depression deepening and the family fortune largely intact, he changed his mind. On his death in the late 1950s, Dos Passos was identified with the political right.

Theodore Dreiser and Emma Goldman both sampled Bolshevik Russia as the alleged panacea for what ailed America. "Red Emma" lived there briefly as an exiled anarchist, before realizing that the USSR was not the answer. Dreiser, on the other hand, was more patient. His **American Tragedy** (1926) remains a haunting and disturbing read about what he believed was wrong with America.

There was even a southern entry: William Faulkner. The first significant writer of the new century from Dixie (thanks to the efforts of **The New Republic's** Malcolm Cowley), he began a career of "summer-and-smoke" novels (**The Sound and the Fury**, 1929) that would do to/for Mississippi what John Steinbeck later would do to/for California.

A discussion of writers in the Twenties would not be complete without mention of H. L. Mencken, the acid-tongued satirist whose lampoons both pleased and infuriated millions of Americans. He introduced words and phrases, like "boob" (meaning idiot; from the French word, *bourge-oisie*) and "booze"(middle-class Americans drinking themselves to death). He wrote about "the great unwashed masses" and "the anthropoid rabble," an homage to Darwin's controversial evolution theories.

Vulgarity, materialism, patriotism, religion; they were all targets. "The patriot," Mencken wrote, "is a bigot, and the man of physical bravery is often on a level intellectually with a Baptist clergyman." On yet another occasion he opined that "civilization was impossible in a democracy, and morality was a monstrosity." "Marriage? If I ever marry," he wrote," it will be on a sudden impulse - like a man shooting himself!" And finally: "Puritanism: the haunting fear that someone, somewhere, might be having a good time."

It is perhaps fitting that the best-selling author of the Twenties was none of these, but little-known stockbroker Bruce Barton, who in 1926 wrote **The Man Nobody Knows.** Its theme? Christ as an early day business executive!

It was, as comedian Fred Allen observed, a decade of wild abandon and bad taste, that despite (or perhaps because of) immense profits, was a harbinger of a less happy, more turbulent time that was to come - one that would have its own fair share of critics.

Archibald MacLeish: The Poet and Politics

One Friday morning in the early 1980s, as I was discussing cultural trends of the 1930s and 1940s in a class in Recent American History, a student informed me that she was a big fan of Archibald MacLeish. After class she pressed me for more information about him. That weekend, I did more than ferret out some source material for her: I wrote the following essay.

When I presented it to her the following Monday, she was crushed. This was more about her "hero" than she wanted to know. My reply - that I was only trying to get her to learn as much as possible about an historic individual - did not help.

The lesson, of course, is an obvious one. Most of the men and women we study are highly complex individuals, with details about their lives that are frequently unsettling, even uncomfortable, to digest.

To the vast majority of people who have little more than a passing interest in the literature and the folkways of the American past, Archibald MacLeish is simply "a poet," a footnote personality whose celebrations of the individual have earned him a place of modest importance in our literary heritage, alongside contemporaries such as Robert Frost and Carl Sandburg.

That, however, suffices only as an overview to his life and career. Like so many creative individuals, much is enveloped in notoriety. In fact, he was one of the most controversial artists of his generation.

To understand him - and especially his politicization - one needs to go back to a consideration of the 1920s, a time that F. Scott Fitzgerald and others heralded as "the lost generation." MacLeish began that decade fresh out of Harvard, but whereas many of his classmates looked blissfully ahead, he saw society through a heavy veil of melancholy. So severe was his disgruntlement with his native land, that he abandoned America for Paris (a favorite "watering hole" of American intellectuals), bemoaning the fact that the "picturesque and romantically conceived past" had given way to "a shoddy and mean-spirited present." (1)

Paris afforded him ample time for soul-searching and "new directions," and, if we are to believe his letters, it was the most stimulating time of his life. Then came the Depression, and a new set of agonies. Many of his fellow intellectuals looked left of center for salvation from that *malaise*, but not MacLeish. He clung to the mechanism of the past. Considering none of Man's current ideological choices "ideal," he opted for capitalism. Despite its faults, capitalism at least permitted a fair amount of "intellectual freedom." This was absent, he argued, in the practice of communism. (2)

This was really no argument at all, replied many of his generation's disenchanted: it was merely conformism; an abdication of his responsibility "to heed the call for constructive social change." Nor did MacLeish endear himself when he penned a scathing attack on - of all things - the Ph. D. thesis, which he saw as a good example of our "moral and intellectual decline." (3) The thesis had become too much a recounting of "dry data." Where was the celebration of the human spirit? To this, a host of *literati* (chief among them Malcolm Cowley of *The New Republic*) gave an answer: though MacLeish was urging the intellectuals to "take charge" of society, he was demonstrating that he was sadly out of step with reality. What MacLeish wanted was what the Lost Generation had failed to get. To many, he was living in the past. (4)

Nor was the debate stilled by his support of social democracy during the Spanish Civil War (1936-39). MacLeish joined a distinguished group of men and women ("The Committee of the One Thousand") who advocated commitment to the Republican forces. (5) Toward that end, with Ernest Hemingway and playwright Lillian Hellman, he sponsored a film, *The Spanish Earth*, which called for the overthrow of General Francisco Franco's fascist *régime.* In one grand step, MacLeish earned the accolades of progressives and libertarians, not to mention American Socialists and Communists who, only two years earlier, had excoriated him as an agent of American fascism. (6)

It was World War II that brought MacLeish into the white heat of the political limelight. In 1942 Franklin D. Roosevelt named him Assistant Director of the powerful Office of War Information. That alienated a large cross-section of the intellectual community. The reason was simple: as a rule intellectuals work alone, without sponsorship or control. To work at the highest level of Government was regarded by many intellectuals with deep suspicion. (7)

Disapproval by his detractors came swiftly. In 1942 MacLeish worked out a sophisticated chart, "to scientifically measure the patriotism of a given publication." If it were not deemed to be "sufficiently patriotic," he and his staff had the power to suppress that publication for the duration of the War. (8) He also urged the country's newspapers to "purge from their payrolls" anyone whose patriotism was questioned. The Left did not see this as the role of the intellectual, and clamored for his dismissal. (9)

Clearly, the War was a turning point for MacLeish. No longer dissatisfied with ideologies (as he had been in the Twenties), he evolved past his love for the Popular Front to become a vehement anti-Stalinist, an anti-fascist, and a staunch interventionist. (10)

There was a modicum of consistency in his political evolution: as he bounced backward, and then forward, in his ideological odyssey, he came to define everything in terms of simple morality and Christianity. The Second World War was proof of our "moral decay"; it never occurred to him that the War's origins were more complicated. At the OWI he sallied forth in his criticism of liberalism, intellectualism, and modern culture, all of which he said were doomed because of that moral decay. (11)

The intellectuals' strongest case against MacLeish concerned his handling of the truth. "Though not prepared personally to advocate fakery," wrote the Yale historian, John Morton Blum, MacLeish nonetheless concluded that the American people "needed assistance in associating their best aspirations with his best reading of the facts." (12) In other words: to win the war, anything goes.

Together with "assistance" regarding the truth, went assistance in the handling of sensitive domestic matters, such as racism. To ingratiate himself with a large Italian-American population, MacLeish proposed in May 1942 that those hyphenates be excluded by the Justice Department in its classification of "undesirable aliens." The FBI was dubious about the merits of that suggestion, and it never got their approval. (13) On the other hand, MacLeish seemed to turn a deaf ear to the plight of native-born blacks, whose disgruntlement with official race policies was leading to substantial domestic woes. MacLeish publicly disapproved of any "corrective action" on their behalf, for that, as he saw it, "would play into the hands of the... Axis." (14) One need not look too far for the intellectuals' reaction to *that* conclusion.

When the war was over and victory had been achieved, MacLeish was far from satisfied. In fact, he may have been more disconsolate about the future than he had been about the recent past. "The peace we will make," he wrote toward the end of that conflict, "will be a peace ... without moral purpose or human interest." (15) It was a familiar theme: a "lost generationist" expressing the same concerns that haunted him a quarter of a century before.

The deep suspicions and resentments that the intellectual community harbored toward him survived the War; many antagonisms would never be resolved. (16) It is important to note, though, that not all of the criticisms were directed at him simply because he had become "a pawn of the Establishment." Witness the editorial remarks of Edmund Wilson, who, as early as 1928 had written to F. Scott Fitzgerald that MacLeish's poetic *"Hamlet"* was just "a piece of bathos." Or later, in 1932, when he stated that his latest poem, *"Conquistador,"* was "lousy"; and a letter from 1940, that called his seminal *"America Was Promises"* "an awful poem." Finally, there exists the damning remark (shortly after MacLeish went to work for the OWI) that he and John Steinbeck were no more than "second and third-rate writers." (17)

Was the resentment mainly attributable to personal jealousies? That is a possibility: he practically vaulted up the ladder of success, leaving many of his fellow *literati* behind. Whatever the reasons - and they must be judiciously studied - the fact remains: as a poet he attracted a small following, while as a man of letters who involved himself in political and ideological controversy, he had a much bigger impact. (18)

MacLeish returned to the ranks of the intellectuals at the end of the war. He wrote poetry and occasional essays until his death nearly two decades later. Time has been kinder to him than to many of his contemporaries, and thanks to America's predictable historical amnesia, he is today remembered more for his romantic verse, than for his sometimes unorthodox political and ideological postulations.

Notes

1. Daniel Aaron, **Writers on the Left** (New York, 1961), p. 264.

2. *Ibid.*, p. 265. For a more intensive scrutiny of MacLeish's thinking in the 1930s, see Malcolm Cowley, **Think Back on Us: A Contemporary Chronicle of the Thirties** (Carbondale, 1967), I, 35-47.

3. William L. O'Neill, **A Better World: The Great Schism - Stalinism and the American Intellectuals** (New York, 1982), p. 33.

4. *Ibid.*, p. 34. The distinguished cultural and political essayist, Edmund Wilson, went even farther, detecting in MacLeish's polemics a call for censorship. Wilson was right: MacLeish later told the American Association for Adult Education that writers should not question "desirable propaganda," even if it proved to be wrong.

5. Larry Ceplair and Steven Englund, **The Inquisition in Hollywood: Politics in the Film Community, 1930-60** (New York, 1980), p. 115. It should

be noted that the Committee was little more than a letterhead group of liberals, "whose chirp was drowned in the raucous din" of those stormy times. By 1948 the Committee was dead. *Ibid.,* p. 290.

6. *Ibid.*

7. *Ibid.* Many prominent scholars (including Malcolm Cowley, whom MacLeish named to his staff) worked in Government during the War. They drew less criticism, for they simply implemented policy, instead of making it.

8. Geoffrey Perrett, **Days of Sadness, Years of Triumph** (New York, 1973), p. 213.

9. *Ibid.* MacLeish did little to defuse criticism. Beginning in 1942, he took part in a weekly radio show, **This Is War!**, extolling the virtues of the American people. That there was nothing on the air opposite it - by design - gave intellectuals another excuse to howl. "MacLeish," charged one, "is no better than [Nazi Propaganda Minister] Dr. Goebbels."

10. O'Neill, p. 37. FDR tried (and failed) to muzzle his OWI Director on several occasions.

11. *Ibid.*

12. John Morton Blum, **V Was For Victory** (New York, 1976), p. 29. There had been earlier hints: before 1939 MacLeish had served as the Librarian of Congress, and in 1939 created a "Democracy Alcove," emphasizing only classical treatments of democracy. No "subversive" literature was allowed. Perrett, p. 123.

13. Blum, p. 153.

14. *Ibid.,* p. 196.

15. Howard Zinn, *A People's History of the United States* (New York, 1980), p. 405.

16. O'Neill, p. 34.

17. Wilson to Fitzgerald, [?], 1928; Wilson to John Peale Bishop, September 30, 1932; Wilson to Thornton Wilder, August 25, 1940; Wilson to Maxwell Geismar, June 10, 1942, in Edmund Wilson, *Letters on Literature and Politics, 1912-72* (New York, 1977), pp. 228, 307, 362, 385.

18. While he was blaming all our moral failings on writers such as Hemingway and Fitzgerald, a number of others who were not members of the intellectual community were gearing up to brand him a heretic. In April 1953 Senator Joseph McCarthy and his staff searched through the USIA libraries abroad (established by MacLeish and others) and found what they referred to as books by "subversive authors." The list was a celebrated one, and included ex-Communist Theodore Dreiser, Harvard's liberal historian Arthur Schlesinger... and MacLeish. The books were taken from the libraries, and burned. Perrett, p. 94; David Noble, *et al.*, *Twentieth Century Limited* (Boston, 1979), II, 400.

Another Side of War: The Home Front in World War II

Recent generations have given more thought and attention to the "war at home" than mine did. For that, they are to be thanked.

"The broadcast put a third grade democracy into tragic confusion. The Americans live under fear of invasion, and upon its announcements, no matter how ridiculous they may be, people start firing guns, drinking poison, throwing themselves from windows, and dashing madly to insane asylums."

That devastating editorial appeared in the official Italian fascist newspaper, **Resto del Carlino**, in reference to a Sunday, October 30, 1938 radio dramatization of H. G. Wells' *"The War of the Worlds."* Its theme? The invasion of America by Martians.

Immediately, apologies pored forth from the New York radio station for the (largely overstated) panic that ensued. It was supposed to be just

47

a harmless Halloween "boo." Weeks later, most Americans had forgotten the broadcast, but in Europe it was not. To Benito Mussolini, and his ally, Adolf Hitler, it showed Americans as gullible, naive, maybe even stupid. It fed their plans for what would be called World War II.

Once the United States entered that war (after the Japanese attack at Pearl Harbor on December 7, 1941), Americans demonstrated that they were anything *but* gullible, naive, and stupid. In the Asian and European theaters of war Americans were tough, determined, and vigilant. On the home front, sacrifices that can only be called heroic were also made, and usually without fuss or protest.

But there are cautions. It is an overstatement to say that "we were all in this together." The internment of two hundred thousand German-, Italian-, and Japanese-Americans starkly exemplified this, not to mention occasional strikes and acts of violence. And this:

"Democracy: a government of the masses. Authority derived through mass meetings and other forms of 'direct' expression. Results in mobacracy. Attitude toward property is Communistic: negation of property rights. Attitude toward law is that the will of the majority shall regulate, whether it be based upon deliberation or governed by passion, prejudice and impulse, without restraint or regard for consequences. Results in demagogism, license, agitation, discontent, and anarchy."

That statement is not from Axis Europe, but from the ***Officer's Training Manual,*** issued to armed forces personnel of the United States at the

48

beginning of the war.

Given all of this, it is extraordinary that the 95% of Americans who never saw a shot fired in anger were able not only to survive, but emerge *victorious,* in the most impactful war in human history.

Mostly, "ordinary Americans" did it by living each day as it came. Nostalgic for an earlier, trouble-free time (their decade of choice: the 1920s), the Forties Generation nonetheless consumed a lot of alcohol, smoked cigarettes (with sexual equality), and - until rationing took over - drove their cars. Rubber, gas and oil were needed for the war effort, so most cars went up on blocks. For many it was a moot point: no cars were made after 1942. Instead, Ford, Chevrolet and other automobile manufacturers made tanks, jeeps, ships, and personnel carriers.

To get around, people used alternate forms of transportation: buses, streetcars, trolleys, bicycles... and their legs. Out of desperation for human companionship, millions unbolted their doors and ventured forth to meet their neighbors. Most of the time their efforts were rewarded, and a tradition of exchanging cups of sugar and passing loaves of homemade bread over the back fence was born.

The new friends walked to stores and cinemas together; many became lifelong pals. For many others, this was simply a manifestation of the "elevator syndrome." After the war - once again free to drive and move about without restrictions - many went back to locking their doors and ignoring their neighbors.

While it lasted, though, it was a building experience. People shared goods (often in contravention of the law). They read more books than ever before: it was the beginning of the paperback revolution. For a quarter they could buy the classics, plus Zane Gray westerns, romance novels, detective stories... anything, in fact, except war stories. They read a lot of science fiction. Still in its infancy as an "art form," readers were introduced to Isaac Asimov, Ray Bradbury, Arthur C. Clarke, and Clifford D. Simak, scribblers who were just beginning careers that would transform their craft from "bug-eyed monster" stories to thought-provoking tales filled with social and political commentary.

Americans went to the movies. For a nickel (or a dime, in big cities) they were treated to two movies, previews of coming attractions, a serial, a plethora of cartoons, and the omnipresent Movietone news. For another nickel they could buy a Coke or a bag of popcorn. Jimmy Stewart, Errol Flynn, Bugs Bunny, Elmer Fudd, Mickey Mouse, and Donald Duck intruded upon Americans for the first time. *Casablanca* was too new to be regarded a *cine* classic, *Fantasia* was far too sophisticated to make money, and Walt Disney had no idea that *Bambi* was written by a Nazi sympathizer.

Music was "swing," with talented artisans like Tommy Dorsey, Benny Goodman, Glenn Miller, and the Andrews Sisters making songs and melodies that would be revered long after their initiators had departed. A young Frank Sinatra seemed always to be using his stage microphone for support, and Bing Crosby mixed crooning with acting, usually with Bob Hope.

Baseball was still America's pastime, but many of its stars (like Ted Williams, Hank Greenberg, and "Joltin' Joe" DiMaggio) were fighting in Europe and Asia. In their absence, makeshift teams played makeshift games. It wasn't pretty, but it took people's minds off the war.

Plastics burst upon the scene... and almost immediately one of them - nylon - vanished. Women were devastated, and struggled with the fact that they would have to wait for war's end to experience smooth stockings again. Nylon was needed in the making of parachutes.

Fighting depression was a full-time job, and "home-fronters" did it by studying their horoscopes, trusting their destinies to palmists, or going to sideshow hypnotists. Kids went to schools that were terrible: many of the younger, talented teachers were gobbled up by the war. When Sally and Johnny came home from school, it normally was to little or no supervision: daddy was fighting overseas and mom was "Rosie the Riveter." Youth gangs were one result, the harbinger of the "street corner society" that would be fodder for sociologists for decades to come. Sally and Johnny sometimes dared to explore their *private* world... and other horrors came their way: venereal disease, teen births, and back alley abortions.

Still, the Forties Generation survived, and became the subject of a reverential work half a century later called ***The Greatest Generation***. At the center of it was that "silent majority," who worked, played, lived, and worried on the home front. It was testimony to one of the most extraordinary eras America had ever experienced, and may never come again.

And the Beat Goes On: Popular Culture and American Society Since 1945

Post-modernists devote a lot of time to the impact of popular culture in American history, and frequently "forget" that it is *not* a new subject. Students have been reading this essay, in various iterations, for more than thirty years.

The Impact of Music

In the fifth century B.C., the Athenian philosopher Plato wrote that "any musical innovation is full of danger to the whole state and ought to be prohibited." The twentieth century parallel of that otherwise open and tolerant society can be found in the United States, to whom the baton of western civilization passed.

Certainly, innovation was not what most musicians had in mind during World War II. The easy-going, big band sounds of Benny Goodman and Glenn Miller relaxed and revivified the American listening public, as did

singers like Hoagy Carmichael, Bing Crosby, Frank Sinatra, and the Andrews Sisters. With civilization being tested by a latter-day Sparta (Nazi
Germany), few dared to rock the boat. Though Woody Guthrie hailed the
trials and tribulations of ordinary Americans, he did so with a guitar that
said "this machine kills fascists."

After the war, and the consequent return to normalcy and traditional
motifs, "message music" grew. In alarmed reaction, a number of notables
(including Art Linkletter and Lawrence Welk) accused these innovators of
a "Machiavellian plot to hypnotize the youth of America." Reminiscent of
the age of Theodore Roosevelt, a half century before, they feared a revolution from below (with the help of Soviet Russia), influenced by the
power of popular music.

In truth, "pop" music has always been tied to politics. Even to Karl
Marx, in the nineteenth century, and to Vladimir Lenin, in the early twentieth, it was seen as the perfect way to instill class consciousness. Americans took their lead from southern music, translating it from rural to
urban themes in the wake of the burgeoning growth of northern cities.
Spokesmen included Will Geer and Burl Ives, whose talent and charisma
made them popular even with mainstream America.

By the 1950s musical innovation was rapidly advancing, thanks in part
to the arrival of television and the huge increase in the sale of phono-
graph records. At first, popular culture struck a moderate pose, with Pat
Boone, *"Your Hit Parade,"* and Ed Sullivan leading the way. Dissidents like

Joan Baez and Bob Dylan were largely ignored.

That began to crumble away in the early 1960s. Elvis Presley scandalized American pop culture with "rock and roll;" Pat Boone gave way to the Beach Boys, who gave way to the Beatles. Traditionalists fought back: Beatles songs were banned (especially in the South). *"Eve of Destruction"* was snubbed, because it criticized the not-yet controversial Vietnam War. Even *"Puff, the Magic Dragon"* was condemned: weren't Peter, Paul and Mary singing the praises of marijuana? In retaliation, Janet Greene and Marty Robbins sang folk songs with patriotic themes. Mainstream compositions of Henry Mancini and Roger Williams provided a high quality, conservative alternative.

The most notable innovation was the pop festival. The first one - in Newport in 1963 - was a modest success. Four years later, a festival in Monterey, California got even more attention, and showed that the age of daring, "anything goes" music had arrived.

Television was slow to follow. One 1960s show, *"Hootenanny,"* was lambasted by activists, because it was not "consciousness-oriented." Cynics called it "Pat Boone with a beat." In 1967 the Smothers Brothers opened Pandora's box, when they defied CBS and invited Pete Seeger to appear on their show. They were promptly fired, but the seed was sown, and pop culture would never be the same.

New themes appeared with explosive force and impressive bravado. From Simon and Garfunkel came "the laments of celebrations of the ordinary," in songs like *"Sounds of Silence," "Scarborough Fair,"* and *"Bridge Over Troubled Water."* Janis Ian had only one hit, but *"Society's Child"* raised questions about racial intermarriage. Some music thundered, and had a much harder edge as the Counterculture took over: the Rolling Stones, Blood, Sweat and Tears, and Jimi Hendrix were examples of that wave.

The Mamas and the Papas urged people "to make your own kind of music"... and your own taboos. The Fifth Dimension borrowed from the hit Broadway play, *HAIR*, and popularized "The Age of Aquarius," where youth and love prevailed (variations of themes already introduced by Bob Dylan). In August 1969 the Counterculture hit its peak at Woodstock: "three days of peace and love." Two months later the musical pendulum moved again, with a violence-riddled concert in northern California.

The Seventies toned down the sociopolitical messages... though not necessarily the volume. More psychic than intellectual were The Who and Pink Floyd. They took rock to extremes, and in turn were counterbalanced by Paul Williams, the Carpenters, and Barry Manilow, who reminded listeners of the softer sounds of the Fifties and early Sixties. This reached an almost folk-pop level, with Judy Collins and the Moody

Blues mesmerizing, even tranquilizing, their audiences.

The Eighties was an almost Dadaistic time: no tone, no timbre, and very little substance. Disco (a garish pop form from the Seventies) gave way to a crude and often inarticulate form of pop music called "rap." Elevator music (*muzak)* also appeared - softer, easy listening music - together with flash dancing and break dancing.

By then, all the messages had been expressed. Fads and freaks dominated the scene: KISS, Twisted Sister, Queen, Michael Jackson, and others. As a new millennium began, memorable tunes were hard to find.

Politics and Film

The immediate post-1945 period saw a return to nostalgic, middle America-type films, with Jimmy Stewart and Gary Cooper dominating box offices with their appeal to the wholesome, boy-next-door image.

The heating up of the Cold War changed that. With McCarthyism running amok, Hollywood accommodated. **Conspirator** (1950) was one of the industry's earliest anti-communist films, three years after the Waldorf statement had declared war on "un-American" movie-makers. **My Son John** (1952), was hysterically blatant in this regard, depicting Robert Walker as a psychopathic communist son of an American Legion soldier... beaten to death with a Bible! Similarly, in **The Red Planet Mars** (also in

1952) the USSR underwent a religious upheaval and threw out communism (after the collapse of the Soviet Union in 1991, the films now seem strangely prophetic).

The Eisenhower years (1953-61) were a low key period, where what "was good for General Motors was good for America." Thus, when *Salt of the Earth* appeared in 1954, just after the stalemated end of the Korean War, the American Legion blocked its showing in Chicago. In another film, *Storm Center* (1956), the DAR gave the producer an award - because the movie's librarian (Bette Davis) burned books on communism.

Sometimes, though, the Fifties produced challenges. Witness *Invasion of the Body Snatchers* (1956), telling us that the Russians were coming... or that we were permitting ourselves to be brainwashed, sanitized, robotized, and dehumanized by our own mores? The Blacklist ended, and talented exiles returned to their labors: *Exodus, Bridge on the River Kwai,* and *Spartacus* were three films that dared to be different.

The explosive Sixties showed the maturation of political films and a sophistication that was ground-breaking. *The Manchurian Candidate* (1962), was one such film: it suggested a communist takeover of America through the electoral process. *Advise and Consent* and *Seven Days in May* similarly caught the popular imagination, attacking the government and the military in ways that had never been attempted. This fueled the youth protest films of the mid- and late Sixties: *The Graduate, Little Big Man, The Strawberry Statement, Easy Rider,* and *Midnight Cowboy*.

Cinema came full circle in the Seventies: the villain was no longer on the Left, but the Right: *The Brotherhood of the Bell* and *Three Days of the Condor* transmitted that suspicion, and *Executive Action* and *The Parallax View* abounded with paranoid images of president-killing.

Predictably, popular culture turned rightward as the nation prospered in the "Weighty Eighties." To critics, a kind of tunnel vision took us over; nostalgia (mostly for the Republican 1950s) was everywhere in demand. To this end, Steven Spielberg made the hugely successful *Back to the Future* trilogy. *Peggy Sue Got Married* showed America in its last blush of innocence before November 22, 1963; and *E.T.* glamorized, and appealed to, middle- and upper-middle class America in a way that was reminiscent of the family films of the 1950s.

Conservative films like *Rocky* and *Rambo* (and their seemingly endless sequels) celebrated blue-collar, hyper-patriotic America. Similarly, the *Star Wars* saga began in 1977, and showed simplistic, cartoon-like characters in easy-to-follow good guys vs. bad guys scenarios. *Raiders of the Lost Ark* and its sequels did the same thing.

Escapist Literature

The Fifties gave us comics and other escapist fare that had little to say between the lines, but were reassuring sugar pills. *"Terry and the*

Pirates," "Blondie," and "Archie," were pitched to a war- and Depression-weary public that wanted nothing more than a few chuckles to start or end the day. In 1950 Charles Schulz introduced the world to *"Peanuts."* That strip turned America into a huge Norman Rockwell print, with characters - Charlie Brown, Snoopy, Linus, Lucy, and others - who became household names. Americans came to identify with them and made *"Peanuts"* the most popular, widely-read comic strip of all time.

In the turbulent Sixties, however, Charlie Brown's America was not everywhere the same: not with iconoclasts like Toffler, Spengler, Marcuse and Mao being read. A sharp edge intruded upon the comics. "Peanuts" was still there, but thanks to Vietnam, the Rights movements, and other concerns, *"Pogo"* appeared, challenging the myth of innocence. To that generation, Walt Kelly's creation made the ultimate pop statement: "we have met the enemy, and he is us."

Starting in the Sixties, *"Doonesbury"* carried criticism to a logical conclusion: excoriating the War, presidential politics, big business, the military, chauvinism, racism, and football (in ways that Schulz would never have attempted). It was a "golden age" for political cartoonists: more than ever before people got their news through the brush strokes of Herblock, Oliphant, and Pfeiffer.

Cult books from World War II-onward dominated, from J. D. Salinger's alienation works of the Fifties (***Catcher in the Rye***), to J. R. R. Tolkien's masterful ***Hobbit*** and ***Lord of the Rings.*** Tolkien's books enjoyed success, for his hobbits were hedonistic lovers of beauty and pretty colors. They resented any intrusion into their "scene," and smoked burning leaves of herbs in pipes of clay. Yet when their quest was done, they returned to find their homeland drastically altered, with a repressive *élite* wielding power via a para-militaristic force in a controlled economy. Who could mistake the way the Counterculture read *that?*

If anything, both comics and fantasies acquired a less humanistic and much sharper edge in the Seventies and Eighties. Comic favorites moved from *"Peanuts"* to *"Garfield"* (a fat, lazy, yuppie-like feline who was the quintessential example of Eighties narcissism), to *"Bloom County,"* where innocence was forever lost, and shock was no longer *nouveau*. Period literature emphasized the cold, the morose, and the horrific (the hugely popular works of Stephen King). Little known Stephen Donaldson wrote the best-selling fantasy series of the time: **The Chronicles of Thomas Covenant, Unbeliever**. In six volumes Donaldson dragged his protagonist (a leper) through unwanted adventures, oedipal fixations, deep self-pity and melancholia.

And beyond? Plato would still be worried about the music, though some artists (like George Winston) presented easy-listening, New Age "elevator music." Much, though, is harsh, loud, and frequently aimed at arousing visceral emotions.

Since the Eighties, the movies have utilized some breathtaking state of the art technology, but state of the past plotting. Simplistic action and adventure films dominate the box office, and a "back to any time" mentality propels Hollywood in the new millennium. Form is more important than substance.

"Peanuts" has stayed with us only in "re-runs," still sowing the verities of white, middle-class values, as a backlash against the relativists. *"Garfield,"* on the other hand, has waned, as the yuppie generation has given way to cynics. Bart Simpson and Beavis and Butthead are their heroes.

"Bloom County" ran out of "good copy" and tried to change. It was transformed into a less than successful, surrealistic *"Outland,"* and went to a comics graveyard. As times changed *"Doonesbury"* lost its message, and its following. Books, likewise, have changed, with Harlequin romance novels and softer-edged fantasy (**Harry Potter, Jody, Ravenscroft, Door to the Shadows, Goblin Tales**) trying to reclaim a generation weened on cynicism and despair.

As we find ourselves in a new millennium, we are reminded of Bob Dylan's remark that "times, they are a'changin'"... but in what direction?

Oriental Tangle: American Foreign Policy vis-à-vis China, Korea, and Vietnam

The nations discussed in this essay are still "hot" topics in academia and government, as the world enters the second decade of the new millennium.

For nearly two hundred years, America's policy-makers have actively pursued an "Asia policy" whose purpose has been to promote trade and ensure the protection of America's interests in the Pacific. There have been many challenges to this policy, and none were greater than those that began with World War II.

China

The first three decades of the twentieth century were not kind to China. Violent resistance to western ideas and practices (the Boxer Rebellion of 1900), a native revolution that ended the Manchu Dynasty, the birth pangs of the Kuomintang, and the ascendancy of ancient rival Japan meant considerable anguish and uncertainty for one of the world's oldest and most storied cultures.

In 1931 imperial Japan took advantage of the chaos of the Great Depression by invading Manchuria, an area essential to Chinese manufacturing. By decade's end Japan's military might had brought colossal suffering to a nation that for years had been struggling with a wretched economy and incompetent leaders. After the Japanese attack at Pearl Harbor, the United States became a player, and asked for China's help in defeating a common enemy. In return, America pledged billions of dollars in aid, and promised not to involve itself in China's internal affairs.

The recipient of this bonanza was Chiang Kai-shek, a warlord who was educated and married in the United States. A fan of American baseball, he was on good terms with President Franklin Roosevelt. He was also the darling of *Time* magazine magnate Henry Luce, a man who loved China. He applauded Chiang for his hatred of Japanese fascism *and* international communism.

In early 1942 Chiang was not living up to America's expectations. U. S. Ambassador Gauss made this clear in a number of reports to the State Department. The American government, however, made it *equally* clear that Gauss had to soften his tone. The reports were not discounted, but it was decided to "look the other way." That, however, did not stop the

Army from dispatching one of its own to monitor the situation. "Vinegar Joe" Stilwell was one of that generation's most talented subalterns. Brash and colorful, he had a no-nonsense approach to life. He found Gauss' concerns to be valid, and in his dispatches indelicately referred to Chiang as the "Peanut." The Chinese leader was spending American money, *not* on the war effort, but on a campaign to rid China of the peasant communist leader, Mao Tse-tung. An infuriated Chiang unsuccessfully peppered Washington with demands for Stilwell's ouster.

Three years and three billion dollars later the war ended, and Army luminary, George C. Marshall (later Secretary of State) made a provocative proposal: he would go to China and ask Chiang and Mao to rule that country together. The suggestion was brilliant, if unrealistic, and fell through - allegedly because *Mao* accepted the offer and *Chiang* rejected it.

By 1949 the American "plan" for China was in ruins: Mao's revolution succeeded, and Chiang fled to Taiwan, supported by more billions of American dollars for years to come. It was unthinkable that the United States could "lose" China, so political heads had to roll. In the **White Paper** for 1949, Dean Acheson (who gives a full account in his memoir, **Present at the Creation**) blamed Chiang, for not instituting the "reforms" that America had requested. Dean Rusk, Assistant Secretary of State for

Foreign Affairs, rebutted this, raising the temperatures of all concerned with the remark that China was "a Slavic Manchuria." That thinly-veiled reference to Soviet communism, ushered in Cold War hysteria and talk of the domino theory.

The situation only worsened: the USSR exploded its first atomic bomb; Alger Hiss was convicted of perjury (but not treason) in a celebrated national security trial; and Joseph McCarthy was entering the foray with a rampage that would lead to a widespread hunt for subversives in his own country. The United States required scapegoats, and the first victims were several so-called "China hands" in the State Department, whose accurate reports on developments in Asia were seen not just as predictions, but as something much more nefarious. *Ipso facto,* in the skewered logic of the time, they were deemed responsible for the "Red triumph," and their careers were forfeit (later rehabilitated, most of them posthumously, by President Ronald Reagan in the 1980s).

For a quarter of a century, America's policy toward Communist China became one of non-recognition, and of economic and political investment in Taiwan. That changed in 1971, when the ultimate Cold Warrior, Richard Nixon, spent a week in Red China, seeing the sights and meeting with Mao. Millions of Americans watched on television in stunned disbelief. The upshot was a *démarché*. Taiwan was evicted from the United Nations and upon Mao's death in 1975 a Marshallesque scenario seemed likely. This was further helped when Nixon, after leaving the presidency, joined the Board of Pepsico, Inc. A noticeable increase in trade - Thomas Jefferson's old dream - became a reality. Everywhere the Chinese could be seen, guzzling American soft drinks, eating *Pizza Hut* pizzas, and playing golf on Robert Trent Jones-designed courses. The Chinese had joined "the Pepsi generation."

As the new millennium began, China was still officially communist, but thanks to the introduction and acceptance of some western-style commodities, it was no longer the ogre Americans perceived it to be. Western-style politics is another matter (witness the Tiananmen Square tragedy in Beijing in 1989), but as the century entered its second decade *Realpolitik*, not fuzzy idealism, fueled America's policy-makers.

Korea

In many ways, America's interaction with Korea was different. Owing to its insularity, its diminutive size, and its paucity of resources, Korea was of little interest to the United States. Well into the twentieth century most Americans were blissfully ignorant of that peninsular nation. A few scholars could address Korea's historic difficulties with China and Japan (especially after Japan's forceful acquisition in the Russo-Japanese War of 1904-05). Beyond that, knowledge was sparse.

That began to change with the advent of World War II. Once again the United States needed help to defeat Japan. This time it was Korea's turn, and deals analogous to those with China were bartered: if the Koreans helped the U.S. (through armed resistance and intelligence-gathering), it would help with post-war liberation. In September 1945 the Japanese were removed and Koreans responded with "free and democratic elections." The results, however, were *not* what President Truman had in mind: a left-wing government had been chosen to chart Korea's future.

Washington insisted that the results be voided, and that new elections be held, with an American-influenced result. The Koreans refused, and the result was friction between the two countries. At that point, the United States put forward Dr. Syngman Rhee to direct Korea's future. Like China's Chiang Kai-shek, Rhee was educated in America (he was a student of Woodrow Wilson at Princeton), married there, was an avid baseball fan, and was a hero-worshiper of FDR. Henry Luce liked him for his virulent anti-communism; like Chiang he was *Time* magazine's "Man of the Year." Rhee received billions of American dollars to "stabilize" his country.

Korea, though, was not China. In the first place, its strategic value was hard to justify, on *either* side of the ideological equation. The Americans did not want to be there; neither did the Soviets. The "real" Cold War in the late 1940s was in Europe, not Asia... and *especially* not in Korea. So in 1948 the U.S. departed, leaving behind the 38th parallel as an invisible dividing line, in the hope that neither the North - a pro-communist entity

68

under Kim Il-sung - and the South, under Rhee, would be foolish enough to test each other.

Rhee's government was no more reform-minded than Chiang's. The United States invested billions, even though Korea was not the focus of our attention. As proof of that, in January 1950 Dean Acheson informed the world's press that to fight the Soviet monolith the U.S. had what was called a "Broad Defense Perimeter," a network of nations, all important to the U.S. and worthy of our help against "the Red menace." Conspicuously absent from that list was South Korea.

Assuming that the North Korean government was paying attention (it is foolish to think otherwise), it was just a matter of time before the "Acheson Doctrine" was tested. In Seoul, Rhee was furious, insisting that if the United States did not stand by South Korea he would not permit the elections that were scheduled for May 1950. The U.S. response was simple and blunt: no elections, no more billions. The elections were held, Rhee was voted out of office... and he voided the results, imprisoned the victors, and ruled by executive *fiat.*

At this point American policy changed, owing partly to the histrionics of Joe McCarthy. On June 18 State Department functionary John Foster Dulles secretly boarded a plane for Seoul and told Rhee that South Korea *was* part of the BDP. Three years later Dulles, nephew of the man who had replaced William Jennings Bryan in 1915 over the **Lusitania** crisis, became Secretary of State in the Eisenhower administration, and became one of America's strongest "commie-haters."

On June 25, 1950, General Douglas MacArthur, head of military oper-ations in Asia, was awakened in his Tokyo residence at 4 a. m. by a junior officer who said that he thought *South* Koreans had just initiated fighting along the 38th parallel. MacArthur sternly informed him that one did not awaken a man of his stature with "he thought." He told the officer to be more precise. Two hours later, MacArthur was awakened again. This time, he was told, the U.S. *knew* that fighting had broken out... and was started by *North* Koreans.

In Washington D.C., President Truman, an "Ag man" from Missouri whose presidency had started with the ordering of the use of the atomic bomb on Japan in 1945, acted promptly, committing the U.S. to South Korea's assistance ... *before* getting the approval of the United Nations. This was an important breach of protocol (especially since the UN was an American creation). It particularly infuriated the Soviets, who made a mammoth blunder: they walked out in protest and were gone for forty-eight hours. Too late, they realized their mistake: it takes a unanimous vote of *members present* on the Security Council to authorize military action. Before they could return, the Council had voted 4-0, in favor of the United States.

In the beginning, American forces went carefully, mindful of China's recent conversion to communism and its growing ties with Moscow. But in late November U.S. forces erred, and drew the Chinese Communists into the conflict. For the next two years the best the U.S. could manage was a stalemate. Along the way the President fired his top general (MacArthur) and discussions raged about whether or not to use the atomic bomb. An armistice (but no treaty) stopped the bloodshed in 1953.

Since then, American troops are still positioned on the southern side of the 38th parallel. Political and economic overtures have netted a sizable, positive change in the South. North Korea is a different matter. It is insulated and solitary and dedicated to communism. It is perhaps the hardest country in the world to know, and continues to concern American policy-makers well into the new millennium.

Vietnam

It is ironic that people today can find so many parallels concerning Korea and Vietnam, for on the surface they are strikingly dissimilar. Vietnam's history includes exploitation and occupation by a major European power (France, beginning in 1882); Korea was never a European target. Vietnam is a veritable treasure trove of materials desired by the industrialized West (gold, silver, tungsten, tin, rubber, manganese, oil); by comparison, Korea is almost resource-free. And yet, parallels there are.

First and foremost, during World War II the U.S. needed Vietnam's help to stop Japanese aggression. Once again, in exchange for promises of aid (armed resistance and intelligence-gathering), large sums of money were offered, together with a pledge that once the war was over, the U.S. would secure Vietnam's freedom by dislodging the Japanese *and* the French.

In 1945 a deal to evict the French was voided because of flareups in the Cold War. The French, who dearly wanted to leave (Vietnam had not been an asset for decades), promised to exit by 1951. They reneged. Ho Chi Minh and the Viet Minh blamed the United States, and called it the real enemy of the Vietnamese. Decades before, in 1919, Ho was in Paris to plead his nation's case. After being denied an audience with President Wilson, Ho, who had scraped out a living as a pastry chef at the posh Carlton Hotel, boarded a train for Moscow and became a communist.

After a disastrous siege at Dienbienphu, the war between the French and the Vietnamese ended in 1954. The U.S. had considered helping the French. Vice-President Nixon and Secretary of State Dulles suggested the use of the atomic bomb; Senator Lyndon Johnson recommended more conventional carpet-bombing by the SAC. In the end, the Joints Chief of Staff, concerned about involvement so soon after America had disengaged from Korea, decided not to act at all.

Dulles was at the peace talks (Geneva, 1955), but only as an unofficial observer. The Accords, ending the War, called for free and democratic elections, in North and South Vietnam, followed by consolidation into a single nation. To Dulles this was ominous. By the end of the year the United States had created SEATO, as a buffer against the extension of communism throughout the rest of Asia.

For the U.S., already embarking upon the most affluent decade in its history, Vietnam quickly disappeared from public view. It remained thus until after the election, in 1960, of John F. Kennedy, a young, energetic New Englander whose anti-communism was the equal of the man he defeated: Richard Nixon. Joseph McCarthy was a Kennedy family friend.

Meanwhile, more military advisors were dispatched to pro-America South Vietnam. That plans were being made (shades of SEATO) to escalate this situation was made public in the summer of 1971, when the *New York Times* printed documents taken by Daniel Ellsberg, a careerist with the Defense Department, in a book called *The Pentagon Papers*.

One of the documents was "Secret Plan 34A," in which American-trained Vietnamese (who hated the communists) were to be parachuted into North Vietnam, under the cover of darkness, storm Hanoi and kill as many high-ranking communists as possible. The Plan was attempted, in August 1964... and failed. Hanoi blamed the U.S., but few people paid any attention.

The summer of 1964 also gave the world the Gulf of Tonkin incident.

Two American destroyers, positioned in international waters off the coast of Vietnam, were reportedly fired upon one night by the North Vietnamese. A thorough search the next morning cast doubts that there *was* an attack. But President Johnson decided he needed more flexibility, should such an "attack" happen again. The result, called the Gulf of Tonkin resolution, was fiercely debated, but approved.

In February 1965 the United States became an active participant in the Vietnam *imbroglio,* when a North Vietnamese attack on an air base at Pleiku, South Vietnam, killed seven Americans. The U.S. retaliated, first with Operation Flaming Dart, and then Operation Rolling Thunder. For nearly three years most Americans supported the conflict. An exception was Sovietologist George Kennan, who spoke against the war in 1966. In 1968 an avalanche of events - the Tet offensive; the murders of Martin Luther King and Robert Kennedy; the election of Richard Nixon - eroded much of that support, and a loud demand for withdrawal, mainly from college-age adults, polarized the nation.

In truth, there were *not* that many protests. Contrary to an idealized, postmodern picture of the Sixties that frequently shows up in books, movies, and documentaries, most college students did or said nothing about the war. As the first "television war," the fish-eyed camera lens distorted the numbers and played into the hands of ideologues and the general public.

President Nixon promised to succeed where the Democrats had failed: to end the war. His administration did that, but only after some detours that resulted in a tragedy that was news all over the world: the killing, by the Ohio National Guard, of four students at Kent State University, on May 4, 1970.

Still, progress toward ending the conflict continued, and ultimately bore fruit. In 1973 Nixon's National Security Advisor, Dr. Henry Kissinger, worked out the details for an end to the fighting, and was a co-winner of that year's Nobel Peace Prize. In the spring of 1975 American troops left Vietnam.

Vietnam's value, even in defeat, was not discounted, and behind the scenes, mostly with stealth and secrecy, U.S. policy-makers worked to reopen Vietnam and make its treasures once again available to America and the West. That started to become a reality in the 1990s.

"The Nasty Nineties"

I gave my first lectures in 1966, when Lyndon Johnson was president. Owing to the explosiveness of the time, I decided *not* to discuss sitting presidents in class. I adhered to that maxim throughout my career. The following essay did not appear until after the beginning of the new millennium.

The 1990s began with a mix of cautious optimism and financial jitters, as the economy - which had attained under Ronald Reagan the highest growth rate since the 1950s - was slowing down. That, coupled with expenditures associated with a foreign adventure (Desert Storm), spelled the end, at least temporarily, of the Republican ascendancy, and allowed a little-known Arkansas politician to be elected President in 1992.

William Jefferson Clinton was a "television president": male-model good looks and a gentle manner reminded the voters of JFK and Jimmy Carter. His immediate message was a middle-of-the road populism, to win over both moderates and liberals in the Democratic Party.

Immediately, it became clear that Bill Clinton was going to be "his own man." A draft dodger in the Vietnam War, he said he would issue an

Executive Order that would require the armed forces to fully integrate gays. That put him at odds with the leadership within the military and marked the beginning of a tepid relationship. The Executive Order never materialized.

In the beginning, he was the darling of militant feminists (or "feminazis," in the words of conservative activist Rush Limbaugh), and various ethnic interests. Jesse Jackson, the ultra left-wing black activist, became Clinton's "spiritual advisor," until sexual misadventures prompted his exit from the Washington scene.

Much of Middle America was appalled by Clinton, and through the Republican-dominated Congress sought an effective counterweight after 1994. The result was the "Contract with America," which neutralized or watered down Clinton's more liberal proposals.

Many Americans were upset with the prodigious amount of lies and distortions that flowed from his presidency. When they had no discernible negative effect, critics referred to him as "Slick Willy," and "the Teflon president" (a label that critics had once stuck on President Reagan).

A poorly-appointed inner circle (mostly leftovers from the failed Carter presidency) continually caused problems. In 1993 one Clinton staffer killed himself. Several Clinton appointments came at the behest of the president's wife, Hillary, whose views were farther to the left than his. Two of her recommendations were particularly noteworthy: Janet Reno as Attorney General, and Madeleine Albright as Secretary of State. Both were firsts for women, and both were disasters. Reno's fortunes faded with the killing of religious dissidents in Waco, Texas. Albright (whom critics called "not-so-bright") badly advised the President on Europe and Africa. After waiting nearly three years, the administration committed the U.S. to an active policy in the Balkans (first Bosnia, then Kosovo), despite an absence of vested interests in that region.

A brief military intervention in Somalia further enraged his detractors, and it was not until four years *after* his presidency ended that Clinton apologized for doing nothing to halt the genocide in Rwanda that cost more than 800,000 lives. His administration all but ignored militant Islam, especially as it impacted Iraq, setting the stage for the tragedy that struck the U.S. at the beginning of the next administration.

A long history of adulterous relationships (dating back to his Arkansas days) made Clinton an easy target of moral Americans. As well, alleged wrongdoing in numerous business ventures (Whitewater, e. g.), coupled with controversial statements before a federal grand jury, led to his impeachment. He was only the second president in American history to be brought to trial in the Senate. Like the other - Andrew Johnson in 1867 - he escaped conviction, but his reputation was tarnished.

And yet, he was lionized by a sizable portion of the American public. The media, for nearly half a century a bastion of left-liberalism, were especially forgiving. CNN was even called "the Clinton News Network." It had been founded by Atlanta communications mogul, Ted Turner, who had married the left-wing actress-activist, Jane Fonda.

Still, the criticisms grew. One of his detractors wrote a book, **Primary Colors**, which savaged the administration. It became a movie. Clint Eastwood, the conservative actor-activist, played upon Clinton's abuse of women with his own interpretation, **Absolute Power**. Even mainstream Hollywood, which otherwise was favorably disposed toward Clinton, presented its disgruntlement in **The American President.** It showed what they had *hoped* he would be.

Meanwhile, the economy supported tech stocks (but little else), and the grumblings continued. Conservatives criticized Clinton for not curbing deregulation. That policy, begun by Jimmy Carter in the late Seventies, was frequently ruinous, especially to the transportation industry. Nor were conservatives happy with his handling of NAFTA. Division within the White House only added to the drama. Clinton's vice-president (another southerner: Al Gore of Tennessee) was even more liberal than his boss, and that added to the friction. The deterioration of their relationship probably contributed to the election of Republican George Bush to the presidency in 2000.

In other areas, the "Nasty Nineties" was a time of little cultural sophistication. Everything seemed keyed to home computers and VCRs. A dark cynicism marred the entertainment landscape: Beavis and Butthead, the Simpsons, and the Mutant Ninja Turtles drove a low-brow culture. Movies disturbed audiences with numbing and excessive sexuality and profanity. Blood-filled action films proliferated (**Jurassic Park, Last Action Hero**), as did race and gender hate films (**Thelma and Louise**). Political correctness, a latter-day, left-wing McCarthyism, was everywhere the norm and dictated a very narrow conformism. It served to put the American mind into an intellectual straitjacket, especially in the field of education. Balance all but disappeared, as the ideologues of the left took over America's classrooms. It became almost impossible to find a conservative counterpoint, except at the private level. Thanks to this "tyranny of the minority," the long-dreaded "dumbing of America" had become a *fait accompli* by century's end.

Television was disappointing, with more mindless sitcoms and dramas than ever before. One of the precious few that was even mildly thought-provoking was *"The X Files."* It was the decade's most popular show and mesmerized audiences with the promise that "the truth is out there." Its creator, Chris Carter, offered an even more starkly realistic look at the times with *"Millennium."* Echoing the Sixties statement that "we have met the enemy, and he is us," it disturbed viewers so much that it lasted only three years.

Two "who-done-it" series of note passed each other in the Nineties: *"Sherlock Holmes"* and *"Poirot."* The former starred Jeremy Brett as the ultimate Arthur Conan Doyle detective, and the latter introduced audiences to David Suchet's rendering of Agatha Christie's Belgian sleuth. Both earned critical praise. The first one ended in mid-decade (with Brett's death); the second was still going strong at the beginning of the twenty-first century.

Another high quality sleuth show, *"Nero Wolfe,"* debuted at the end of the decade, but lasted only two seasons. British television offered *"Murder Rooms,"* with Ian Richardson as the inspiration for Holmes. Brilliant and well-received by critics and fans alike, it lasted long enough to give viewers five memorable stories.

The other high-quality offering was *AMC's "Remember WENN,"* but that finely-acted, finely-scripted, award-winning show about commercial radio in its heyday did not make it into the next century. "The times were a-changin'," as Bob Dylan famously remarked, and *A&E, AMC,* and other networks reflected those changes, regardless of howls of protest from indignant viewers.

Historians are sharply divided on the Clinton legacy. Liberals tend to be forgiving in their assessment, emphasizing his efforts on behalf of women and minorities. Conservatives, on the other hand, are more harsh (one has called Clinton "an amoral sociopath and a pathogenic liar"). In the last poll taken during his presidency, ordinary Americans were asked *their* opinion. Seventeen per cent said he deserved an A... but thirty-five per cent awarded him an F.

American History and the Movies: An Interpretation

The way history is portrayed in the movies has intrigued historians for decades. This essay - and the one on Western Civilization that concludes this collection - dates from the late 1970s. It has been revised many times, most recently in 2010.

History - ours or someone else's - has been a favorite viewing pastime for nearly a hundred years. It has always been easier (especially now, with VCRs and DVDs) to spend two or three hours watching the spectacle and pageantry of a *Gandhi* or a *Gone With the Wind*, than to take the time to read about them in books and magazines. Hollywood has long recognized that fact, and has tried in every conceivable way "to bring history to life," in an effort to maximize profits... regardless of accuracy.

The purpose of this essay is to show how Hollywood has treated American history, and how it frequently has adapted historical fact to contemporary political, ideological, and social considerations. Along the way we will make note of some good films - and a lot of *bad* ones - and comment on the times in which those films were made, and why they were made the way they were.

Admittedly, this effort can be no less subjective than any other. The difference (and it is doubtless a small one) is that it springs from a historian's mind, not a journalist's. A lot of selectivity is involved; not every film that touches upon our heritage can be discussed. Still, the essay strives to be honest and fair, without making any claims to "winning over" everyone. For that, the reader will have to go elsewhere.

Early America

The least-explored period in American history is also perhaps the least understood... which explains, in part, why Hollywood has done so little to expand viewer awareness of it. Early American history - from the Colonial period through the Revolutionary War, and ending with the birth of the Republic - is almost virgin territory. One reason may be that too close a scrutiny invites controversy: that the War for Independence was not just a war for democracy; that it did not propel us into the fore-front of western civilization.

Ideologically, there is likely a subtler, more basic reason, one that pervades not only Movie America, but the real one, too: the centerpiece is "revolution" (albeit one that was only half-baked). Our Founding Fathers did not act very altruistically, but mostly out of consummate greed and self-interest, and set up a state that can easily be recognized as the fore-runner of money capitalism and the multinational corporation (Franklin, Jefferson, Adams, and Washington were all notoriously wealthy men, who never considered sharing their wealth with the masses).

Traditions, beliefs, and legends mask the earliest period, obfuscating reality and giving us so few examples of cinematic *vérité* as to make the entire period almost unworthy of our attention. To cite an obvious exam-ple: Puritanism, that seventeenth century strain of fundamentalist intol-erance, first reared its ugly head in a 1926 screen adaptation of Nathaniel Hawthorne's 1851 classic, ***The Scarlet Letter***. It was but one of a hand-ful of films in that silent era (sound did not intrude upon movies until 1927) that glorified romantic sacrifice in the 1600s, treated Indians as little more than parasites, and sold heroic individualism to the mostly contented white, middle- and lower-class movie audiences for whom those films were made.

The Indian, who was occasionally brutalized by American colonists, was emasculated in ***The Last of the Mohicans*** (1920), ***Drums Along the Mohawk*** (1939), and ***The Deerslayer*** (1958). In ***Mohicans***, we encounter a reproduction of James Fenimore Cooper's early nineteenth century story, originally a stodgy compendium of turgid prose that drew the ire of Mark Twain. "Cooper had," he wrote, "all the qualifications of a great American writer, except the simple ability to write." Especially cumbersome was Cooper's (and, subsequently, Hollywood's) infantilization of those early residents. "In the matter of intellect," observed Twain, "the difference between a Cooper Indian and the Indian who stands in front of the cigar store is not spacious." *Mohicans* was an affirmation of that. It was a one dimensional view of pre-Independence America, a harbinger of the dash toward manifest destiny, and the extolling of white-Christian supremacy. The film came at a time in our history when a spate of such films was offered, partly to ease the pain of America's just-ended participation in World War I.

Two decades later, the specter of yet another war was on the horizon, and Hollywood again turned to ragged, emotional appeal to sell its 1939 epic, *Drums*. It was an unabashed patriotic undertaking, with recently-discovered Henry Fonda serving as the spokesman for Movie America. It was, as well, a pastoral piece, melding the people with the land of the 1770s (an antidote to the turmoil that rocked the country in the 1930s: the antics of Huey Long and Father Coughlin, the hard times of the New Deal, and the distending international realities involving Hitler, Mussolini, and Stalin). It was nothing less than a reaffirmation of the American dream.

This sugar pill was so pleasing to the pallet that even the day's historians tended to be sympathetic; gains in the name of "progress" that had been earned before the 1920s were replaced by a resurgence of reaction. William Faulkner volunteered to write the screenplay, and John

Ford (who soon would mold John Wayne into the personification of Movie America) made *Drums* a tapestry of populism by portraying ordinary people in their struggle for values: the celebration of the family.

Drums was "for fans who like the war whoops bloodcurdling and their arson Technicolored." It sublimely linked the Indians with the present-day evils of Nazism. Worse, in a huge revision of reality (for which Hollywood - right *and* left - is consistently notorious), the battle that ended the movie never really happened.

Hollywood also demonstrates that prejudice is generational. In the early 1990s the public mood was toward "justice and cultural fair play." When *Mohicans* was remade in 1992, it was politically correct: measurably more sensitive to the (now) Native American subculture than the original film. That, too, spelled failure: it was a dishonest interpretation of Cooper's novel. Nowhere did it show the savagery (less its "nobility") that is the fact of history, for Indians *and* whites. It was, in effect, another sugar pill, but for a different generation.

As for the "happening" of that period? To date, only four films have dared to tell that story: *1776* (made in 1973, in anticipation of the forthcoming Bicentennial); *Revolution*, a 1985 British production; *Sweet Liberty*, done in 1986; and *The Patriot* (1999). The first was a musical, and an aesthetic failure; the second was a gloomy Al Pacino-Donald Sutherland dullard that bombed at the box office; the third was a tongue-in-cheek Alan Alda-Michael Caine satire. The fourth was an offense against reason: a politically correct "freedom flick" from Mel Gibson which failed every test for getting the history right, and along the way demonized the British. It also strained Anglo-American relations, at a time when Britain was a partner in a war that America was fighting in Iraq and Afghanistan.

From almost the beginning, American presidents have been ill-reported by Hollywood. The first one to have been given cinematic treatment was Andrew Jackson. But don't look too deeply: in *The President's Lady* (1953), there was no mention of Jackson's messianic behavior, or of his dislike of the Indians. The focus of the film was Jackson's wife, Rachel (an oddish character, played too prettily by Susan Hayward). "Old Hickory" was played by Charlton Heston, in the first of his many god-head roles, a year before his role as Moses in the epic remake of *The Ten Commandments*.

Post-revolutionary New England has always been good copy, especially considering the fact that by the 1860s there were few Indians left or any Redcoats to be tarred and feathered. It was 99% white, insulated, and visually breathtaking. In Hawthorne's *House of the Seven Gables* (1940), George Sanders lent his tweedy British accent to a quasi-realistic depiction of a New England family whose stereotypical statements about caste delighted moviegoers everywhere. The original screenwriter, Lester Cole, wanted a script that was unkind to Hawthorne's aristocracy, but the studios objected and fired him. He did not reemerge in the headlines until ten years later, as one of "the Hollywood Ten" that was blacklisted for harboring left-of-center political preferences.

The seminal film of the period remains *Moby Dick*, from Herman Melville's 1851 classic. In 1953, when the movie was made, the Korean War was winding down and America was getting ready for the "happy days," from which it would not escape for nearly ten years. Science fiction writer Ray Bradbury composed the script for John Huston, who wanted to show the vigor and the majesty of whaling in the New England of the 1840s.

Unfortunately, the film did not do justice to the book that English departments everywhere were calling "the great American novel." Amiable Gregory Peck as the villainous Captain Ahab and meek-mannered Richard Basehart as the Richard Henry Dana-like sailor were glaring examples of miscasting, and the white whale that was the object of the quest was embarrassing to watch. If nothing else, the film inspired Peter Benchley, who, together with Steven Spielberg, two decades later gave the world *Jaws*.

The Civil War

Hollywood has treated the Civil War period with grudging respect, even admiration. Nowhere is this better demonstrated than in the 1939 release of *Gone With the Wind*. It faithfully followed Margaret Mitchell's soap opera (written while she was recovering from a broken ankle), and was floridly wrapped up in all the *cliches* and sobriquets imaginable. Mention it to anyone, and visages of Clark Gable and Vivien Leigh spring to mind, together with images of the "Old South," mint juleps, honor, grace, charm, and anything else that can be associated with the *ante-bellum* era. That, of course, was what Hollywood had in mind, at a time when the world was drifting closer and closer to yet another war.

In reallty, **GWTW** was a classic sham: a grotesque distortion of the way things were; a propagandistic bombast in support of a discredited and bankrupt American myth. It was also poorly made, with acting and dialogue so juvenile that could *only* have come from the 1930s. It featured cardboard characters who wandered through four hours of torment, in blissful ignorance of the War, the times, and themselves. Above all, it packed a message that, in the strongest possible terms, urged on "the American ideal," and anything else in the name of flag-enveloped myopia. Its success and attendant hero-worship were understandable: **GWTW** was what most Americans wanted to believe, and belief nearly always wins out over fact. "There is evidence," wrote the **New York Times** in early 1940, "that historical truth is not at a premium at the box office." The comment was directed at the makers of **GWTW**.

Hollywood has reeled off a long list of Civil War "epics," mostly made in a distorted vein. Audie Murphy dragged us through Stephen Crane's **The Red Badge of Courage** in 1951; Fess Parker traded in his Davey Crockett gear to help Disney make **The Great Locomotive Chase** in 1956; and John Wayne and William Holden had us ride along with them in the disappointing **Horse Soldiers** in 1959.

As early as 1915, filmmaker D.W. Griffith treated America to a fondness for War-related racism in **The Birth of a Nation** (which was Woodrow Wilson's favorite film; remade in 1975 as **The Klansman**). On the other hand, only once (thankfully) has the War been played for laughs, and that effort, **Advance to the Rear** (1964), is remembered mostly for a pop song ("*Today*") that played throughout the film.

Interestingly, one *does* get a glimpse of realism in **The Good, the Bad, and the Ugly**. This 1968 Clint Eastwood-Eli Wallach film was made not in Hollywood, but in Spain, by maverick Italian director, Sergio Leone. One film tried so hard for realism that it forgot about everything else: 1990's politically correct **Glory**. Critically acclaimed and well-received at the box office, it nonetheless suffered from a number of flaws, including the miscasting of Matthew Broderick. That's typical of Hollywood: it zeros in on a footnote character and a minor incident, and plays fast and loose with "the way it was."

Home life in the Civil War is rarely mentioned in our literature, and among the few who have dared, no one has done it better than Louisa Mae Alcott. Her 1868 novel, **Little Women,** is a safe story about motherhood and the hearth, and Hollywood has cashed in with two versions: in 1933, with Katharine Hepburn, and in 1949, with Elizabeth Taylor. The theme? While the men are away at war, life goes on back home, with the girls dreaming of fame and fortune and repatriation with loved ones, once the dreaded conflict is over. As one critic put it: it was a place "where men would return to wives who had not aged." It reminds us of life in a glass menagerie... the subject of another Hepburn film, a decade later.

The Old West

Arguably, Hollywood's favorite arena has been the "Old West," and just about every conceivable kind of cowboy and Indian yarn has been made - almost all of them sure-fire winners at the box office, ostensibly without ideological overtones. But beware!

The classic statement may have been made in *Red River*, the 1948 potboiler that had John Wayne sanitizing the frontier. It depicted "The Great Myth," and was, as one critic pungently observed, a film that "tingles all the nerve endings but never touches the brain."

Other films in that vein include *The Alamo*, in which John Wayne and his buddies distorted the facts and substituted Mexicans for Indians in the tale of Texas' battle for independence in the 1830s. It was just as poorly remade, along politically correct lines, in the late 1990s. *Chisum*, a boy-meets-bovine film, was released in 1970; and *The Shootist*, the

"Duke's" last performance, came in 1976.

There have been a few honest westerns. For example, see **Shane**, a low-budget Alan Ladd sleeper (1953), and **Cowboy** (1958), Willa Cather's hard-edged story of cattle barons that effectively refuted the Turner thesis about the democratization of the frontier. The debunking continued in the Sixties, first (oddly enough) by Clint Eastwood, through his "spaghetti westerns" (**A Fistful of Dollars, For a Few Dollars More, Hang 'em High**), and in the Seventies, with **The Great Northfield, Minnesota Raid** (1972) and **The Missouri Breaks**. The latter (1976) showed Marlon Brando and Jack Nicholson in grim proportions. All proclaimed the primacy of the anti-hero and the seamier side of life.

The Sixties also gave us whimsical release, inspired largely by that generation's irreverence in politics. (1) **Cat Ballou**, a 1965 Jane Fonda film, was funny and satirical (and a better sell than the 1976 "sequel," **Great Scout and Cathouse Thursday**). At the end of the Sixties Robert Redford and Paul Newman planted tongues firmly in their cheeks and made box office gold with **Butch Cassidy and the Sundance Kid**, based on the antics of some real-life desperadoes. James Garner, who rose to fame on the strength of the late Fifties television series, *"Maverick,"* came up with another irreverent and atypical hero in the 1969 hit, **Support Your Local Sheriff** (and later, **Support Your Local Gunfighter**).

Humor, taken to extremes, becomes parody, and in 1974 that was what Mel Brooks dropped on the world, in his wildly hilarious **Blazing**

Saddles. After that, it seemed impossible to do an "old-fashioned" western. Even John Wayne yielded to the changing times in 1976, when he allowed his character in **Rooster Cogburn** (first introduced in 1970's **True Grit**) to be bossed around by feminist Katharine Hepburn.

Through it all, the Indian began to gain respectability in Hollywood's version of historical reality. To be sure he has come a long way from one-dimensional efforts, such as **Broken Arrow** (1950), **Apache** and **Apache Rifles** (both 1954). Thanks primarily to the influence of the Counterculture, he finally arrived - quite literally - as a "human being," in the 1970 masterpiece, **Little Big Man**.

It is difficult to find a more poignant film. Arthur Penn's superb direction of Dustin Hoffman (as Jack Crabb) was the signature piece of the Woodstock Generation. It was a powerful indictment, by extrapolation, of America's involvement in Vietnam. Hypocrisy, greed, expansion ... all are vividly represented.

Perhaps the most fitting statement comes via the film's grandfather figure,"Old Lodgeskins" (played with dignity by Chief Dan George). To the Indian, he tells Hoffman's character, "everything is alive;" but to the white man, "everything is dead." We also see the first accurate cinematic depiction of General Custer. He comes across as an insane, would-be President, who believed in the Jacksonian view that the only good Indian was a dead Indian. This was a far cry from the Custer-as-hero rendered by Ronald Reagan twenty years earlier.

Two decades later, Hollywood "upscaled" Penn's film, this time calling it **Dances With Wolves**, with Kevin Costner in the lead. Made when the American Indian Movement had all but vanished, and a more conservative ethic had won, **Wolves** had its protagonist leaving doomed Indians to fight their last battle against white civilization alone. Aesthetically pleasing and well-paced, it suffered the plight of many politically correct films: the Indians were seen as more civilized than they really were.

The Gilded Age

The time down to the eve of World War I was explosive and dynamic. It was essentially a dark and stormy period, with corporation-building ("Robber Barons"/"Captains of Industry"), expansive militarism, and labor horrors. It was, as Mark Twain so caustically wrote, "a gilded age," that soiled nearly everyone.

Hollywood has thoroughly enjoyed that era, first with Twain's **Tom Sawyer** (1930), an expression of innocence and pastoral *naiveté* that was not Twain's intention. Genteel Boston? **The Bostonians** was a failed work of fiction, written by Henry James in 1886. It became a failed motion picture in 1984, plodding along under the weight of Christopher Reeve. Strong scents of sarsaparilla abound: witness the 1962 crowd-pleaser, **The Music Man**, with Robert Preston playfully conning the good people of River City (a euphemism for middle America); and **Paint Your Wagon** (1969), with Lee Marvin and Clint Eastwood merrily singing their way through the California gold fields. 1969 also gave us **Hello, Dolly!**, a musical extravaganza that cast Barbra Streisand in her first important role. On the periphery is another Christopher Reeve effort, **Somewhere in Time** (cruelly lambasted by the critics when it appeared in 1980), a small film that tenderly and tear-jerkingly took the viewer back to 1912, to find eternal love (played by Jane Seymour).

Not so delightful was **McTeague**. A muckraking novel written by Frank Norris in 1899, it was turned into **Greed** by Hollywood in 1925 - a pastiche that its author would not have recognized. It was "like looking at a mangled lover in a morgue," wrote one critic. Equally bizarre was the treatment given Theodore Dreiser's **Sister Carrie.** Hollywood waited until 1952 to tackle that property, and not without controversy. The House Committee on Un-American Activities tried to bury it via charges that it was "flagrant Communist propaganda." Ginger Rogers' mother grabbed the spotlight, telling the HUAC that she forbade her daughter to appear in that, or any other, film that had "subversive leanings." The female lead went eventually to Jennifer Jones, a much more accomplished actress. Shortly thereafter, Rogers bowed out of the film business.

Why the flack? Carrie used Social Darwinism to explain America. Free will was an illusion; conventional morality was meaningless; loneliness and dissatisfaction were the true by-products of the American dream.

Add to that the fact that Dreiser once had lived and written in the Soviet Union, and it's no wonder there was such a howl of protest.

Also wrapped up in ideology is *The Wizard of Oz*, L. Frank Baum's "children's tale" of the 1890s that has produced a spate of Hollywoodizations (including a box office flop, *The Wiz*, that alienated white America in the Seventies because of its all-black cast). *The* version was the 1939 blockbuster, produced by avid right-winger, Louis B. Mayer of MGM, and offering Judy Garland as the pubescent Dorothy... plus those charming supporting characters. (2)

Was it simply a children's story? On the surface, yes; it was the kind of movie that Disney could have made, but... go to the *Oz* books for a history lesson - they will read like a study of corruption: the farmers vs. the railroads, Wall Street, and an ineffectual president (anybody from Grover Cleveland to William McKinley). Insert Baum's characters and, presto! Oz becomes a political satire, *à la* **Gulliver's Travels**, or **Alice in Wonderland**.

Of course, MGM didn't make it that way, so you'll just have to squint your eyes, know your Baum, and trust your instincts. Examples of satire? How about when patriotism was mocked and courage was clothed in silly uniforms and cheap medals (remember the "doctor of thinkology" scene?). There *is* a counterpoint: *The Dreamer of Oz*. Made for television in 1990, it tells the story in a vastly different, non-political way. John Ritter was superb in that one as Baum.

Another alarmist, Jack London, gave the world *The Sea Wolf* in 1904, and by 1941 Hollywood finally dared to put it on the screen... and failed. The film version, which featured perennial tough guy, Edward G. Robinson, and John Garfield, was made into a sharper denunciation of the "superman idea" (because of Hitler) than London had in mind. Also evident in the film (but not in the book) was the glorification of self-sacrifice (the affirmation of democracy). London's strong anti-capitalist message was wholly absent.

Expansionism in the post-Civil War period has always been handled with kid gloves. The only movie ever made about the Spanish-American War [*The Rough Riders*] did not appear until the 1990s - to very small audiences. *Diamond Head*, a 1963 vehicle for Hollywood favorite, Charlton Heston, glamorized Hawaii as an 1880s paradise. Also in 1963 came *55 Days in Peking*, a bastardized Charlton Heston-Ava Gardner fiasco about the Boxer Rebellion in China (1900). It was a critical flop, complete with westerners playacting as Chinese.

The prize for "The Most Clever Distortion of History" surely must go to a 1975 MGM release, *The Wind and the Lion*, in which Sean Connery exchanged his 007 trappings for those of a North African Berber bandit, in order to kidnap an American woman (Candice Bergen) and antagonize Teddy Roosevelt (Brian Keith). Based *very* loosely on a real incident in 1904, *Wind* gave viewers the opportunity to see Connery really act (and to see Keith's "bully" performance as TR). The problem? In real life the kidnap victim was Greek, not American... and not a woman, but a man! Not a single critic caught the gaffe.

World War I

The first World War has always been something of a problem for Hollywood (attest the dearth of films about that conflict). How can one keep shooting westerns-as-war movies without arousing suspicion and disgruntlement, in even the least discerning viewer? By shooting only a few... and with as little real history as possible.

Early on, the majority of those films flattered the military and trumpeted the wonders of democracy. *The Big Parade* (1925) is one example, in which the American doughboy was depicted in heroic proportions and the Germans were painted in very dark colors. *Parade* ignored the possibility of Allied war guilt, effectively leaving audiences feeling smug and superior. It was a hit, and inspired Gary Cooper and Helen Hayes to cash in with *A Farewell to Arms* in 1932. Dissident views on that "war to end all wars" are hard to find. Perhaps the first film to dare another perspective was *All Quiet on the Western Front*, an award-winner that for years was nearly the only film to downplay the notion of glory in the trenches.

In 1952 Hollywood presented two treatments of that *debacle*: *The African Queen* and *Viva, Zapata!* The first was a schmaltzy Humphrey

98

Bogart-Katharine Hepburn film, that cast Germans in 1914 Africa as oafs. It scored with movie audiences and became a screen classic. The second one did not fare as well. *Viva* was a propaganda flick, made by Jack Warner to show that democracy was alive and well in the Mexico of 1914 ... and 1952, when our relations with Mexico had hit an ideological low. To show his good intentions, Warner turned Emiliano Zapata into a reformer and a champion of democracy. That, said State Department Advisor Nelson Rockefeller, would be well-received by both Mexican *and* American audiences. The early Fifties, though, was the heyday of the HUAC, and not a few of its investigators thought that Zapata was a communist. This delighted screenwriter Lester Cole... until he was axed (thanks to the HUAC) and replaced by John Steinbeck, whose radicalism stopped well short of his.

The HUAC brought pressure on Steinbeck, and subsequently it was someone closer to Cole's views - Elia Kazan - who finished the script. In the final analysis, what began as an endorsement of Zapata's revolution ended up as a plea for the *status quo*. An outraged playwright named Lillian Hellman called it "pious bullshit" - and was investigated by the HUAC.

One consequence of this was that the Mexican government refused to cooperate with the filming. It accused Hollywood of being unfair to Zapata, and extracted assurances that remarks about the Catholic Church's extensive land holdings be deleted from the script. If that wasn't enough, the dreaded Breen Office of Censorship pressured producer Darryl Zanuck into removing any offensive remarks about the American military.

Reminiscent of the furor over *Viva* was *Reds* (1981). For many years Warren Beatty had wanted to bring to the screen the story of John Reed, an American Socialist whose eyewitness account of the 1917 Bolshevik Revolution (*Ten Days That Shook the World*) became a literary classic.

Beatty waded through a plethora of obstacles. Hollywood was nervous about any project that sympathized with Lenin and company. So he bankrolled the film himself, bringing into the cast with him Diane Keaton, as Louise Bryant; Edward Hermann, as Max Eastman; Jack Nicholson, as Eugene O'Neill; and Maureen Stapleton, who won an Oscar for her portrayal of Emma Goldman.

Though perhaps overlong, it was a critical hit, a slightly altered telling of a story about ideology and love, and a liberal alternative to the more popular and commercial *Doctor Zhivago* (1965). Alas, *Reds* was not a hit with the public. It came out at the wrong time, just as a conservative president was taking office. (3)

Only one other film about the first World War has enjoyed some lasting popularity. Made in 1957, when McCarthy was finally gone, *Paths to Glory* escaped the scissors of the Breen Office, even though its anti-war message was clear. It was an important film that showed off Kirk Douglas' versatility. For Stanley Kubrick, who a decade later would give the world his cinematic masterpiece, *2001: A Space Odyssey* (and twenty years after that, *Full Metal Jacket*, which found fault with another war), it was a personal triumph. The American military condemned **Paths**, and one of America's wartime allies - France - banned it.

The Twenties

A much safer era for Hollywood has been the 1920s, which most Americans believe "roared" and gave everyone a good time. Tinseltown has certainly glamorized that period: with **Funny Girl** (1969), the modestly-altered story of entertainer Fanny Brice, which paired Barbra Streisand and Omar Sharif; **Thoroughly Modern Millie** (1967), a wonderfully breezy film with Carol Channing, Julie Andrews, and Mary Tyler Moore taking liberties with 1922; and **Lucky Lady** (1976), a look at bootlegging (Liza Minnelli), that was anything but lucky for its backers.

Then there was **The World's Greatest Lover**, a 1978 farce with Gene Wilder clowning his way through life as the legendary Rudolph Valentino. And keep saying "romance" long enough to a Twenties *aficionado*, and F. Scott Fitzgerald's **The Great Gatsby** will come to mind.

Hollywood has treated the public to two odd editions of "Scotty's" best known story (which he thoroughly despised). The first was made in 1949, and went largely unnoticed, but it is the 1974 remake that stands out... generally amidst a great howling. Robert Redford misplaced his talents in that glitter fest, and Mia Farrow, who was obviously still recoiling from **Rosemary's Baby**, gave one of the worst performances in the long history of film-making.   One critic went so far as to call it "nightmarish," and a testimonial to "incipient stupidity." Regardless, **Gatsby** is a look at the up-from-poverty ritual that Americans love to celebrate.

There are heavier treatments of the Twenties, but few have filled the coffers of the major studios. Certainly, an adaptation of Dreiser's **An American Tragedy** did not exactly "pack them in" when it was released in the 1930s. It was an attack upon the insensitivity of the legal system, and a psychological study of someone acting out the myth of the self-made man. It was also a criticism of evangelism, urban poverty, petty opportunism, and ruthless competition. A considerable part of Dreiser's book never made it to the silver screen.

Main Street, written by liberal Sinclair Lewis in 1920, was so caustic and irreverent (poking fun at the small town as the "home of the purest democracy") that Hollywood watered down just about everything in it, so as to bring it to the screen in 1936. Even the title was changed: would *you* expect to see a muckraking commentary on life in the 1920s with a title like *I Married a Doctor*? Just as well: all mention of woman suffrage, race problems, radicalism, or the World War, were cheerlessly omitted. The film staggered into theaters as a camouflaged reactionary vehicle, a relief to the disillusioned masses, instead of an honest reminder of the recently departed "good old days."

In 1922 Lewis wrote another book, **Babbitt**, and that entered our libraries and our lexicon as few have, before or since. It was deeply resented by the middle class, for the book dissected its morality, mores, and institutions. Pundit H. L. Mencken liked it, though, and was inspired to coin the word, "booboisie." By the time the book made it to movie houses (two versions, in 1924 and 1934), much of the message - about America's "barbaric lack of culture" and its "grasping materialism" - had been erased. Rather, the films pushed conformity (what David Riesman, in the 1950s, would call "the outer-directed man"). To Hollywood's displeasure, the message reached few people: the films fizzled.

Finally, mention needs be made of three films that deal with specific aspects of the history of the 1920s: *Inherit the Wind*, a 1961 Spencer Tracy-Frederic March feast for the soul (as opposed to the woeful 1990 remake) that fascinatingly (if not very accurately) examined the 1925 "monkey trial" on evolution and found the South guilty of stupidity; *Sacco and Vanzetti*, a 1972 undertaking that indicted America for ethnic and ideological intolerance; and *Matewan* (1989), with James Earl Jones boringly re-enacting a Harlan County (Kentucky) coal mine dispute. It was factual, but buried in political correctness.

The Thirties

The 1930s is a festival ground for movie-makers ... so long as not

103

too many boats are rocked. One which was - in Socialist Upton Sinclair's *The Wet Parade* (1931) - advocated revolution... and quite predictably flopped at the box office. Likewise, *Chinatown* (1974) presented Jack Nicholson in John Huston's study of water politics and corruption in southern California. It was based on a true story (but of a much earlier period) and was followed by a weak sequel, *The Two Jakes*, in 1990. On the other hand, in *Paper Moon* there was no hope, only despair; there was no meaning to a yet unwritten future.

One can find a similar kind of bluntness in *Citizen Kane*, the 1940 bio-pic that broke new ground and heaped *kudos* on its youthful creator, Orson Welles. *Kane* was a lightly-camouflaged *exposé* of William Rand-olph Hearst, America's most vociferous newspaper publisher. Hailed by liberals as a film masterpiece (and condemned by conservatives), *Kane* remains one of the most powerful indictments of abused power in Amer-ican history. It is also a very hard film to follow, and thus not much of a treat for the viewer.

John Steinbeck was the severest critic of the period. The film of his book, *Of Mice and Men* (1939), introduced Burgess Meredith to movie audiences and showed the hopelessness and despair of the Thirties. But it was *The Grapes of Wrath* that cinched Steinbeck's reputation as a muckraker. It, too, was made into a motion picture in 1939 (with Henry Fonda in the role of his career), and caused consternation throughout the movie industry.

Its message was so disturbing that 20th Century Fox and Chase Manhattan Bank (the principal backers of the film) put extraordinary pressure on mogul Darryl Zanuck to kill production. Zanuck, a staunch Republican, was hardly in sympathy with Steinbeck's anti-capitalism, but he *was* an advocate of moderate social change. He also saw the potential for making a lot of money - so he corralled liberal Fonda, while fellow conservative John Ford watered down the script (one never actually sees the Joads *working*), shot the movie...and laughed all the way to the bank.

Also stolid in its portrayal of Depression America was **The Day of the Locust**, a 1975 depiction of societal disintegration and prospects for class warfare in the Thirties. Leftist author, Nathaniel West, wrote the book in 1939 as a protest against fascism; that message was antiquated, resulting in a story that wandered in search of a purpose.. and failed miserably.

Another "hard" treatment deserves mention, though its story spanned three decades: **The Way We Were** (1973), with Redford and Streisand making tired liberal protests and charging the individual with the responsibility for changing the social fabric by non-violent means. It remains an over-the-top reminder of dreams gone awry in those turbulent times.

Of course, the Thirties was not all "Russian realism" in the movies. Witness the Redford-Newman classic, **The Sting** (1973), which has real audience staying-power. It has endured as one of the most enjoyable gems in movie history. And if cardboard concepts of Good and Evil are your cup of tea, check out the extremely popular **Raiders of the Lost Ark**

(1981), and its sequels, with Harrison Ford (as Indiana Jones), treating us to a fantasy-packed romp through that same highly-charged period.

World War II

The Second World War took up only half of the 1940s, but for most people the Forties means little else. That conflict has commanded our attention as has no other. There has been no dearth of films from Hollywood to underscore that fact.

In 1942, for example, Hollywood made *For Whom the Bell Tolls*. Based on Ernest Hemingway's prize-winning 1940 novel, it examined the Spanish Civil War of 1936-39 (a dress rehearsal for the war that America had just entered). The studio signed Gary Cooper and Ingrid Bergman to play the main characters, and applauded the novel's "a-political" nature. Nowhere were evolution and left-wing ideology (the book's main themes) even mentioned. Even fascism was ignored, thanks largely to the fact that the United States did not wish to offend a war-time partner, Francisco Franco of Spain. The film, then, was a cop-out. Hollywood selected arch-reactionary Sam Wood, as its director. Hemingway, an occasional liberal with strong anti-fascist leanings, was furious with the changes, and spent years, unsuccessfully, seeking redress.

That was not the only controversial film of the War. In fact, *Mission to*

Moscow, made in 1943, may be the *most* controversial film of all time. For the historian, it is a textbook lesson in distortion by design. **Mission** was based on the memoirs of America's wartime Ambassador to the Soviet Union, Joseph Davies. It was made with Soviet assistance, in the hope that a friendship would be stimulated, and thus help both countries defeat Hitler. So where's the controversy?

In the first place, it grossly distorted the picture of life in the USSR, showing only an idyllic, happy people, struggling heroically in defense of western civilization. Stalin was lionized, and Trotsky came across as a pro-Nazi villain. Berlin howled over that one. Hitler's Propaganda Minister, Josef Goebbels, lambasted the producers for being "dangerous ignoramuses." Absurdities were everywhere, all of them with the approval of FDR, who had suggested the project. The Soviet Embassy in Washington read and approved the script, and Stalin saw to it that a Russian language version was shown everywhere in the USSR (to Warner Brothers considerable financial joy).

Once the war was over, though, conservative Jack Warner had to backtrack: the HUAC accused him of being a "Commie" stooge... and worse. To make amends, his studio made *I Was a Communist for the FBI* (1951), an anti-Soviet effort that overjoyed the HUAC and its despotic champion, Joe McCarthy. Still, **Mission** has left a bad taste, having so easily misinformed the American people about "real life" in the Soviet Union. Educator John Dewey called it "totalitarian propaganda for mass consumption," and even liberal journals, such as *The New Republic*, treated it to a roasting that was without equal. Gratefully, the movie quickly disappeared from the scene, and can be found only infrequently on the late show, or in video shops that cater to offbeat films.

Three other controversial films about the War came a few years later. *Catch-22* (1970) was a surrealistic nightmare, based loosely on Joseph Heller's best-selling book about alienation and greed. *Slaughterhouse-Five* (1972) was Kurt Vonnegut's bizarre trip through space and time. It was merciless in its condemnation of war (especially the American fire-bombing of Dresden, a non-military target which Vonnegut witnessed as a soldier). It was the third film, though, that received the most attention: *Patton*, the 1970 box office hit that pleased doves and hawks alike. To some, George C. Scott's character was a conceited, romantic warrior, lost in modern times. On the other hand, President Richard Nixon credited it with influencing his decision to invade Cambodia.

Most other films have been the simple "blood-and-guts" type, with little to commend them: *Stalag 17* (1953), which inspired a tasteless 1960s television sit-com called *"Hogan's Heroes"*; *The Bridges at Toko-Ri* (1955); *The Longest Day* (1963); *The Battle of the Bulge* (1966); *The Dirty Dozen* (1967); *The Bridge at Remagen* (1969); and *A Bridge Too Far* (1977), to name just a few. Only *The Bridge on the River Kwai* (1958) dared to show the unwisdom of war - thanks, in part, to a script that was written by a recently rehabilitated victim of the Blacklist (though he was not mentioned in the credits).

The lamentable, but predictable, attack at Pearl Harbor was given an early whitewash by Hollywood (*From Here to Eternity*, 1953), but was effectively interpreted in *Tora! Tora! Tora!*, a 1970 docudrama, filled with an all-star cast. Despite a roasting by some critics, it is the only film about that *debacle* to make judicious use of the documents, and to tell the story from both sides. On the other hand, a hugely expensive release from 2001, was a disaster. Starring youthful liberal Ben Affleck, *Pearl Harbor* was one of those politically correct nightmares that were so frequent after the collapse of Soviet communism. Ridiculous dialogue, *Star Wars*-type fighter scenes, and a complete disregard for the facts, made it one of the worst films ever made.

Touching the War just peripherally are *The Caine Mutiny* (1954), the Humphrey Bogart classic about a naval hero gone mad; *The Court Martial of Billy Mitchell*, the 1956 Gary Cooper study of an army officer gone bad (he dared to suggest in the 1920s that we were vulnerable to an attack from Japan); and *Judgment at Nuremburg*, a Spencer Tracy-Maximillian Schell treatment (1961) of the War Crimes trials. *Raggedy Man* (1981) was one of a scant few films dealing with the Home Front. It concerned the lonely life of a woman whose GI husband had been swallowed up by the War. It was superior to 1971's *Summer of '42*, in which Jennifer O'Neill's character adjusted to loneliness by leading a local teenage boy through the rites of passage. Highly recommended is *The Inci-*

dent, a made-for-TV drama (1990) about a small-town lawyer (Walter Matthau) who is forced to defend a German POW in Colorado.

The immediate aftermath of war is studied in *The Best Years of Our Lives*. Made in 1946 - a year replete with strikes, slowdowns in the economy, and a host of evils, real and imagined, at home and abroad - *Years* was about those who came home, and the difficulty they had readjusting to civilian life. It was prophetic, but it was also pure Hollywood: the real problems of post-War America were glossed over. James Agee of *The Nation* called it "a long, pious piece of deceit and self-deceit, embarrassed by hot flashes of talent, conscience, truthfulness, and dignity." It was a sugar pill, well-received by a society tired of the horrors of war.

Not all patriotic films were heavy-handed: witness *Casablanca* (1942), the much-explained Bogart-Bergman effort that was directed against the evils of fascism. (4) Two years later came *To Have and Have Not*, based on just the first few pages of a Hemingway book. That one introduced Bogart to his future wife, Lauren Bacall. It, too, was an escapist film, and played well in Peoria.

Perhaps the award for "Most Doctored Script in the Name of Propaganda" should go to the producers of *The Human Comedy*, a 1943 bit of silliness that deliberately subverted author William Saroyan's message that war was the manifest symbol of mankind's many failures. Nowhere in the film (which starred Mickey Rooney) was there even the slightest mention of the high juvenile delinquency rate, VD, food-rationing, the internment of Japanese-Americans, and labor strife that was everywhere in the novel. Saroyan was not entirely blameless. "For the good of the country" he put aside his values, and applauded Hollywood. Today it is hard to find a copy of that dismal film.

Korea and Vietnam

No sooner was World War II over, than Hollywood discovered the Cold War, an American invention (said the Soviets) designed to keep munitions makers counting their profits, to keep hysteria at full boil, and make sure of large and lucrative box office receipts.

After a spate of late 1940s anti-Soviet films, Hollywood was presented with the highly salable Korean quagmire in 1950. Hollywood outdid itself in presenting second-rate, machoistic, highly vituperative films, that ennobled war and showed geopolitics in glorious black and white. *The Red Ball Express* and *Fixed Bayonets* (both 1952), *Mission Over Korea* (1953), and *Pork Chop Hill* (1959) are examples of that. In 1962 a rare masterpiece was added: *The Manchurian Candidate*, a mesmerizer that chilled audiences with its depiction of brainwashing. A stellar cast, with Angela Lansbury in the "dragon lady" role of her life, made it an instant classic. Not so fine was the 2004 remake, more proof that politically correct films do more harm than good.

In 1977 liberal Gregory Peck transcended both World War II and Korea with an unusually sympathetic interpretation of Gen. MacArthur. *M*A*S*H*, made seven years earlier, offered a meaningful counterpoint; just as important was the television series of the same name, which, for nearly a decade and a half showed that war was not good for children and other living things.

The television series succeeded because it helped debunk a more recent conflict: the one in Vietnam. That war, which seriously divided America, at first had Hollywood's stamp of approval. There was the bland and apolitical *Saigon* (1948), which featured Alan Ladd. America's early active involvement was highlighted by two gung-ho interpretations: *The Seventh Dawn* (1964), with William Holden; and *The Green Berets* (1967), with John Wayne.

But Vietnam was not Korea, and Movie America was to show the dark, ugly side of that conflict in ways that broke new ground. As early as 1958, Eugene Burdick and William Lederer had teamed up to write *The Ugly American*, and by the time a major studio hired Marlon Brando to star in the movie version (1963), their prophecy about misunderstanding Asian politics came true. Three harsher films cinched the case against the War: *Hearts and Minds* (1975); *Apocalypse Now* (1979); and *Platoon* (1988). Note the dates: all three came after the war had ended.

Hearts and Minds was a documentary which angered a huge number of people, including Frank Sinatra and Bob Hope, who lambasted it "for its treason" the evening that it won an Academy Award. Thirty years later, Michael Moore, "Minister of Propaganda and Enlightenment for the Democratic Party," would insult even more thinking Americans, with his left-wing trashing of another war (*Fahrenheit 911*). *Apocalypse Now,* another Brando film, was Francis Ford Coppola's display of America's interest in Asia. In that one, he borrowed Joseph Conrad's story, *The Heart of Darkness,* which dealt with British imperialism in Africa. *Platoon*, an attempt at realism by maverick Oliver Stone (who had seen duty in Vietnam) added even more to the debate about why we were there.

Powerful commentaries about life after Vietnam can be found in *Coming Home*, a 1978 drama that gave Jane Fonda and Jon Voight a chance to show what happened to returning Vets. Contrast that with *The Deer Hunter*, also 1978, a macabre treatment of the same alienation and frustration. By the early 1980s America's historical amnesia about Vietnam had come full circle, and the presence of a conservative president (who called Vietnam "a noble crusade") sent a signal to Hollywood that it was all right, once again, to revise reality. *The Killing Fields* (1984) and all the *Rambo* films are examples, as was a late 1980s television series, *China Beach*. Only Robin Williams was able to channel some opposition. His *Good Morning, Vietnam* (1987) concerned Vietnam in 1965, as seen through the eyes of a flipped-out Air Force disc jockey. Made by Disney (under the Touchstone label), it was irreverent, but also funny.

Politics and the Cold War

Politics in the post-1945 period is a charged arena for Hollywood. Straight political films that are more for enjoyment than enlightenment are numerous. Among these have been ***Advise and Consent*** (1962), Otto Preminger's liberal adaptation of Alan Drury's very Republican novel; ***The Best Man***, a 1964 primer of presidential politics, scripted by liberal Gore Vidal and featuring Henry Fonda and Cliff Robertson; ***The Candidate*** (1970), with Robert Redford dissecting the brief political career of California's John Tunney; and ***All the President's Men*** (1976), with Hoffman and Redford blowing the whistle on Nixon.

Eliciting substantial controversy was ***All the King's Men***, Broderick Crawford's claim to fame in the movies. It was a thinly-disguised 1949 rendering of presidential aspirant, Huey Long, that reminds one of ***Citizen Kane***. Based on Robert Penn Warren's fine novel, it was the object of an intensive investigation by the HUAC. In 2009 it was remade, this time with radical activist Sean Penn, and bombed badly. Then there was ***The Last Hurrah*** (1959), a Spencer Tracy film that was far too soft on Boston's old ward political establishment to be effective.

Some political films have been almost hysterical in their portrayal of ideology, both right and left. Starting in 1949, with ***The Fountainhead*** (from the book by Ayn Rand), one sees red almost everywhere. Nancy

Davis, who in the "Weighty Eighties" would live in the White House under another name, used her small talents in the making of **The Next Voice You Hear**, a 1950 yawner that literally brought God into the resolution of the problems then facing western civilization.

Also appearing in that first year of the Korean War was **The Conspirator**, a propaganda vehicle weighed down by Robert and Elizabeth Taylor, who simply warned audiences to be wary of strangers. The "stranger theory" got an even weirder processing in the 1952 dementia, **My Son John**, with Helen Hayes' character standing by while her American Legion husband (Dean Jagger) beat to death their Communist-sympathizing, atheistic son (Robert Walker) with a Bible! Peter Graves added to the idiocy with a 1952 dullard, **Red Planet Mars**. In that one, Communist Russia was won over to a Christian revival just before the world came to an end!

Science fiction seemed the perfect medium in the Fifties for exposing the "red menace." Certainly the 1951 classic, **The Thing**, qualified: its concluding message ("watch the skies!") could just as easily be directed at Russians as Martians. Thirty-one years later, it was remade, this time without the propaganda or the superfluous love interest, and was more faithful to J. W. Campbell's story line.

One remake that produced a different effect was **The Invasion of the Body Snatchers**. The 1978 version was depressing in Technicolor; the 1956 black and white release (later "colorized") was vivid and stark. It was a statement about paranoia and conformity, and it drew a lot of fire from the HUAC.

The Fifties, as depicted in the movie, was suburbanized, bureaucratized, complacent, consensus, and secure - not alienated, disturbed, rebellious, or chaotic. At least, that's how Hollywood chose to see it. So on came the "pods," and we were all replaced, swiftly and efficiently, minus our free will, our feelings, and our individuality. In other words: perfect conformity. It was not a film about Communism; it was about what *we* had done to ourselves, in the name of technology and intellectual myopia. In the original version, it was also about a man going insane. (5)

The year after *Invasion*, Joe McCarthy died, and the fright tactics of those turbulent times reached their peak. Bette Davis starred in *Storm Center*, whose central concern was the necessary burning of a library - because it contained a solitary book on Communism! The DAR loved it. There were still conspiratorialists, but their offerings were not as blatant. Witness Alfred Hitchcock's *North by Northwest.* That 1959 tingler was brilliant, with so many fine performances (including Cary Grant, James Mason, Leo G. Carroll), and was filled with so many of "Hitch's" tricks (the crop-dusting scene, the chase across Mt. Rushmore), that one easily forgets it was another film about "us vs. them."

Much like *NBNW* was *The Prize*, a 1963 adaptation of Leon Uris' best-selling book about Nobel week in Stockholm. Paul Newman and Edward G. Robinson dominated the feature, but lovable old Leo G. Carroll was there, too - just before performing as Alexander Waverly, in the tongue-in-cheek spy-vs.-spy television series, *"The Man from U.N.C.L.E."* In many ways, **The Prize** was a clone, but from Hollywood's ever-growing left-liberal perspective.

After that, movies began to soften considerably, thanks in no small part to the "thaw" in early Sixties U.S.-Soviet relations, the rise of the Counterculture, and the fact that we had not yet gotten bogged down in Vietnam. So, we could be charmed by *Charade*, a 1964 Hitchcock-like film, with Cary Grant (once again) and Audrey Hepburn getting involved in non-ideological intrigues in Paris (against a young Walter Matthau), and lulled along by the dreamy music of Henry Mancini. The satirical touch was also to be found in a slew of Ian Fleming stories that burst upon the silver screen: **Dr. No, From Russia with Love, Goldfinger,** and many more. They were very lucrative, easy to watch, and made a star out of Sean Connery as James Bond. James Coburn's star also rose in this age of re-discovered innocence: **Our Man Flint** and **In Like Flint** pushed satire all the way to parody, and did well at the box office.

A more somber tone was what Michael Caine offered in **The Ipcress File**, called "a thinking man's **Goldfinger**" when it first appeared in 1964. A sequel (**Funeral in Berlin**) failed to match the original, partly because by 1968 the real world had become dangerous, with the Vietnam War tearing the U.S. apart and the Soviets invading Czechoslovakia for the second time in a generation. Regrettably, the third - and last - chapter of Michael Caine's series was highly improbable. **The Billion Dollar Brain** told the tale of a zany Texas billionaire (a thinly disguised reference to H. L. Hunt) who tried to invade the Soviet Union! If that was not dumb enough, otherwise believable Gregory Peck made *The Chairman* in 1969. Its story? Get close enough to kill Mao Tse-tung with a powerful bomb ... which was planted in the head of Peck's character!

This love affair with spy flicks seemed almost without end. *Ice Station Zebra*, set at the North Pole, showcased the talents of Patrick McGoohan (on loan from *"The Prisoner"*). It was billionaire Howard Hughes' favorite movie. Disturbing to watch was *The Kremlin Letter* (1970), even though it had a wonderful part for Richard Boone. *The Groundstar Conspiracy* (1972) painted red streaks everywhere, with a better than average story (but ghastly music) and a twist. George Peppard's character emerged as a fascistic voice of authority ("if I had my way, I'd bug every bedroom in America"). In the Reagan Eighties Hollywood released a truly scurrilous film called *Red Dawn* (1984), suggesting a Russian invasion of America, beginning in Kansas. (A takeoff of sorts - *"Jericho"* - briefly came to tele-vision in 2006.) Suitably, the Soviet newspaper, *Izvestia*, declared that *Dawn* was fit only for "limited intellects." (6)

One needs to watch 1966's *The Russians Are Coming, The Russians Are Coming*, a film that strikes a balance by pointing out just how dumb *we* could be, and how human the Russians could be. Alan Arkin was at his best in that one, as a befuddled Soviet submarine officer.

Not all of our paranoia has been outer-directed: *Seven Days In May* was a thought-provoking chiller from 1964 that prophesied a military takeover of the U.S. That one featured two of Hollywood's better-known liberals, Kirk Douglas and Burt Lancaster. Also watch *Mirage*, the 1965 sleeper with an amnesiac (Gregory Peck) seeking his true identity, and instead running afoul of the military-industrial complex. In 1971, when Nixon was moving America to the Right, Hollywood responded with *The Brotherhood of the Bell*, a scary tale with Glenn Ford's character blowing the whistle on a super secret group that was trying to run the country. A less believable remake, *Skull and Bones*, came two decades later.

The fear of the Right was expressed (also in 1971) in *WUSA*, with Paul Newman warning America about the influence of the reactionaries in the southern media (unusual, since the media was in reality moving to the left). In 1973 we were embarrassed by *Executive Action*, a seldom-seen entry that had Burt Lancaster (again), Will Geer, and Robert Ryan explaining that JFK was assassinated not by Lee Harvey Oswald, but by right-wing Texas businessmen, because they suspected the president was about to disengage the U.S. from Vietnam and embark upon a radical civil rights policy. A year later, Warren Beatty was equally silly with *The Parallax View*. It probed the aftermath of a JFK-type killing. In 1975 Redford gave the world *Three Days of the Condor*, a chiller which assured us (thanks in part to Max von Sydow's stellar performance) that the enemy was our own CIA. By the time the Right had hit its peak (with Reagan), the message of a John Carpenter horror film (*They Live*, 1988) was clear, as was the disturbing **Betrayal** (1988), based on the real-life assassination of a liberal radio talk show host by white supremacists in the western United States.

None of those, however, produced as much fallout as Oliver Stone's **JFK** (1991), which reopened the wounds left by a president's murder a quarter of a century ago. Nominated for Best Picture (which showed how far to the left Hollywood had gone), maverick writer-director Stone rubbed audience nerve endings raw with a three hour, rapid-fire *tour de force* that themed, like **Executive Action**, that the deed was done by someone other than Lee Harvey Oswald. In this version, the CIA and other agencies of the Federal government... and maybe even LBJ ... ordered the hit. Hollywood's liberal-left community was highly visible, with cameos by Edward Asner, Jack Lemmon, Donald Sutherland, and Walter Matthau. Kevin Costner projected one of his better screen efforts as New Orleans District Attorney, Jim Garrison - who was also in the film ... as Chief Justice Earl Warren!

JFK touched off a firestorm of protest, much of it orchestrated by the Government, but much, too, by the historical profession, which accused Stone of tampering overmuch with the facts surrounding the killing. The last word? Hardly, as attest 1993's psychological thriller, **Line of Fire**, with Clint Eastwood playing a Secret Serviceman who failed in 1963 and, now, thirty years later, is given another chance to stop a presidential assassination (by John Malkovich, in the role of a lifetime).

1992 was an election year, and it surprised no one that Hollywood chose to release films that addressed both external and internal political concerns. **Patriot Games** dealt with the former: a post-Cold War thriller that showed the philosophy and the actions of the IRA (Irish Republican Army). Based on the book by Tom Clancy, it was a fast-paced, disturbing commentary on the world of terrorism.

The other film, **Bob Roberts**, dealt with domestic politics, and was no less explosive or controversial. All of the elements for high drama and social commentary were there: disaffection with entitlement programs, anger toward an ineffectual Congress, decline in traditional morality, and widespread acceptance of sloth in the marketplace. Enter Bob Roberts (liberal Tim Robbins), a guitar-toting, right-wing folk-singer (son of western singer Marty Robbins), who pushed all the right buttons to win a Senate seat... which included a faked assassination attempt.

Bob Roberts was a fast-paced nightmare: allusions to George Wallace, H. Ross Perot, and Bill Clinton are unmistakable. Barry Levinson produced it, giving it a liberal stamp of forewarning. It's hard *not* to sympathize with the neo-fascistic protagonist.

As the Clinton presidency sputtered and waffled, at home and abroad, Hollywood turned up the heat. Early on, **The War Room** (1993) eclectically pointed out some inconsistencies in the new President, and by the end of his first term even the liberal community was becoming disenchanted with its man in the White House. Michael Douglas made this point in *The American President.* It showed what the left hoped Clinton *would* be. Disgruntlement was joined by embarrassment - thanks to the sex scandals in his second administration. In response, Dustin Hoffman and Robert DeNiro struck a nerve with the 1997 hit, *Wag the Dog*. This one themed an incumbent president being bailed out of his extra-marital affairs by his advisors, who stage a phony war. Clint Eastwood's *Absolute Power* took fictional shots at Clinton, with liberal Gene Hackman playing the guilty president (1996). *Primary Colors* excoriated everyone in the Clinton White House. All in all, the Nineties had more negative movies about a sitting president than any other decade in the twentieth century.

Doomsday

Closely linked with our never-ending appetite for paranoia and poli- tics flicks has been the doomsday drama. It has seldom been done for laughs (Mickey Rooney, as a peanut butter sandwich-eating hero in *The Atomic Kid*, 1955, is the only one that comes to mind); usually it's been done to produce a variety of visceral emotions.

In that regard, we've certainly been warned enough times: *The Day the Earth Stood Still* (1951) did it via vintage science fiction. In that one a visiting alien (Michael Rennie) tried to warn Patricia Neal and her fellow Earthers against taking nuclear weapons into space. *Them!* (1954) had lovable old Edmund Gwenn (Kris Kringle in the original **Miracle on 34th Street**) investigating mutational effects of atom bomb blasts on ants - with predictably terrifying results. The ultimate thriller may have been Michael Crichton's **The Andromeda Strain** (1971). That one juxtaposed the problem of the Unknown with our space probes.

We've also warned ourselves: **Dr. Strangelove**, the epic 1964 black humor-fest in which Peter Sellers (who played three parts) urged us to protect ourselves against our own worst intentions. It satirically attacked the military, which for years had been treated with kid gloves. The early Sixties gave the world the ill-starred Bay of Pigs disaster and the Nuclear Test Ban Treaty, so Hollywood simply played to the prevailing mood swing. Historian Lewis Mumford called it the "first breakthrough" in Cold War thinking. The military was not amused: General Curtis LeMay bank-rolled a rebuttal called **A Gathering of Eagles**.

Despite **Strangelove's** flaws (it was *not* an entirely honest assessment of what might go wrong), it was better than **Fail-Safe**, an extremely dark 1964 Henry Fonda study about the same subject.

The story about the men in the missile silos has been done more than once: with a lot of histrionics and muddled acting (Lancaster, again!) in **Twilight's Last Gleaming** (1977); as a stern warning about the vulnerability of sophisticated computer systems (**WarGames**, 1982); and as pure fantasy wrapped up in a child's pledge to get rid of nuclear weapons (**Amazing Grace and Chuck**, 1986). Only **War Games** did well at the box office. Critics were hostile to **Chuck**, and that drew angry denunciations from co-star Gregory Peck, who publicized the film all over the country. He should have reconsidered; it was a silly film.

Where else might the problem be? In the non-explosive nuclear reactors, of course. That prompted Jane Fonda, Michael Douglas, and Jack Lemmon to make the compelling **China Syndrome** in 1979. Three weeks after its debut, the Three Mile Island reactor almost *did* melt down, thus fulfilling prophecy and insuring the film's commercial success.

Doomsday has been the subject of quite a number of movies. In 1983, there was ABC's made-for-TV 1983 horror show, **The Day After** (which, if anything, underplayed the terror of nuclear confrontation). ABC followed the airing with a panel discussion, hosted by Ted Koppel, and a "cross-section" of opinion on the nuclear issue that included Henry Kissinger.

Usually, Hollywood has been content to take a low key, low budget look at doomsday: in **Beginning of the End** (1958) the dropping of the Bomb didn't even produce changes in the environment; whereas in **Damnation Alley**, George Peppard raced all over an upside-down-world, fighting impossibly mutated vermin in his quest for survivors. Compare those with Hollywood's first serious statement on the Day After theme: Gregory Peck (again), fatalistically accepting the end of the world in Stanley Kramer's **On the Beach** (1959). The military disliked that one and refused to cooperate in the filming.

Not nearly as disheartening was **The World, the Flesh, and the Devil**

(1959). It employed biological, not nuclear, weapons, thereby explaining why there was no extensive property damage (shades of the neutron bomb?). That theme was reinforced in *The Omega Man* (1971), with Charlton Heston in yet another of his god-head roles - this time standing up for science against a world in which mutation had become the norm. It was remade, with Will Smith, in 2008. Three small 1980s presentations concentrated on biological catastrophes: *Endangered Species* (1982), *Warning Sign* (1985), and *Impulse* (1986). Just before the Millennium, Hollywood did two more: *Outbreak*, with Dustin Hoffman chasing down an Ebola-type virus, and *The Patriot*, with Steven Seagal trying to vanquish a similarly powerful virus being spread by ideological fanatics.

Ecological disaster has also been prophesied. *Silent Running* (1972), with music by Joan Baez, saw the last forests being cared for on a spaceship by a friend of the earth (Bruce Dern) and three 'droids. When disaster played havoc with Maine, the result was *Prophecy* (1979); when it ruined our cities the example was the dark *Soylent Green*, a 1973 story in which Charlton Heston and Edward G. Robinson (in his last role) tried to get enough to eat in post-catastrophe New York... only to discover that the delicacy that everyone craved was recycled people.

George Orwell's chilling novel, *1984*, required neither nuclear nor biological decimation: just conventional warfare run amok, triggered by ideological frenzy. The book has had two film interpretations: in 1960, with Michael Redgrave, and 1984 (appropriately enough), with John Hurt and Richard Burton (his last role). Orwell's widow disliked the first one so much that she was able to halt its showing in syndication.

A dark future is not just an Orwellian idea. Ray Bradbury's brilliant *Fahrenheit 451* was brought to the screen in 1967 by the French director, François Traufault. In it, Montag (played by Oskar Werner) was a fireman whose job was to burn books. Julie Christie played two parts: Montag's air head wife, and the book-lover who convinced him to rebel.

An antiseptic dystopia was what George Lucas had in mind when he made *THX 138* in 1971. (7) Robert Duvall and Donald Pleasance provided the acting in that somber, thought-provoking study. *Rollerball* (1976) depicted one man's stand against the system, in the not-too-distant future, and *Blade Runner* (1982) brought dark reality to Los Angeles in the twenty-first century. In that one - which rekindled interest in the stories of Philip K. Dick - Harrison Ford's character eliminated androids in the name of corporate democracy. Arnold Schwarzenegger (of *Conan* fame) has cashed in on this theme, too, via five variations on that theme: *The Running Man* (1987), which also was a biting criticism of the media; *The Terminator* (1984), which was a criticism of machine technology; *Terminator 2: Judgment Day* (1991), which held out some hope for the human race; *Terminator 3: Rise of the Machines* (2003), which destroyed that hope, and *The Sixth Day* (2000), which took the cloning controversy into the doomsday category. The city as dystopia was the subject of *Logan's Run* (1976). Not particularly well done, it was nonetheless memorable for the scenes stolen by the "Old Man" (played by Peter Ustinov). See also *Fortress* (but not the sequel), in which Christopher Lambert explains what can happen if the government dictates procreation.

Finally, there is *Planet of the Apes*, the 1968 hit scripted by Rod Serling (of *"Twilight Zone"* fame) that had Charlton Heston (who else) as an astronaut who lands on a world where Darwin's evolutionary theories have gone askew. Its imaginative ending, plus some fine performances, made this a classic (which is more than one could say for its sequels, or the inexplicable remake, in 2000). Like *2001*, it is a story that would be forever identified with the Sixties Generation.

Social Commentary

As the Sixties took hold, the studios turned their attention and their energies to social commentary, taking note of the changes in lifestyle, politics, and leisure. In particular, they cashed in on the increasingly large numbers of college-age movie-goers (supplanting the middle-aged and older patrons who had been the dominant group of customers).

Lifestyles

The most pungent commentary was the one that dealt with how

people really lived, and on that score movie audiences were bombarded with soap opera morality (first inspired by the 1957 release, **Peyton Place**, and its sequel); **Where the Boys Are** (a 1960 bit of fluff that may have signaled the end of innocence, regarding boy-girl get-togethers); the first frank discussions of lesbianism (**The Fox**, in 1968, with Sandy Dennis and Anne Heywood); male homosexuality (**The Boys in the Band**, 1970); marital swaps (**Bob and Carol and Ted and Alice**, 1969); free love (**Carnal Knowledge**, 1971, with Jack Nicholson and Art Garfunkel); incest (**The Savage is Loose**, 1976, with George C. Scott and Trish Van Devere); transvestism (**Tootsie**, with Dustin Hoffman; **Victor/Victoria**, with Julie Andrews, 1982); and men having babies (**Junior**, 1994), with Arnold Schwarzenegger as the first man to be so honored.

Along the way, Audrey Hepburn was a call-girl-turned-good-girl (with George Peppard's help) in Truman Capote's **Breakfast at Tiffany's** (1962), and feminism was subtly evident in the innocent Sixties comedy, **Sex and the Single Girl** (1965). During the Seventies a lot of these themes got more earnest treatment, as in Jane Fonda's **Klute** (1971), and **Deliverance** (1972). **Klute** was a frank and intelligent look at the world of a prostitute, and earned Fonda an Oscar; **Deliverance** shocked many moviegoers (and critics), with its hard-hitting commentary on the subject of male rape. There are the changing lifestyles of the nuclear family in Dustin Hoffman's **Kramer vs. Kramer** (1979), which introduced viewers to the modest talents of Meryl Streep. There were some disquieting looks

128

at what happens when "scorned women" get even: Glenn Close's *Fatal Attraction* (1987) and Michael Crichton's *Disclosure* (1995).

Alienation

At the heart of social commentary was alienation, for the Sixties ripped society apart, first with numerous political killings, then the war in Vietnam, and finally the controversial "drug scene." *On the Waterfront*, Marlon Brando's springboard to fame, was the obvious precursor, and by the Sixties there was alienation aplenty, from Rod Steiger's *The Pawnbroker* (1965), to Mary McCarthy's *The Group* (1966), to Burt Lancaster's *The Swimmer*, to Jacqueline Susann's drug-infested *Valley of the Dolls* (1968).

Homelessness has been topical only in recent years. It has been dealt with tastelessly (Mel Brooks' *Life Stinks*), and eclectically (*The Fisher King*), both 1991. In the latter, Robin Williams misplaced his talents in a quasi-sympathetic look at homelessness by exhibiting a character whose wanderings were part Zen and part hooey. *Midnight Cowboy* effectively opened Pandora's box in 1969, and all heretofore socially unacceptable themes paraded across the screen, urged on by brilliant performances from Dustin Hoffman and Jon Voight. They were passed over for Best Actor in favor of John Wayne (*True Grit*).

Perhaps as an Establishment "rebuttal," Hollywood offered *The Last Picture Show* in which Ben Johnson showed, in black and white, the decadence and stagnation of a small Texas town, but in such a way as not to challenge the fabric of American society (1972). An early Steven Spielberg farce, *The Sugarland Express* (1974) countered that, lampooning Texans and consequently getting boycotted in a number of Texas towns. He learned it was not nice to poke fun at The Big Wide Wonderful.

The pinnacle of alienation films, though, may be *The Big Chill* (1984), which displayed a reunion of Sixties mavericks two decades after their radical days at the University of Michigan. One soon discovers, however, that their ideals have been sacrificed, some in the name of greed. It was imminently salable in the Weighty Eighties.

Counterculture

The "in" word of the Sixties was "Counterculture," and many studios cashed in on "the movements" (whatever the times fashioned them to be). Inspired a decade earlier by James Dean's *Rebel Without a Cause* (1956), there was the celebration of shocking amorality (*Blow-Up*, 1967), which was crucified by the Catholic Legion of Decency; some confusion about life after college (Dustin Hoffman's *The Graduate*, 1968); and Richard Benjamin's free-wheeling and very erratic *Goodbye, Columbus*

(1969). There was also Arlo Guthrie's **Alice's Restaurant** (1969), and the seminal "statement film:" **Easy Rider** (also 1969). That was the low budget/ big return flick with Peter Fonda (Jane's brother), Dennis Hopper, and Jack Nicholson looking for the "real America," and finding it... at the business end of a shotgun, down a rural road in the deep South.

Easy Rider was tame, compared with **Zabriskie Point** (1970). While Fonda and Hopper had been content to find America, the creators of **ZP** wanted to reconstruct It along very radical lines. It was nothing less than a call to political revolution, and was heatedly investigated by the U.S. Attorney's office. Staid old MGM took a lot of heat: the Right believed the studio went too far in its pronouncements; the Left was just as sure it did not go far enough. Crew members testified that the production was anti-American, and the director admitted that he made it to conform with his Marxist leanings. Before it was finished, MGM made cuts, then released the film without fanfare ... and breathed a sigh of relief when it died at the box office. Trying to find a print anywhere is sheer wizardry; it has never been shown on television.

1970 was the year **Woodstock** made its way into movie houses. That extravaganza, which chronicled three days of peace and love (and some marvelous music), has been shown only infrequently on television, with major cuts. Like **ZP**, your best bet is to buy or rent a copy.

If **ZP** angered Hollywood, then **RPM** (1970) brought quick relief. That sluggish and improbable Anthony Quinn-Ann Margret exercise showed campus militancy, but in such a sophomoric way (by design) that it was an embarrassment to students everywhere. Diehards responded with *The Strawberry Statement* (1971), depicting the student takeover of Columbia University in 1968. In the same year came *Billy Jack*, which quickly became a cult favorite and helped promote Indian pride... even though it almost didn't make it to the theaters. The Powers That Be at first decreed it to be too anti-law and order (they didn't want another *ZP*). Only when the wife of the president of Warner Brothers openly embraced it was it released. Those who opposed the decision rejoiced when a 1975 sequel had nothing to commend it... and was a flop.

The hair-pulling continued, as Peter Fonda revved it up one more time (in 1974) with *Dirty Mary, Crazy Larry*. By 1975, though, the fire had gone out, and the Sixties Generation had yielded to "the 'Septic Seventies," and that group's preference for Calvin Klein jeans, Gucci loafers, and stock portfolios. When Dustin Hoffman made the grossly irreverent *Lenny* in 1975 (to memorialize Sixties humorist-activist Lenny Bruce), it fell on deaf ears. So, too, did *HAIR* (1979). Beautiful music notwithstanding, it just didn't have the electricity of the 1960s Broadway play.

Psychological Considerations

This was also a breakthrough time for history's "dark side." In 1957

Hollywood presented *Fear Strikes Out*, about the mental breakdown of popular Boston Red Sox baseball star, Jimmy Piersall. It was buried in a syrupy, traditional love story. In the early Sixties Hollywood began to mature. In 1963, for instance, comic actor Jack Lemmon proved his versatility with a riveting performance as an alcoholic, in *The Days of Wine and Roses*. It effectively made the statement that alcoholism is a disease. In 1968, with the Vietnam War escalating, urban crime shooting upward, and traditional morality going to hell, audiences cheered *The Heart is a Lonely Hunter*, starring Alan Arkin. Still, the producers managed to play a few tricks on everyone. Carson McCullers' 1940 book, upon which the movie was based, was a study about the horrors of the Depression: labor unrest, bigotry, fascism, and anti-Semitism. All of that was glossed over in the film version. Only the reality of poverty was left intact (for it alone knows no season).

Ideological concerns played no part in the making of the 1969 classic, *Charly*, the performance of a lifetime for Cliff Robertson. *Charly* was the story of a mentally-retarded young man, who doctors try to bring to normality with a "wonder drug" - only to learn that the drug's effect is temporary. Charly, who had become bright and articulate, ends as he had begun: a child in an adult's body. William Hurt's heart-rending *Children of a Lesser God* (1987), Dustin Hoffman's masterful *Rain Man* (1988), Harrison Ford's *Regarding Henry* (1991), and Robert DeNiro's *Awakenings* (1992) similarly touched audiences. The Nineties also produced a bumper crop on the subject of autism: *Silent Fall*, with Richard Dreyfuss, *House of Cards*, with Tommy Lee Jones, and *Mercury Rising*, with Bruce Willis.

Insanity has become a popular theme in our age of Future Shock. Carrie Snodgrass drew rave reviews as a victim, in *The Diary of a Mad Housewife* (1970), and two decades later Barbra Streisand disappointed patrons with her performance in *Nuts* (1989). In *The Hospital* (1972), George C. Scott and Diana Rigg awkwardly translated Paddy Chayevsky's fine play to the silver screen.

The ultimate "asylum films" are *One Flew Over the Cuckoo's Nest* (1976) and *The Ninth Configuration* (1984). In the first, Jack Nicholson gave a soul-crushing performance as McMurphy (8), and in the second, Stacey Keach turned in the finest job of his career... just before going through his own, real-life mental problems.

Race

Hollywood "discovered" race in the Sixties - or so it seemed. Heretofore (with the exception of the heavily censored and boycotted *Native Son*, in 1951), Hollywood was content to have audiences watch banal stereotypes of the "Amos and Andy" type. That began to change in 1962 (a year before Martin Luther King's presence was felt) with *To Kill a*

Mockingbird. That one was about Gregory Peck's character defending a southern Black man accused of murder. Following that was *Lilies of the Field*, which launched Sidney Poitier's career. Next came the tender and very touching *A Patch of Blue* (1966), with his character befriending an abused blind white girl. But 1967 was *the* year: Michael Caine and Jane Fonda opened the year with an awful film (*Hurry Sundown*), and Poitier reached the peak of his powers with three blockbusters. The first, *To Sir, With Love*, showed him as a teacher in a poor section of London; the second was *Guess Who's Coming to Dinner?*, wherein he played opposite Spencer Tracy (in his last role) and Katharine Hepburn, informing them that he was going to marry their daughter. Very thought-provoking was *In the Heat of the Night*, a masterpiece in the race debate, set against the backdrop of a sleepy southern town. Rod Steiger was at his best as the bigoted sheriff, and deserved his Oscar for Best Supporting Actor.

But then, something happened. King was assassinated, the Kennedy clan was similarly reduced, and racial enlightenment - which never was a high priority in America - slipped back a notch or two. *Shaft*, made during the law and order Nixon years, offended mainstream America (because of its "Black-is-beautiful" message), and not even the proto-historical "*Roots*" (a television series, which its creator later said was a sham), the fictional *Autobiography of Miss Jane Pittman*, or *Sounder*, were enough to take the edge off racial disgruntlement. Still, interested parties kept trying. Edward James Olmos burst upon the scene in the 1980s as one crusader, first with a look at the L.A. riots of 1943 (*Zoot Suit*, 1981). Next was *Wolfen* (1985), which made a statement about the plight of American Indians, and *Stand and Deliver* (1988), a not very well done story about how hard it was to teach Hispanics. Predictably, liberal director Steven Spielberg made a contribution. *The Color Purple* (1987) showed the degradation that Blacks suffered in a much earlier time. Since it was told from a woman's point of view, it could also seen as a feminist film. In *Driving Miss Daisy* (1990), Jessica Tandy and Morgan Freeman downplayed racial differences and pleased general audiences. (9)

Commercialism

Certainly of importance in the alteration of history by Hollywood has been commercialism. Perhaps Woody Allen said it best in 1969: *Take the Money and Run*. Irreverence of the Almighty Dollar got a huge boost from Spielberg's *Jaws* the 1975 Moby Dick-reincarnation about summer money in the beach town of Amity. Cuba's dictator Fidel Castro called it his favorite film. To him, it showed America's true perspective on values. A stellar cast (Richard Dreyfuss, Robert Shaw, and Roy Scheider) told a classic horror story, with one notable departure from Melville's tale: in *Moby Dick*, Ahab was the real villain. One almost feels sorry for the Great White Whale. In *Jaws*, no one shed any tears over the demise of the

Great White Shark, even though it, like Melville's behemoth, was simply living (and feeding) in its natural environment. In both cases, man was the intruder.

Nashville appeared the same year, and that biting criticism, aimed at the banality of country music, infuriated the good people of Nashville so much that they declared director Robert Altman *persona non grata*. In 1976 the studios opened up another controversy, with **Network**. That one, with William Holden and Peter Finch handling most of the acting chores, was an attempt to expose the heartlessness and the ruthlessness of the television industry. Not nearly as effective were **Broadcast News** and **Switching Channels** (both 1988), which conspiratorialists believed was the media's attempt to water down the controversy.

In 1977 Hollywood tried to explain what happened to people when slowdowns in the economy cost them their jobs. The result was **Fun With Dick and Jane**, a well-done bit of black humor, with Jane Fonda and George Segal coming up with a creative (and funny) resolution to their dilemma. The climax to this reinvestigation of values may have come in 1981, with **Arthur**, a romp through New York's aristocracy, with Sir John Gielgud getting a much-deserved Oscar for his portrayal of a butler who had to put up with the juvenile behavior of a spoiled, rich alcoholic (Dudley Moore). If Castro liked **Jaws**, he must have loved **Arthur**.

Law and Order

Hollywood has liked this category almost as much as it has liked westerns, for it transcends history, politics, and sociology. Most films in this genre have been unabashedly pro-establishment, but by odd circumstance two early entries glorified the criminal: *Little Caesar* (1930), with Edward G. Robinson, and *Public Enemy* (1931), with James Cagney. The Cagney film outraged the Establishment so much that the Catholic Legion of Decency was created in its wake as a public censor.

It is not surprising that we do not encounter any noteworthy law and order films for more than two decades; and when they did appear, they are pro-Establishment: *The Asphalt Jungle* (1950), *Blackboard Jungle* (1955), and *Big House, U.S.A.* (1955). All three condemned gangs, rebellious youth in school, and youth who ended up in prison.

The lone quality law and order flick of the Fifties appeared in 1957 and was called *Twelve Angry Men*. It melded a superb cast into a search of their souls for the determination of the guilt or innocence of a young man from the other side of the tracks. Prejudice, bigotry, and narrow-mindedness are all laid bare as the twelve jurors struggle to do the right thing. It has become a screen classic. It was remade (badly) as an homage to political correctness.

Our fascination with crime increased in the 1960s. *Cape Fear* (1962;

remade 1993), *In Cold Blood* (1968), and *The Boston Strangler* (1969) held no glory for anyone. As the Counterculture reached its zenith, so did Hollywood's empathy with change. A good example of that is *Bonny and Clyde*, the 1967 Warren Beatty-Faye Dunaway retelling of the notorious Clyde Barrow gang of the 1930s. With its gangster-as-folk-hero theme, most of the press railed against it, led by *New York Times* critic, Bosley Crowther. The public protested his attacks so loudly that the *Times* fired him. (10)

Alas, the Establishment has never given ground easily. In the Nixon Seventies traditional interpretations of law and order returned, and movie audiences did an about face and asked for reactionary vehicles like *Dirty Harry* (1972), and other Clint Eastwood murder and mayhem celebrations (such as *Magnum Force*, 1974, and *The Dead Pool*, 1988).

Charles Bronson rode the crest of this latest wave, becoming a star in mid-life after decades of bit parts in wholly forgettable "B" pictures. Films like *Death Wish* (1974) and *Telefon* (1978) lined his pockets and those of the studios. The Right enjoyed the antics of *Walking Tall* (1973, plus its sequel). Al Pacino's *Dog Day Afternoon* (1976) was also well-received.

In 1991 *The Silence of the Lambs* won the Best Picture award for its chilling look at an FBI agent tracking down a psychopath. Jodie Foster played the FBI agent (a coup for the women's movement), the Establishment was portrayed as not overly compassionate, and the medical profession (about whom so many Americans had come to distrust) was shown to have slipped a cog or two. It was extremely uncomfortable to watch - until you realized that the story did not make much sense and everyone was over-acting badly. It became really funny (and was spoofed as *The Silence of the Hams*).

So where do *The Godfather* (1972) and its sequels (1975, 1990) fit into this discussion? Probably more as transition films than as law-and-order nightmares. That triptych tried to tell as honestly as possible the rise to power of one immigrant family, and in many ways reminded us of the first law and order films (gangster-as-hero). The first two films delivered superb writing (Mario Puzo), direction (Francis Ford Coppola), and acting (Marlon Brando, Al Pacino, Robert DeNiro, Robert Duvall, and James Caan), and showed us the "human" side of organized crime.

Unfortunately, the long-awaited final installment of the saga was disappointing. Stripped of much of its original cast, it limped along with a poor script and second-rate acting, and obfuscated much of what had gone before. Collectively, the films have given both historians and sociologists much to think about. To be sure, wherever they may belong, the *Godfather* epic has produced history's most lucrative "good guy/bad guy" films.

At this point you probably still have a lot of questions (which is as it should be). Some answers might be found in the following:

Cagin, Seth. *Hollywood Films of the Seventies* (1984);

Fraser, George. *The Hollywood History of the World* (1988);

Gardner, Gerald. *The Censorship Papers: Movie Censorship Letters from the Hays Office, 1934-1968* (1987);

Klein, Michael. *The English Novel and the Movies* (1981);

Mintz, Steven. *Hollywood's America: U. S. History Through Its Films* (1993);

O'Connor, John. *American History/American Film* (1980);

Peary, Gerald. *The Classic American Novel and the Movies* (1977);

_____ , *The Modern American Novel and the Movies* (1978);

Sayre, Nora. *Running Time: Films of the Cold War* (1982);

Shindler, Colin. *Hollywood Goes to War* (1979);

Sklar, Robert. *Movie-Made America: A Cultural History* (1975);

Notes

1. Hollywood has always been divided along ideological lines. Performers of the liberal-left persuasion have included Warren Beatty, Shirley MacLaine, Jane Fonda, Peter Fonda, Donald Sutherland, Jack Nicholson, Walter Matthau, Glenda Jackson, Charles Laughton, Katharine Hepburn, Spencer Tracy, Dustin Hoffman, Ed Asner, Burt Lancaster, Kirk Douglas, Michael Douglas, Will Geer, Marlon Brando, Robert Redford, Humphrey Bogart, Darryl Hannah, Melvyn Douglas, Orson Welles, Paul Newman, Woody Allen, Sidney Poitier, Barbra Streisand, Tommy Lee Jones, and Jason Robards. A sampling of the conservative-right will turn up John Wayne, Frank Sinatra, Mickey Rooney, Ronald Reagan, Gary Cooper,

Helen Hayes, Jimmy Stewart, William Holden, Glenn Ford, Errol Flynn, Clint Eastwood, Lee Marvin, Walter Brennan, Buddy Ebsen, Shirley Temple, Charlton Heston, Charles Bronson, Sylvester Stallone, Bruce Willis, Arnold Schwarzenegger, Cary Grant, Sean Connery, Audrey Hepburn, Jon Voight, Steve McQueen, Tom Selleck, Chuck Norris, Mel Gibson, George C. Scott, Robert Duvall, Ward Bond, Wilford Brimley, and Gary Sinise.

2. Mayer wanted Shirley Temple for the role, but contract problems kept America's "little sweetheart" from getting it. As for the smallest stars: the Singer midgets played the Munchkins, and were a violent and vicious bunch that had to be constantly supervised. (That subplot was the subject of a tasteless, seldom-seen Chevy Chase-Carrie Fisher film, *Under the Rainbow*, made in 1982.) And, yes: Mayer and the other brass *did* almost cut "Over the Rainbow" ... because they thought the song was too slow!

3. *Reds* lost out at the Academy Awards to *Chariots of Fire*, an esthetically pleasing film that trumpeted traditional beliefs and values. A cry of "foul" was heard all the way to Moscow, but in vain: *Chariots* was a better film.

4. The writers and actors made up *Casablanca* as they went along, not knowing until the last day how it would end. Ronald Reagan was considered for the lead (after tough guy actor George Raft had turned it down), but contractual difficulties prevented that from happening.

5. The Donald Sutherland-Leonard Nimoy remake played some tricks on the audience. Thirty minutes into the film, Sutherland's car almost strikes a wild-eyed pedestrian, who's screaming, hysterically, that "they're coming." His identity? Kevin McCarthy, who played the lead in the first screen version. And the cab driver who later takes Sutherland to the airport? Don Siegel, the first movie's director.

6. *Dawn*, together with the *Rambo* films, inspired the Soviets to make

Solo Voyage, a 1986 rebuttal that showed the U.S. as the "evil empire" (cf. with the Arnold Schwarzenegger hit, ***Red Heat***, in 1988). It was never made available for viewing in the U.S. Similarly, ***Gorky Park*** (1987) was trashed in the USSR, and only the success of *glasnost* and Gorbachev made Hollywood change just slightly the film, ***The Hunt for Red October*** (1990). It featured Sean Connery as a Soviet submarine captain who did not wish to start World War III. Otherwise, the novel by Tom Clancy ("the author laureate of the Pentagon") was avowedly anti-Soviet. So was ***The Russia House***, a Connery film (that flopped), also in 1990.

7. Lucas, who gave the world ***Star Wars*** six years later, had a hard time selling ***THX***. He succeeded only after making extensive budget cuts, and requiring much of the shooting be done in the not-yet-completed BART tubes in San Francisco. If you look closely, you'll see a car in ***American Graffiti*** sporting the license plate, THX 138.

8. Jack Nicholson almost did not get the role. Director Michael Douglas wanted his father, Kirk, for the part (he had done the role on Broadway in 1963). Kirk was considered "too old" (he was 60, whereas Nicholson was just 39), so Jack got the part... and subsequently the Oscar for Best Actor. Nine years later, the elder Douglas got the role, substituting a nursing home for the asylum in a film called ***Amos***.

9. In 1984 Hollywood gave racism a twist in ***A Soldier's Story***, dealing with segregated Army units in the South. The ultimate "Eighties treatment," though, may have been ***Mississippi Burning*** (1988). In that one, the FBI was seen as more interested than they really were in solving a racial murder in 1963. Six months passed, in fact, before public pressure motivated them to investigate.

10. Beatty wanted his sister (Shirley MacLaine) to co-star. Director Penn balked (too close to incest?). Still, the film won numerous awards, and (save for Crowther) critical acclaim, despite the bloodiest climax scene moviegoers had ever seen.

II. Europe

Culture, Civilization, and History

Since the late 1920s, Will Durant has delighted readers with his accounts of history and philosophy. Among his many books was *The Story of Civilization*, an eleven volume treatment that took half a century to complete.

What follows is a summation of his views on the nature of history and civilization, taken from Volume I (*Our Oriental Heritage*), and his views of history, with the help of his wife, Ariel, in *Lessons of History*.

Civilization is social order promoting cultural creation. It is comprised of four elements: economic provision; political organization; moral traditions; and the pursuit of knowledge and the arts.

Civilization suggests the city: it is the habit of civility. It is not a great people that makes civilization; it is great civilizations which make people.

Economic elements of civilization start with hunting - the quest for food and wars for security and mastery, besides which all wars are but a little noise. Agriculture is next (a discovery made by women). After that is industry, beginning with fire. Last is trade.

The economic organization of civilization means that people, both primitive and modern, own land. Communal ownership is ancient, and is called communism. It offers security, whereas individualism can bring wealth, insecurity, and slavery. It intensifies competition and makes man feel poverty with bitterness. Communism invokes the idea of a simpler and more equal life.

As for the political elements of civilization: man is *not* willingly a political animal; he dares not love society so much as he fears solitude. Wars make for the existence of politics, the enslavement of prisoners, the subordination of classes, and the growth of government.

Law is something that comes with property, marriage and government. Primitive societies learned to get along without it. The first step in the evolution of law was revenge (Hammurabi); the second was the substitution of damages for revenge. Then came the obligation to prevent and punish wrongdoing.

There are moral elements in civilization: marriage is the association of mates for the having and caring of offspring. Individual marriage came through the desire of the male to have "cheap slaves." Consequently, polygamy was predominant in the primitive world. Romantic love was late in coming (the Middle Ages). Virginity changed from being a fault to being a virtue with the institution of property (to the Greeks, the word "virgin" pertained only to women). "Morality is the sum of the prejudices of a community," wrote Anatole France. Dishonesty is not as ancient as greed, for hunger is older than property. Dishonesty rose with civilization, because there are more things to be stolen, and "education makes man clever."

On the subject of religion: fear, said Lucretius, was the first mother of the gods (the fear of death). Most human gods were idealized dead men. Gradually, the cult of the ghost became ancestor worship - and was to be feared. Religion arose not out of sacerdotal invention or chicanery, but of persistent wonder, fear, insecurity, hopefulness and loneliness. The moral function of religion is to conserve established values, not create new ones.

ÐÐÐÐÐÐÐ

In 1968 the Durants published *Lessons of History*. The points they made are summarized below.

History and the Earth. The Durants begin with a definition, regarding history as simply "the events or record of the past"... whose first lesson is modesty. Man's place in the cosmic arena is transitory, especially when confronted by the elements of geology, geography and climate. "All of those limit our actions," but they also inspire us: for "man, not the earth, makes civilization."

Biology and History. History is a "fragment of biology": the laws of biology are the fundamental lessons of history. In particular, man is subject to the processes and the "trials of evolution," that allow only the fittest to live. From that, it follows that the first biological lesson of history is competition. Cooperation is important, but survives only "because it is a tool of competition."

The second biological lesson of history is that life is selective; that we are all born *unfree* and *unequal* and must always be proving ourselves, especially as civilization becomes more complex. "Freedom and equality are sworn and everlasting enemies," for it is only the person who is below average who desires equality... and after that "equality" has been achieved he or she wishes to be higher still.

The third biological lesson is that life must breed, yet carefully. If man is reckless, then famine, pestilence and war will undermine that lesson. Balance in breeding is imperative, but man has not been very intelligent in that regard. Even if the existing agricultural knowledge were everywhere applied and could feed twice the present population, there would soon be the paradoxical problem of too many mouths to feed. To remedy this, parentage should be based on the principle of health (*à la* ancient Sparta), and not "sexual agitation." Intellect is discounted as a determinant: "philosophers are not the fittest material from which to breed the race."

Race and History. Racism is the norm in history, and no civilization is immune. In 1899, Houston Stewart Chamberlain espoused white racism for the British; seventeen years later Madison Grant was doing the same thing for America. Grant's contained a warning: if certain "measures" were not soon taken, the Nordic race would fall from power by the year 2000, with western civilization being supplanted by one from the East. "History is color-blind." Civilization can be developed "under almost any skin."

Character and History. "Society is founded not on the ideals but on the nature of man." How much? Though there has been some change through the centuries, history shows little alteration in the conduct of Mankind. The means change, but the motives and the ends remain the same.

Morals and History. Man's numerous moral codes "are negligible." They differ in time and place; they have to be adjusted to historical and environmental conditions. Man has problems with codes. "Man has never reconciled himself to the Ten Commandments."

Religion and History. This is the longest and most substantive chapter. Only when priests used fear and ritual to support morality and law did religion become both "a force vital and rival to the state." Thereupon, the state told the people that the local codes had been dictated by the gods, thus giving us the origins of theocracy.

Although the Church often has served the state, one must note the frequency with which it has claimed the "right to stand above all states." Espousing divine origin, the Church offered itself to man as a "last court," yet most of its leaders were "biased, venal or extortionate," riddled with more fraud than their pagan predecessors.

History has justified the Church in the belief that the masses desire a religion that is "rich in miracle, mystery and myth." The Church dares not alter the doctrines "that reason smiles at," for such changes would disillusion those millions who have been given a singular view of life.

Is there a god? "If by God we mean a supreme being, history does not support a god." Indeed, history remains an act of natural selection; and if history were to select any supernatural agent, it most likely would be the dualism of Zoroaster: there is not just the contest between 'good' and 'evil,' but a *different* perception of those terms. Good is that which survives. "The universe has no prejudice in favor of Christ as against Ghenghis Khan."

Since Zoroaster, there have been numerous attempts to define man's role *vis-à-vis* God. The Deists made God vague; the Protestants of the sixteenth century exposed the "miracles" of the Catholics. The propaganda of "patriotism, capitalism or Communism" succeeds due to the inclusion of a supernatural creed and moral code. Catholicism survives because it appeals to imagination, to hope and to the senses. It has sacrificed intellect, especially in modern times when most converts seem to be won to satisfy ideological crusades. "As long as there is poverty, there will be gods."

Economics and History. The earliest economics revolved around agriculture, and soon that meant the creation of slavery. All civilizations have experienced that combination: all have suffered from its abuse. It contributed to the death of some civilizations (like Rome), and the restructuring of others (like the United States).

Essentially, it was a natural phenomenon, for it was an important way of concentrating wealth. The individual concentration of wealth is the norm; the redistribution of wealth is not only hard to find, but an almost impossible scenario, given the nature of man.

Socialism and History. Socialism is not a modern invention - it has always been a factor in Western Civilization. The Ptolemies in Egypt were devotees of state socialism. Diocletian was a Roman Socialist who oversaw a perpetual war economy. China has had innumerable attempts: Wang Mand, was a millionaire who scattered his riches to the poor in 20 A.D.; he nationalized farms and made low interest loans. The longest-lasting socialistic society was that of the Incas.

Nowadays the Church tends to disapprove of socialism, but this was not always so. Preacher Thomas Münzer recruited an army of peasants in the Reformation, inspired them with tales of Communism among the Apostles, and led them to battle. Anabaptists followed this example by practicing communism for nearly one hundred years.

Marx and Engels expected that socialism would first come in industrial Britain. It came instead to proto-industrial Russia. Ultimately, as Marx observed, "East is West and West is East, and soon the twain shall meet." History is on the side of the socialists.

Government and History. The first condition of freedom "is its limitation," and it is the prime task of government to establish order. Given the primacy in history of the government over the individual, we find that monarchy is "the most natural" form of government. Democracies, by contrast, "have been hectic interludes," existing really only in modern times as a lasting force. Even during Pericles' time the aristocracy ruled, and the American Revolution was not only a revolt of colonists against a distant government, but also an "uprising of a native middle class against an imported aristocracy."

Democracy is the hardest form of government to achieve, because it requires a "wide spread" of intelligence, which, historically, is "perpetually retarded by the fertility of the simple." Ignorance thus becomes a mixed blessing : one can fool enough of the people enough of the time to run a large (democratic) country.

History and War. This is the bleakest of all the chapters, for it centers around the incontestable fact that in all of history only 268 years have seen no war... and the not entirely incontestable belief that man, therefore, delights in the promulgation of war.

"War, or competition, is the father of all things; peace is an unstable equilibrium."

Growth and Decay. If, as the Durants define it, civilization is "a social order promoting cultural creation," history is largely a copycat (though it repeats itself "only in outline"). Every year is an adventure, with the question asked: are we going forward, or backward?

The nineteenth century writer Saint-Simon was sure that socialism would begin a new organic Age of unified belief, organization and stability. Oswald Spengler took his ideas and looked backward to a nobility ruling the twentieth century. When civilization declines, it is because the political or intellectual leaders "fail to meet the challenges of change." There is a caution: civilizations do not really "die;" they continue under someone else as "the generation of the racial soul."

Is Progress Real? Man has produced no substantive changes in his nature. With that in mind, all of his technological advances have to be written off as just new means of achieving old ends. Progress is "the increasing control of the environment by life. If the present stage is an advance in the control of that environment, then the progress is real. If it is not..."

Finally: if education is the "transmission of civilization," then we are progressing. We have not yet surpassed the "selected geniuses of antiquity," but we have raised the level of knowledge beyond any age that has ever had.

Principal Political Philosophies
of the Modern World

Probably the most heated discussions and debates of the twentieth century concerned political philosophy. Summarized below are the most important and influential political philosophies that impacted that century, as defined by their creators.

Socialism/Communism. *Marxism:* after Karl Marx and Friedrich Engels, 19th Century.

To cancel out human misery and to ensure universal happiness, Marx and Engels believed it was necessary to abolish private property, and redistribute it in a spirit of collectivization. They believed it was necessary to end all class distinctions (upper, middle, lower); abolish the church and its hierarchy (but not religion); and to realize the concept of community, via the eventual abolition of the State.

To accomplish this, there must be a community of goods and services, in which a perfect equality of conditions would prevail (*"to each according to one's needs"*). This must necessarily be anti-capitalist, because capitalism historically has divided people, producing misery, disharmony and abject poverty for the greater number(*"that mode of production in which human labor power has become a commodity"*).

Society evolved from feudalism, through mercantilism, to capitalism, and to socialism (a temporary step, ruled by a benevolent "dictatorship of the proletariat"). At some undefined point in the future, a revolution by workers and peasants will bring about true communism - which Marx defined as a classless, stateless society.

This scenario ("scientific Marxism") exists only in theory, partly because compromise with dissident groups is necessary to unite working people in common cause; and partly (according to opponents), because it fails to consider the non-ideological nature of man.

Leninism: **after Vladimir Ilich Ulyanov, Bolshevik champion of the Second Russian Revolution of 1917; ruler of the USSR, 1917-24.**

Lenin discarded the ideas of several nineteenth century Utopians (Fourier, Owen, St.-Simon), and modified Marxism: *"communism is socialism plus electricity."* He embraced Marx' idea of economic determinism - arguing that man's material wants are "his great curse." It's the purpose of a strong state (acting in behalf of common people) to "cleanse" man of this "failing."

154

Unlike Marx, Lenin saw that class consciousness must be instilled in the people through "re-education" (indoctrination). Unlike Leon Trotsky (Menshevik opponent; later Bolshevik comrade), Lenin did not see the need for "world communism" until after communism first had been consolidated in Russia.

Russia (after 1921, the Soviet Union) was to be ruled by the Communist Party: an *élite* (less than ten per cent of the populace) that was to be an *"elastic superstructure"* to act in behalf of the people via unanimous consent. The primary focal group was to be the proletariat; peasants were not to be trusted, owing to their traditional conservatism.

Lenin believed in the sacrifice of "basic freedoms" until communism could be achieved, and the transitional state (Socialism) was no longer necessary. When? In Marx' view, the State will "wither away;" but not even Lenin knew when that would be. Ideologically, Leninism aimed at a more practicable adaptation of Marxism.

Stalinism: after Josef Vissiaronovich Djugashvili; ruler of the USSR, 1928-53.

Not quite the intellectual that Lenin and Trotsky were, Stalin was often preoccupied with semantics. In a rightward move away from Trotsky (his main rival after Lenin's death), he espoused the idea of "socialism in one country." He called Marxism a "science," and periodically "modi-fied" it, to bring it in line with ever-changing conditions.

Collectivization of agriculture was essential. It was to be enforced ab-solutely (e. g., the elimination of *kulaks*, or "rich peasants"). Opposition - by peasants or anyone else - was considered "counterrevolutionary," and was to be repressed via systematic purges.

Unlike Lenin and Trotsky's quasi-isolationism, Stalin believed that a precise and thorough interaction with other socialist states was vital (*Comintern*), and would lay the groundwork for revolution in "backwards areas" (a concept which was foreign to Marx). Stalinism ultimately dis-solved into a "cult of the personality," and thus more resembled tsarism than Bolshevism.

Italian Fascism: after Benito Mussolini, Socialist in World War I; in power, 1922-45.

Mussolini provided fascism with its philosophical basis. This included *élitism*, with a subservience to the will of *Il Duce* ("the leader;" a Hegelian concept). He attempted to reconstruct the "glorious Roman past," with the assistance of modern ideas such as futurism.

No opposition to the fascist party was tolerated. The State would rule, through a partnership with big business (corporatism), and the Catholic

Church (for legitimacy). At bottom, fascism was a hodge-podge of ideas that failed the test of a consistent ideological philosophy.

German National Socialism [Nazism]: **after Adolf Hitler; in power, 1933-45.**

This was another "pseudo-ideology," born out of Imperial Germany's defeat in World War I. Like Italian fascism, it drew much of its support from the urban middle class, for whom vengeance (*Dolchstoss)* was a motive force.

The concept of Herder's *Volksgeist* ("national spirit [destiny]") was reinforced by a strong belief in Germany's mythic past. To achieve this it was necessary to institute cultural and racial purity (which was largely absent from Italy). It was aimed primarily at the Jews, who allegedly profited from Germany's plight and were instrumental in the country's downfall in World War I.

Nazis despised the West for the creation of the liberal Weimar Republic (1918-33), and for supporting Zionism and tolerating communism. Anti-Semitic tactics included popularizing the fraudulent ***Protocols of the Elders of Zion.*** Both Jews and Communists were excoriated in Hitler's ***Mein Kampf*** (*My Struggle*).

In Nazism, *Der Führer* ("the leader") was the voice of all Germany, guided by a *Führerprinzip* ("leader-principle"), much like Italy. Hitler saw himself as a messiah to racially pure, Aryan Germans. Nationalism and imperialism were vital for Germany's rise to domination.

Toward these ends, Hitler engineered consolidation (*Gleichschaltung*), via terror tactics, such as the employment of a State police (*Gestapo)*. All opposition was crushed.

Communism and Fascism: *Similarities*...

Both Left- and Right-wing ideologies were authoritarian in practice; Stalin even attempted total personal control (totalitarianism). Both ideologies demonstrated a strong and powerful *élitism*. Both were monolithic: one political party represented the whole; both were passionately anti-democratic. In both, the economic system depended on the political system, and was dictated by it.

...and Differences.

Communism has a definite theoretical basis, grounded not in emotion but in reason; essentially, fascism is an emotional non-ideology. With the exception of Stalin, communism does not rely as much on charisma as fascism does. Theoretically, communism abhors materialism in all its forms; fascism restricts materialism, but glorifies the individual.

Communism trumpets the equality of man; fascism despises egalitarianism. Communism requires a definite break with the past and is optimistic about the future; fascism rekindles the past. Communism draws most of its support from workers; fascism's main support is from middle and upper classes. Communism aims at the complete dissolution of the state; fascism strives toward a strong, eternal state that will act in the people's behalf.

The Grand Enigma: Continuity and Change in Russian History, from Peter the Great to the Present

Russia has mesmerized and befuddled historians for centuries. This essay began taking shape in 1970, and has been rewritten too many times to count. The current iteration takes the story down through the Putin years of post-Soviet Russia.

In the late 1820s, the French Comte, Alexis de Tocqueville, came to the United States to study our customs, our institutions, and our beliefs. The upshot of that study was **Democracy in America**, a book which continues to sell well on both sides of the Atlantic nearly two centuries later.

In that book - which was written primarily to explain why our revolution had worked, and what France might learn from it - Tocqueville made a bold prediction. "Two nations," he wrote, "would have a mandate from heaven to rule the world in the next century." One, not surprisingly, was the United States. The other was Russia.

By making that forecast for the twentieth century, Tocqueville unwittingly added his name to a long list of "Russia-watchers:" scholars, politicians, statesmen... all of them fascinated, intrigued, bewildered, and even frightened by the Russian bear. It is a subject that has only gained in intensity as the developments of that century bore out his predictions as prophecy.

Especially since 1917, this interest (some say "obsession") with Russia has magnified. During the 1920s, Russia (renamed the Soviet Union) was an object of curiosity. Its internal situation was regarded by the West as unstable, and its plans abroad aroused fear. In the Depression-ridden 1930s, the USSR astonished many with its resiliency and its surge toward international power. During World War II it lost more than 20 million people, yet emerged victorious.

After 1945, the Cold War rose and fell in varying degrees of intensity, with Russia still no less quixotic (and no less interested in world power). The questions (at least among the truth seekers) remained the same that had been asked for at least two centuries: how did Russia get to this point? Was modern Russia noticeably different from Holy Russia? Or the same?

The following essay seeks some answers to these questions. Necessarily brief, it does not endeavor to treat all areas of Russian history with equanimity. Many areas are not treated at all. Rather, the purpose is to inspire curiosity, in the hope that the reader will want to learn more about what Britain's Prime Minister, Winston Churchill, called "a riddle wrapped up in a mystery inside an enigma."

ℛℛℛℛℛℛℛ

For more than two centuries there has been no letup in the outpouring of information on Peter the Great. His reign has been identified either as one signifying a break with the past, or one that had a camouflaged attachment to the *status quo*. (1) To more than a few students of Russian history, Peter belongs in the progressive camp. He was a ruler who, at a "great divide in history," earnestly sought to eliminate Russia's backwardness by utilizing the technical advances that had propelled western Europe into the modern world. (2) In that regard, his aims were clear: "to use the West to overcome the West" - and to overcome Russia. (3)

To this school of thought, foremost in the effort toward modernization was the establishment of Russia as a power, a goal which eluded his predecessors. Peter built an army (comprised of all classes of the population) and the nucleus of a navy (with the help of Holland and Britain), via some rigid tax policies. (4) This helped Russia establish a fledgling empire, but it is noteworthy that the populace - and especially the peasants - paid heavily for this. It was a foretaste of continuity that one

162

would find throughout the rest of the Romanov dynasty and beyond.

In terms of form, nearly everything changed in Russia. A law of 1707, for example, divided the country into eight provinces, each controlled by governors who were answerable only to the tsar. (5) This adjustment in the administrative process - which survived until 1917 and facilitated the collection of mammoth taxes - fell into disrepair. Through this "adjustment," the individual office-holder was far more influential than ever before, but corruption, an old acquaintance in Russian history, escalated. (6) Opposition, from top to bottom, stalled much of this "reform spirit."

It was in the area of thought and culture that Peter made a major directional change. Though Russia and Europe had much in common during the Middle Ages, isolation had cut Russia off from the development of scholasticism and the rekindling of science that propelled Italy, France, Holland and Britain into a Renaissance that Russia never had. Peter embraced these ideas, and helped Russia create the nucleus of a system of modern education. (7) It was not really progressive, though: the main beneficiaries of a western-type schooling were the soldiers and sailors of his army and navy, and the purpose was functional rather than academic. Most Russians would have to wait a long time for a universal educational system. (8)

Regardless, these steps alarmed the Russian Orthodox Church, an institution which for centuries enjoyed absolute control in instructional matters. Influenced by aftershocks of the schism of the 1660s, the

163

Church treated Peter's entire "westward conversion" with contempt. He became the "anti-Christ," bent on forcing westernization at the sacrifice of Russia's "glorious past." (9) In the end, though, the Church was unable to motivate the Russian people against their tsar, and by 1721 had become an integral part of the bureaucracy. (10) Tsarist control in that area appeared to be complete. (11)

Perhaps most significant was the effect that these reforms had upon the *dvoriane* (landed gentry). Peter drew more and more young men from that estate into military service, often placing them alongside serfs (much to the gentry's displeasure). (12) To clarify the gentry's position *vis-à-vis* the tsar, Peter created a "Table of Ranks," establishing a tradition of "glorified government service" which lasted, despite numerous attacks, until 1917. (13)

It can be argued that Petrine reforms did not so much push Russia ahead, as it *pulled* Russia within view of its more advanced, western neighbors. Thanks to a desire for autocracy at home and for power on the international scene (wars with Sweden, *e. g.,*), gentry and peasants alike tended to be suspicious and non-supportive. Peter tried to check this, and to dispel growing unrest, with another bureaucratic agency: the secret police. He thus communicated that he would use any device to insure "a new legitimization of the Russian autocracy through western absolutist methods." (14)

The seventy-five years following Peter's death - the "era of palace revolutions" - offered serious departures from, as well as imitations of, Peter's reforms. Almost immediately, Catherine I sought to appease a highly alienated nobility as a *quid pro quo* for her own modest designs. When that failed, she won support with the actions of the Guards regiments and the secret police. She tried, and mostly succeeded, in keeping the opposition in check. (15)

Her reign was brief and was followed by Anne, whose chief innovation was the creation of a cabinet (in lieu of a council), which relied heavily on Germans and other foreigners. Peter had good luck with *his* foreign advisors (especially the Dutch), but Anne's cabinet did not enjoy a long life: it was terminated during the next *régime*, in line with Elizabeth's policy of restoring Peter's administrative order (with the Senate as the central organ). (16) Supported by the Guards, Elizabeth, like Catherine and Anne before her, did little to further the modernization of Russia. (17) Meanwhile, the martial philosophy - once so well executed by Peter - continued to captivate the attention of the House of Romanov. There were several campaigns, resulting in a pattern that would be repeated down to 1917: no enduring victories, a heavy drain on the treasury, huge increases in taxation, and the increased antagonism of the *dvoriane*. (18)

As foreign policy became less attractive and productive, Elizabeth tried to ameliorate the nobility. She did this by abolishing the secret police and reducing the price of salt - an act of generosity that was canceled out by the badly-managed Seven Years' War. (19)   Only in the cultural sphere was Elizabeth able to move ahead. (20)

Catherine II (who followed the brief and inconsequential rule of tsar Peter III) had more ability and resources than the previous four sovereigns, yet failed to make Russia "forward-thinking." Historian Michael Florinsky ascribes to her a "confused liberalism," which, on the one hand, sought to revitalize the pre-Petrine law code, and on the other tried to embrace too many European concepts that could not work. (21) Her "idealism" notwithstanding, she did not give in to any demands for radical change. (22)

That Catherine was no revolutionary may best be seen in her policy toward the nobility *and* the peasants. Though an elaborate instruction of 1768 announced her desire to promote "the glory of the citizens, of the state and of the monarchy," there was little change in Russia's interior situation. She still awarded privileges to the upper classes in exchange for fealty. Peasants and serfs - still not legally defined as human beings - saw their lot become steadily worse. (23) Consequently, her reign became known as the "golden age of the aristocracy"... truly a misnomer, when one realizes the inevitable dependency that class had upon the monarch. (24) Importantly, Catherine's efforts in placating the nobility were but a more polished endeavor to achieve what others before her had failed to accomplish: monarchical security. (25)

To further strengthen the monarchy, Catherine continued a policy initiated by Peter: she dispossessed the Church, closed down many monasteries, and increased secularization. (26) Ostensibly, this was in line with Enlightenment pronouncements (making the incorporation of western ideas - such as secular education - much easier). In reality, education now was the special province of the state, with little regard for any kind of "enlightenment." Disgruntlement magnified, and resulted in the development of an anti-tsarist intelligentsia. (27) Too concerned with other matters, Catherine left education to Ivan Betsky, who insisted that the main object of the schools was "to build character," not to impart knowledge. (28)

Catherine *was* somewhat innovative in instructions regarding towns. In 1785 she actually suggested a plan for local government that went well beyond proposals of the Petrine era. Received with little enthusiasm by the bureaucracy, her idea went nowhere. Only the monarchy and the nobility, therefore, showed any real gains. As Georges Vernadsky notes, "the monarchy ascended to its zenith while serfdom reached its apogee." (29)

In foreign affairs, Catherine had some measure of success. She strove to fulfill Peter the Great's dream of gathering the lands into one union, and of developing Russian trade with its neighbors. Here, too, one sees continuity: like her forbears, Catherine failed to vanquish an old enemy, Turkey. Moreover, imperialistic adventures in that sphere were costly, slowing Russia's modernization. (30) Yet, most observers agree that in foreign affairs she made at least one small step forward. Quite rightly, B. H. Sumner has written that by the end of her rule, Russia was "politically and militarily a European power" for the first time. (31)

In 1797, Paul followed his mother to the throne. Early voicing a belief in enlightened despotism, Paul has been a disappointment to historians. He is known for eliminating most of Catherine's reforms (especially the privileges given to the nobility in the Charter of 1785). (32) Also, he tried to bring the *dvoriane* into line by restoring the collegial system. Finally (in a move reminiscent of Elizabeth), he ordered serfs to pledge fealty to him, with no mention of future emancipation. Instead of bringing the aristocracy and the monarchy into a more compatible relationship, Paul antagonized an already poor situation. His behavior has raised questions among historians as to his mental competency. (33)

Following Paul's five-year reign came a ruler of even greater puzzlement. Called by historians "the enigmatic tsar," Alexander I early on was surrounded by an impressive circle of advisors. At first, he encouraged a path toward modernization. Guided by his teacher, the Frenchman La Harpe, and by his *confidant*, a Pole named Czartoryski, Alexander probably was in earnest about reforms. He advocated a rule of law (a kind of *Rechtsstaat*), thought seriously about serf emancipation and a constitution, and - like Catherine II - wanted a thoroughly revamped tax system. (34) However, just as Florinsky calls many of Catherine's suggestions "stillborn," so, too, does he regard Alexander's approach to progress as "sterile." (35) Monarchical insecurity remained; the tsar's suspicions of a potentially strong, challenging nobility stayed until the end of his reign in 1825. (36)

Roughly the first dozen years of Alexander's rule may be referred to as his "liberal" period. During this time he proposed the abolition of the secret police and the collegial system. He re-established the Senate as the highest organ of judicial and administrative control. He likewise made a concession to the serfs: by the law of 1803 a landowner could free an entire village, if he promised to give some of his land as a condition of that emancipation. (37) To no one's surprise, the measure met resistance from the less liberal nobility and was never carried out. (38)

The aristocracy's continued opposition was one of two factors which turned Alexander away from modernization. The other was Napoleon. Employing an outmoded enlightened despotism that demanded foreign as well as domestic security, Alexander's differences with the "child of the Revolution" contributed to the Napoleonic Wars. Turning inward to escape the harshness of the conflict, Alexander was aided by charlatans and mystics (as would Nicholas II, a hundred years later). This angered the Orthodox clergy: it feared the tsar would take suspicious counsel and "rebuild an imperfect world according to Christian morality." (39)

Alexander's imbroglio with France, not unlike the many conflicts of his predecessors, produced unbalanced trade, huge debts, and a listless industrialization policy. This further alienated the nobility. Paradoxically, the tsar's resistance to Napoleon earned him a modicum of respect *outside* Russia. Even more than Catherine II, he was able to elevate his nation's standing in world affairs. (40)

The clamor of the intelligentsia probably would have been strong even if Alexander had not become involved in the wars. Almost with *dejà vù*, he restored (in 1807) the secret police. With the help of the ministry of education, he tightened censorship and promulgated the notion that Catherine would have decried: schools were to be places of "nationalistic fervor, anti-foreign and anti-western." (41) Reaction brought an end to the Enlightenment.

Amidst the tumult of resentment toward a tightened administration, the "first Russian Revolution" (as Anatole Mazour calls it) occurred in 1825. Led by a small group of army officers and some intelligentsia, the uprising came at a time when Russia had no tsar. (42) It failed, chiefly because it had little popular support, poor leadership, no unity, and an absence of revolutionary technique. The result, predictably, was a further tightening of the autocracy. (43)

This "Decembrist Revolt" impressed upon the new tsar the need for a firm hand. Under Nicholas I, Russia became a bastion of conservatism in Europe. One of his advisors, Uvarov, made Russia identical with the concepts of "Orthodoxy, Aristocracy and Nationality." Russia would initiate reforms only when necessary, and would swiftly repress western revolutionary ideas. (44)

An uneasy cooperation between the tsar and the nobility remained. Nicholas moved cautiously, and especially on the delicate peasant-serf question. He regarded serfdom as an evil which had to be dealt with, but he moved slowly, so as not to alienate the nobility and the moderate intelligentsia. To the nobles' demands for an amicable resolution, Nicholas offered Kiselev's suggestion of a *mir*-type, self-governing, economically advanced commune. (45) He achieved little success when his recommendation for serf freedom met with resistance from influential landowners. (46)

Although the bureaucracy tried to stifle the influx of western ideas, Nicholas' reign became (not unlike Elizabeth's) a "golden age" in literature. Pushkin, Lermontev, Gogol and Turgenev added important chapters to Russia's literary heritage, despite the official pronouncement that a person should be educated only in accordance with one's "station." Nicholas did his part, expanding the art collection of the Hermitage more than any tsar, before or since.

Universality was not yet a feature of Russia's intellectual growth. (47) Uvarov impeded westernization by insisting that "the perpetrator of fear and ignorance" - the Orthodox Church - should exist simply to "monitor... morals and conduct." To disregard that would be blasphemy. (48)

Amidst all this, alienation increased among the intellectuals to a point where there were numerous groups of intelligentsia, each with a different point of view as how best to serve Russia. (49)

Conservative attitudes dominated both domestic and foreign policy during Nicholas' reign. Poland, which under Alexander I had briefly enjoyed a taste of liberty, attempted a nationalistic rebellion in 1830-31; it was quashed. The area was reorganized under an Organic Statute, which, as Barbara Jelavich writes, made Poland "an invisible part of the Russian empire." (50) As well, Nicholas drew Russia into an intensification of the ancient struggle for control of the Near East. Poor management led to the ruinous Crimean War at the end of his rule. (51)

Predictably, the ascension to the throne of Alexander II in 1855 was greeted with delight by those Russians who had disliked the repressive atmosphere of his predecessor. Just as predictably, Alexander dismayed those who believed modernization would proceed at a quickened pace.

Historians have called Alexander the "tsar-liberator," for his edicts concerning the serfs. Sharing Nicholas' conviction that serfdom was an evil that needed to be ended, he at least made a first move. But Alexander granted the edict of emancipation (1861), principally because he was a *Realpolitiker*: he wished to prevent a peasant revolution. He sought to keep the nobility - "the mainstay of the throne" - under control. He granted emancipation to stave off political and economic dislocation.(52)

Emancipation was to be accomplished over a long period of time. It weakened the rights of neither the nobles nor the monarch; nor did it alter the forms of prior land tenure: the commune (*mir*) was already a reality, and was the basic unit of peasant organization until 1917. (53)

Even the granting of local government, embodied in the many *zemstva* (rural councils) - which Mikhail Speransky had envisaged during the rule of Alexander I - had but a limited effect on modernization. The *zemstva* were concerned with local economic needs, and suffered from a lack of funds and the necessary cooperation with the security police. Charles Morley calls this "the first experiment in Russian democracy." In spite of that, Russia "remained essentially an old *régime*, founded on sharp class inequalities and a lack of significant social mobility." (54)

The rural reforms were received with little enthusiasm. As Alexander Gerschrenkon has written, the liberated serfs were bewildered and confused, and finally disappointed: the best lands stayed with the gentry. (55) Economic backwardness, widespread corruption, and a variety of other ills made emancipation an unattractive alternative. The gap between the masses and the government widened, as the institutions of the "new freedom" proved to be a sham. (56)

It would be wrong, though, to attribute imperial disintegration solely to the incomplete change in the status of peasants. The growing importance of capitalism should not be overlooked. The nobility and the growing middle class found more rewards in industry and commerce than in farming. It is not without reason that Soviet historians denoted 1861 as a dividing line between feudalism and modernity, despite the fact that hired labor had been replacing servile labor at a steady pace since the rule of the first Alexander. (57)

The other reforms of Alexander II have received less attention, even though many of them were more successful than his rural decrees. His 1864 edict that modernized the Russian courts stands out as "the most western of all the Great Reforms." (58) It created district courts, a jury system, and reduced judicial corruption. There was also some tolerance of free speech (though only in the courtroom); this was a first in Russian history. A dramatic example of the limitations can be found in the much-maligned field of foreign affairs: though Russia's reverses were not as frequent, the government routinely suppressed any remarks that were uncomplimentary to the *régime*. (59)

Disappointed by the incompleteness - and seeming insincerity - of the reforms, the intelligentsia increased its role as critic. It produced a major revolutionary movement. Better organized than its predecessors, this one committed its energies to the stabilization of the socioeconomic structure. (60)

Alexander III, whom Melvin Wren calls "a man of small mind and of small deeds," ascended the throne after the assassination of Alexander II. Seeking reprisals, he listened to the political Right: he tightened censorship, expanded the secret police, and moved Russia in the direction of deep reaction and intransigence. (61)

Interruptions in Russia's modernization took the form of "counter-reforms" that effectively stifled liberal voices. Echoing the "Orthodoxy, Autocracy and Nationality" of Nicholas I, the new tsar gave the bureaucracy substantially larger power. All popular representation was clearly discouraged. (62) Thanks to the counsel of Konstantin Pobedonostsev, Alexander believed that the "basic evil" confronting Russia no longer was serfdom, but constitutionalism. (63) The lower classes posed little threat. They responded to the "voice of orthodoxy, said Pobedonostsev," and were the principal supporters of the government. The real challenge to authority came from the new urban proletariat and the ever-present intelligentsia. (64)

As disgruntlement grew, so did conservatism. In measures reminiscent of the days of Nicholas I, educational opportunities once again were awarded on the basis of class. The monarchy showed a religious intolerance that hearkened back to earlier periods, as *pogroms* against the Jews became more and more frequent. (65)   Also continuous with the flow of nineteenth century politics was the strengthening of the Russian military and the secret police. Right-wing politicians heralded Russia's imperial schemes and criticized detractors as alien to Russia's "destiny."

Alexander's death in 1894 left Russia in the hands of the most enigmatic and chronicled tsar since Catherine the Great. Nicholas II shared his father's hostility toward representative government, but lacked the ability to deal with that institution in a manner that would ensure domestic tranquility. The last and perhaps saddest of the Romanovs inherited a paradox: on the one hand the gradual evolution toward industrialism meant a huge surge upwards in the nation's economy; on the other, the intelligentsia blamed increasing impoverishment of the masses on the same growth.

Nicholas entrusted two advisors with the task of modernizing Russia. From Peter Stolypin came a request to liberate peasants from bondage to the communes; from Sergei Witte came plans for a bigger commitment to industrialization, by way of a rigid tariff system, and the suggestion that Russia be organized in favor of the peasants. (66) Both men tried to prevent revolution. Their combined energies, Florinsky writes, were "the last attempt" to understand the "forces of change." (67)

The intelligentsia that spearheaded opposition to tsarist policies were identified (especially after 1890) as Socialist Revolutionaries, Bolsheviks and Mensheviks (after 1903). All of them envisaged, through different means, an end to the autocratic rejection of constitutions. (68) Chances for violent revolution increased; industrial ills led to student protests and strikes. Commonplace was the armed repression of those strikes and the secret police's infiltration of labor organizations. (69)

Apart from the middle-class intellectuals, to whom revolution seemed akin to a "pastime" (Florinsky), lower-level changes in thinking were taking place. In the *zemstva*, local representatives wanted the monarchy to give way to a representative format. (70)

It is not true that the first real germination of revolution on a broad popular base took place only after Russia's disastrous war with Japan in 1904-05, but that did contribute a spark. (71) Nor is it true that after the Tsushima disaster Nicholas' reforms were the result of frantic efforts to stave off insurrection. Witte's program of 1905 was discussed three years before, and had been tabled, because it would have met stern opposition from prominent conservative forces. (72)

Predictably the 1905 reforms changed very little. Urban workers, who sought by example to influence their rural counterparts, experienced problems that went back before Peter the Great's time: illiteracy and the suspicion of new ideas. Nor was the urban proletariat immediately receptive to radical change. (73)

177

The "October Manifesto" of 1905 gave little hint of self-government, for it allowed no mass political parties, and did nothing to lessen the influence of the bureaucracy. (74) Perhaps most disappointing of all was the nature of the *duma* (legislature). Though the first one had enough peasants, the proletariat and intellectuals were slighted. In fact, none of the *dumas* were the legislative bodies once envisaged by Speransky. (75)

Georg von Rauch has pointed out that before the creation of the Manifesto one had to look with patience before finding anyone who truly had benefited from the tsar's policies. (76) Some capitalists had prospered (thanks in part to Witte's programs), but the tsar himself was not fond of capitalism. Also, the industrial modernization of Russia brought the once-favored landlord class into a state of decline, and no one was forecasting peasant actions with any degree of certainty.

The Manifesto, with all its inadequacies, was Russia's first "social contract," and introduced the "constitutional period" to the empire. The era, however, was short-lived: Constitutional Democrats (Cadets) were a big influence in the first *duma*, and opposed the tsar. (77) Distressed by the intensity of their opposition, the government changed the nation's electoral law in 1907, making the *duma* more conservative and "cooperative." (78)

Bureaucratic changes did not end displeasure with the government. Just prior to World War I, twenty-five percent of the peasant class left the communes for the cities, and constituted a new group for revolutionary infiltration. (79) In terms of education, the nation had become fairly progressive, despite extremely conservative ministries. The universities - many as modern as their western counterparts - became centers of organized protest. (80) That does not mean, though, that they were the "breeding grounds" for the 1917 revolutions. The "logic of events" was leading Russia to collapse: the war in 1914. (81)

Certainly one of the things that *did* spark the Bolshevik takeover in late 1917 was the poor judgment of the Provisional Government, which took power in the Spring revolution of that year. (82) Its most important official, Alexander Kerensky, acted without a thoroughgoing plan, calling for the Russian people to rally behind the new government in the prosecution of the war effort. (83) A lack of public support and trust (84), plus an ignorance of the true nature of Bolshevism, brought an end to the Provisional Government's power that November. (85)

Consistent with Russian history, an immediate concern for Vladimir Lenin and the new Bolshevik *régime* was centralization. (86) Organized much better than the Whites (counter-revolutionary forces which sought to unseat the Bolsheviks), the new government used old ideas in new guise to win a civil war that lasted until 1921. The *Cheka* (secret police) was very effective: it maintained order through intimidation and repression. At the same time, the Red Army (under Leon Trotsky's initial guidance) helped in the consolidation of Socialist power. (87)

The insistence by some scholars that Lenin's victory simply improved upon tsarist institutions is at best naive. Lenin's highest accomplishment, according to E.H. Carr, was the introduction of the Communist Party as the USSR's ultimate ruling body. (88) The Communist Party has no true parallel in tsarist Russia. (89)

The transformation of Russia after 1917 is one of the turning points in modern history, and took many forms. A first step was the New Economic Policy (NEP), "a tactical retreat from Communism" that sought the free cooperation of the peasants, in order to forge a link between them, the proletariat, and the Party. (90) Departing from war communism, the Soviet government allowed peasants to keep what they had produced (after taxes). Some peasants, such as the *kulaks*, prospered from this measure; in addition, there was a new class of small businessmen (*Nepmen*), ensuring that some form of capitalism was not unattractive as a means of achieving national solidarity. (91)

Josef Stalin, who advanced to the Party leadership in a power fight after Lenin's death in 1924, disliked the NEP, and particularly the profits that *kulaks* and *Nepmen* were making. (92) His answer to this was the first Five-Year Plan. One of the most ambitious modernizing attempts in Russian history, it was nothing less than a social revolution. (93) Important to the first Plan was the collectivization of agriculture, which German scholar Reinhard Wittram calls "an extremely deep revolutionary change." Expressing the hope that Soviet Russia soon would be able to run its farm operations on an efficient basis, Stalin knew that seventy-eight percent of the peasants belonged to collectives. (94) A centrally-planned industrialization completed the Plan, producing "the most effective means of squeezing all available capital from Russia." (95) For the first time, industrial workers were Russia's largest social class.

The new state was extremely ambitious. Motivated by the same kinds of desires, tsarist efforts in this direction encountered few obstacles: no well-developed middle-class existed as late as Alexander III; there was no sizable urban proletariat until tsar Nicholas II; and at no time was Russia able financially to resolve internal difficulties... thanks to a growing number of foreign adventures. (96)

As the tsars relied on the secret police, so, too, did Stalin. It arrested anyone who challenged the purpose of the Party (which is to say, Stalin). He developed a paranoia that ultimately set Russia backward, believing that enemies were all around him. He dealt with them in purges which punished Russia's most gifted artisans, political leaders and military men. Censorship bore a nineteenth century imprint, and labor camps filled to overflowing. (97)

"Next to getting a victory from the world revolution," writes Ossip K. Flechtheim, "the greatest aim of Soviet power [was] not being a socialist island." (98) This pronouncement of Soviet foreign policy largely explains the rationale of Lenin, and then Stalin, in the creation of the Communist

International (*Comintern*), to achieve the former, and an active participation with western non-Communist countries, to get the latter. (99)

Though many Soviet foreign policy objectives were continuations of Russian historical policy, the *modus operandi* was different. (100) People in tsarist Russia's foreign office often exercised a fair amount of initiative in the formulation of policy. In Soviet Russia, foreign policy was dictated by Party councils. Unlike the Nesselrodes and the Gorchakovs of tsarist times, Gregorii Chicherin and Maxim Litvinov did not hold high ranks in the Soviet hierarchy. Seldom were they asked for advice; in reality, they were figureheads. (101)

Soviet Russia's new course was dictated by *Realpolitik*. Because its economy was in terrible shape after the Revolution and the Civil War, the Soviets sought a *rapprochement* with the West. Nonetheless, it was with some surprise that the victors of the Great War learned of the USSR's *détente* with Weimar Germany in 1922, and the Non-Aggression Pact with Hitler seventeen years later. (102) The first added to western fears that the Soviet Union had embarked upon a journey to "turn the free world into a communist lake," and the second added confusion to the West's understanding of right- and left-wing ideologies. (103)

New, too, was the people's attitude toward the nation in time of war. Peter the Great was never able to arouse a defense of the Motherland the way Stalin did when Hitler's army invaded the USSR in 1941. Nor was Nicholas II able to sustain national support for World War I as Stalin was able to do in the "Great Patriotic War." (104) Stalin also had little diffi-culty in promoting what he called "a defensive position" in the first years of the Cold War. (105)

In the first years after Stalin's death, Party leaders rejected many of his deeds. Nikita Khrushchev denounced him in a 1956 speech that would have been unthinkable in tsarist Russia. In his opinion, Russia's evolution from Socialism to Communism had gone awry. Thus, Issac Deutscher refers to the post-Stalinist era as the "twilight of totalitarianism," in which the USSR moved to prevent the recurrence of a strong leader by transferring more power to the Party. (106) For a time, there was a collective leadership, "designed to prevent any one leader from using a particular institution as a vehicle for obtaining a political supremacy." (107)

Being put back on the road to a workable communism also meant that certain institutions which were strong in Stalin's time became weaker. The secret police (most usually called the KGB) was not as oppressive as the earlier NKVD; nor were the labor camps as full or as cruel as they had been in the 1930s and 1940s. Legitimate protest from various seg-ments of the population was voiced (*e. g.*, the Jews), but this, too, was indicative of the maturation process: minority protests were not allowed at all in Stalin's time. (108)

The Soviet economy did not progress fully in accordance with the many Five-Year Plans which survived Stalin. To the end of the Soviet period, production remained uneven: heavy industry made large strides forward, but commodities were woefully scarce. Though the farm situation was not as bleak as in preceding generations, neither was much encouragement given to the cultivators of the land. (109)

It would be a mistake, though, to pretend that the "great socialist experiment" did not produce meaningful social change. The gentry, landlords and clergy disappeared as a group; so, too, did bankers, financiers and industrialists. The *petite bourgeoisie*, needed briefly when Lenin created the NEP, faded away after 1928. The Church, whose influence had been a factor in Russian affairs since the Middle Ages, was removed from the ruling hierarchy. It had been, as Deutscher put it, "the great enemy of a rational, socialist society." (110) Meanwhile, the workers and peasants - in whose name the Revolution was consummated - accepted the basic tenets of the new order. The Soviet analysis of the Revolution made clear that the Bolshevik victory ended the massive alienation that workers and peasants had endured under tsarism. (111) In the view of West German historian Klaus Mehnert, "Soviet man" came to "accept the authority of the State, the primacy of discipline and wisdom of the ruling group." (112)

On the other hand, Yugoslav Communist scholar-politico, Milovan Dji-las, wrote that a "new class" had evolved in the USSR: a group of *élitists* distinguished from the masses by their education, managerial ability, and unswerving devotion to the State. (113) They were the descendants of workers from the revolutionary era, or were themselves workers, yet no longer kept any ties to their origins. More gifted than any "special class" existing before the Revolution, they were different in one important aspect: they earned material benefits, but could not bequeath their jobs. In the USSR, all positions of public responsibility had to be earned. (114)

One of the most enduring Soviet reforms was in the field of education. Whether at the public school or university or technical school level, the State insisted that each citizen be educated to his or her fullest capacity. Since the incentive was government-directed, Russian students tended to work more productively than students in other countries. (115) Their task was difficult, but in just over seventy years they made solid progress - more, arguably, than any other large country in the same period of time. (116)

The literary record was good, even though a strict censorship kept much of that treasure from the people. Common to much of Soviet writing was "socialist realism," which took the form of narrating the rewards of a total commitment to Marxism-Leninism. Scholars who challenged the system, in part or in whole, had their works "restricted" - not unlike Gogol and others, in nineteenth century Russia. The prohibition of full literary freedom to poets like Anna Anakmatova and novelists like Boris Pasternak and Alexander Solzhenitsyn, deprived the Russian people of a meaningful counterpoint. (117)

The end of the Soviet Union in 1991 presaged a period of flux that had Kremlinologists scurrying to their books for even more clues into the identity of history's most famous enigma. Eerily, the seventy-four-year Soviet experiment was seen, for the first time, to be just another step in Russia's evolution. Putting it, for the first time, in the past, like all other epochs, was vexing.

Mikhail Gorbachev's brief reign (half a dozen years) corresponded to a global shift away from the left. A *Realpolitiker* (not unlike Khrushchev), he responded with *glasnost* (openness) and *perestroika* (restructuring). He was a dedicated Communist, but saw in the world of the 1980s a reason to depart (at least for awhile) from Marxism-Leninism's message. This was appreciated in the West, where he was embraced by a Cold War-weary public and a conservative American president. Inside the changing USSR his successes were less inspiring... mindful of other times, when international success meant domestic deprivation.

When another revolution overthrew Gorbachev in the summer of 1991, westerners and Russians alike were not sure what to expect. Boris Yeltsin, a Gorbachev *confidant,* took the lead, and continued the spirit (if not the substance) of Gorbachev's reformation. He even introduced the first electoral democracy in Russian history: citizens, with no restrictions, were allowed to vote for a president. Yeltsin won that first election, and then proceeded to oversee a complex restructuring of his own. At least on paper, a multitude of republics (and their diverse populations) won autonomy, with Russia (the largest republic) keeping most of the military and commercial power.

Problems erupted almost immediately. The Communist Party was still powerful, but for the first time since 1921 it shared the political spotlight with dozens of other parties. All jockeyed for position, as the region's economy - so used to state support - crumbled in a flurry of experiments. Free market (western) ideas were introduced, and met with little success. As food lines grew, disgruntlement escalated. On the far right, Vladimir Zhirinovsky emerged with a bold plan to rekindle the monarchy, reestablish the old empire (including Alaska, to the chagrin of the United States), and to have, once and for all, a "final solution" to the Jewish and Muslim "problems." (118)

The rest of the world regarded the Russian bear with new alarm, prompting many to rue the day that once-hated Soviet Communism had failed. Russia's "re-structuring" had not resulted in international tranquility; resurgence in Russia's traditional outward-looking made the 1990s a disquieting time on the world scene, especially in the Balkans, where two wars tested the diplomatic skills of Russia *and* the West.

As the new millennium began, Russia's situation was bleak. Organized crime (the Russian *mafiya*) was a clear and present danger at home, and had begun to be a problem abroad. Morale was so poor that ordinary Russians did not know which way to turn. When Yeltsin's programs did not succeed, it was no surprise when the next leader reminded many of "Old Guard" Bolsheviks. That man was Vladimir Putin, head of the KGB.

Putin turned out to be a *Realpolitiker.* Once more the world had moved to the right (conservative George W. Bush was the new American president), and moderation was the byword. It was clear, to both Russia and the U.S., that their nations' many domestic problems (as well as the world's) would have to be dealt with slowly and cautiously. As the world was hit with a new and vituperative wave of terrorism in 2001 (inspired by militant Islam), conservatism was in peril. Russia-watchers looked for clues: which way would Russia turn? Would the answers be found in an examination of the past... or spring from something new?

In the final analysis, neither modernization nor revolution have ended in Russia. It has simply reached another stage in its long evolution. Every day domestic and international events shape its future and the lives of its people. Russia has "westernized" to a point of assimilation; but it cannot become "more European;" it cannot follow the lead of the countries that authored its first liberal tendencies - for Europe is no longer the leader.

Russia has reached a point where its own dynamism and powers of creation have equaled (and in many cases surpassed) the influence of its continental teacher. Change must have a distinctly Russian flavor.

Russia has made enormous strides since 1689. What many skeptics (like George Kennan) do not always appreciate is the change that has taken place since 1917, a span of less than a hundred years. Leadership has been varied and domestic frustrations have been many. Yet the dedication to an ideal (however remote and perhaps unworkable) has never changed: there will always be a "Russian presence." To those who scoff, it should be pointed out that the acceptance of the *American* ideal is based upon a not very different optimism: that *its* system will "mature" and evolve until it, too, is copied by the rest of the world.

Notes

1. A best-selling interpretation of the Eighties sidesteps the controversy and concentrates on the personality of the man: Robert K. Massie, **Peter the Great: His Life and World** (New York, 1980). Another popular rendering (by Serge Yakobson, "Peter the Great: A Russian Hero," **History Today**, July 1972), adds even less, save for the widely-held view that modernization was forced on Peter by the "necessity of the hour." Reinhard Wittram also rejects the thesis that Russia changed much under Peter. He doubts that Peter created "a new social basis" for Russia. **Peter I: Czar und Kaiser** (Göttingen, 1964). In the early 1970s Melvin Wren argued that modernization had been "on the way" for 250 years, with Russia being so firmly committed that "later attempts to reverse the trend invariably failed." **The Western Impact Upon Tsarist Russia** (New

York, 1971), p. 57. This complements Georges Florovsky, who noted that there was continuity "from the very beginning." "The Problem of Old Russian Culture," *Slavic Review* (March 1962), p. 1.

2. Lionel Kochan, *The Making of Modern Russia* (London, 1962), p. 115.

3. *Ibid.* Or, as Vasily Kliuchevsky noted, "he sought western techniques, not western civilization." Michael Florinsky, *Russia: a History and an Interpretation* (New York, 1947), I, 321. Though the terms "westernization" and "modernization" are used interchangeably, the latter is preferred because of the present writer's belief that modernization has been a constant theme in Russian history. Westernization is a term chiefly applicable to Russia before 1917.

4. Kochan, p. 100. Before Peter, Alexis wanted a navy, but never got it. Kliuchevsky, *Peter the Great* (New York, 1958), p. 15. C. E. Black noted that henceforward Russia had four aims: stability of the frontier, favorable conditions for economic growth, unification of lands considered to be Russia's, and short-term international alliances. "The Pattern of Russian Objectives," *Russian Foreign Policy*, ed. Ivo J. Lederer (New Haven, 1962), pp. 6-7. Werner Markert has traced these aims as far back as the Tatar period. See *Osteuropa und die Abendländische Welt: Aufsätze und Vorträge* (Göttingen, 1966), p. 62. Kliuchevsky, p. 170, calls this the "soul tax." Another scholar has traced this to a 1719 law in which the state for the first time assumed direct authority over peasants. Until that time they were the lords' private property. After that their status declined. Georges Vernadsky, "Le Servage en France, en Allemagne et en Russie," *Relazioni del X Congresso Internazionale di Scienza Storiche* (September 1955), p. 267.

5. Florinsky, I, 367. This replaced the medieval *kormlenie,* whereby governors kept all or part of the revenues.

6. *Ibid.*

7. *Ibid.,* I, 405-06.

8. Wren, pp. 48-49.

9. Peter made it clear that the Church was to be subordinate to the state. To the charge that he was "anti-Christ," Peter accused the monasteries of being "hotbeds of debauchery and centers of subversive activities," and replaced the Patriarchate in 1721 with the less vocal Holy Synod. "Thus the Church became a part of the bureaucracy at the mercy of the emperor." Florinsky, I, 414. Peter also created a collegial system (to replace central governmental departments, called *prikazy*) as a means of checking corruption. He established a Senate, which was to be mainly a tax-collecting agency (*not* a legislative body), which would act for him when he was absent from the capital. The colleges crumbled "because Peter did not take into account the differences between large Russia and Sweden [on whose model the system was based]." Moreover the Synod's creation strained Church-State relations: Peter named bishops directly. Though it endured until 1917, the Senate went through many battles, involving real and imagined power. Wren, pp. 30-33.

10. The Great Schism of the 1660s was concerned mainly with the conflict between Patriarch Nikon and "Old Believers" (traditionalists). Nikon pointed out errors in Orthodox ritual and was accused of radicalism by the "Old Believers," who wished to see no changes at all. At bottom, the schism produced a meaningless debate, over who was more powerful, the Church or the State. See Wren, p. 36. As Wittram notes, Peter was responsible for the decline of the Church's political fortunes. Reinhard Wittram, **Russia and Europe** (New York, 1973), p. 17. Cited hereafter as **Russia**.

11. Florinsky, I, 410. The Church had reason to worry. The Senate got the right to attack the less "progressive" tenets of orthodoxy. As one scholar has written: "the Church thus became a propaganda agency for [Peter's] political views and his reform projects." Georges Bissonnette, "Peter the

Great and the Church as an Educational Institution," *Essays in Russian and Soviet History*, ed. J. Curtiss (New York, 1968), p. 17. The Church's loss of power in education was not much: schools rarely had been centers for learning before the edict. Wittram, Russia, p. 11.

12. Kliuchevsky, p. 16.

13. The chief duty of the *dvoriane* was to perform military service, in exchange for the privilege of getting hereditary title to land. "Service," wrote one historian, "became the most natural way to retain wealth." Marc Raeff, *The Origins of the Intelligentsia: the 18th Century Nobility* (New York, 1966), p. 17; Otto Hoetzsch, *The Evolution of Russia* (New York, 1966), p. 90. There is some disagreement about the table of ranks. Florinsky states that despite the rewards offered by State service, nobles often tried to evade service (I, 419). Raeff notes that their displeasure evolved slowly (finally taking root in the genesis of an intelligentsia), pp. 10, 109, 153. Importantly, Peter's table broke a personal bond between tsar and the gentry, which consequently worsened the lot of peasants and serfs. Peasants now "fled into the woods," to avoid labor or the draft. This angered the nobility, who blamed the tsar (Wren, p.58).

14. Markert, p. 64. What was really new about Peter's reforms, Wren writes, "was less the reforms themselves than the spirit with which he imposed them" (p. 66). Kliuchevsky (pp. 54, 85) calls the "reforms" continuations of earlier policies. "Westernization" did not assist the development of local, representative government, and class divisions increased. Kliuchevsky faults Peter for a lack of judgment.

15. To ensure stability, she created a Supreme Privy Council. Under the direction of Baron Menshikov, it was much like Peter's Senate, save that Catherine permitted it a firmer hand in national affairs. Florinsky, I, 437.

16. *Ibid.,* I, 454.

17. Florinsky notes, *e. g.,* that a clamor for a constitution in 1730 fell on

deaf ears. *Ibid.,* I, 455.

18. There was a conflict over the Polish Succession (1733); more problems with Turkey (1735-39); another dispute with Sweden (1741-42); and the Seven Years' War (1756-63). Having sampled some privileges, the nobility used Russia's wars to press for more recognition and power.

19. Florinsky, I, 498-99.

20. Wren, pp. 74-75, observes that "progressive" education drew some attention, with some consideration being given to making a real learning atmosphere. He cautions, however, that despite the increase in the number of schools, the dearth of capable teachers and qualified students remained a problem. For the few who were able to appreciate it, there was a "golden age" of sorts, when Mikhail Lomonosov and others rose to literary success.

21. One is reminded of Peter's anxiety and oversight: of trying to implement Swedish institutions on Russia.

22. The monarchical principle remained rooted in strict observance of existing law. Florinsky notes (perhaps correctly) that those ideas of the Enlightenment which might have appealed to the sub-monarchic estates remained a fantasy. Even if created, new organizations would have been ignored. Florinsky, I, 550.

23. Catherine, for instance, permitted no debate on the question of serf emancipation. Wittram, *Russia*, p. 64.

24. Her Charter of the Nobility (1785) stated that nobles were free from compulsory service and direct taxation, and had the right to dispose of property (including serfs) as they chose. Raeff reasons that she wished to transform the service nobility into a class of landowners, locally-rooted individuals who would strengthen the nation economically and be

grateful to the monarch. Raeff, p. 105. Kochan prods further: he suggests that the less than equal footing between monarch and nobility was to prevent monarchism from devolving into oligarchy. Kochan, p. 11. Florinsky calls this "a false sense of security," as the charter for the first time created a group with many privileges and no feeling of loyalty to the state. The *dvoriane* became the chief instrument of the bureaucracy, and a future danger to the state. Florinsky, I, 605.

25. *Ibid.*

26. *Ibid.,* I, 549; Wren, p. 10.

27. Since there were very few educated Russians independent of the autocracy, the old systems (especially in education) remained in disrepair. Yet, under the cloak of indifference, an intelligentsia did grow, with Kantemir ("the father of Russian literature"), Lomonosov and Sumarokov being active.

28. Wren, p. 92.

29. Vernadsky, p. 269. Since at least Peter's time, peasants had come to bear a heavier tax burden (the poll tax) and the *obrok*. At Catherine's death, peasants were regarded as permanent features of the landed estates. The serfs - unlike the slaves of Old Muscovy, in that they weren't chattel and not taxable - could be sold with, or apart from, the land. The emancipation of the *dvoriane* made peasant and serf conditions more difficult. Peasant rebellions (such as Pugachev's, in 1773) became frequent, dramatically demonstrating the inequities of Russia's social and economic order. The rebellions, as Wren notes, shook "monarchic security," and inspired the growth of the intelligentsia. Confrontation between the monarchy, the peasants and serfs was "a peculiar feature of Russian social history." *Ibid.,* p. 270; Wren, p. 99.

30. Florinsky, I, 604.

31. B.H. Sumner, "Russia and Europe," *Oxford Slavonic Papers*, II (1952).

32. Paul reminded the nobles of their obligation to pay taxes, imposed social restrictions and dissolved their provincial assemblies. Wren, p. 113.

33. In early 1972 a group of academicians formed the "Group on the Use of Psychology in History," whose purpose was to bring psychology and history together to help in the study of the individual. One of the Group's first subjects was Paul. Subsequent studies have included Belinsky, Dostoevsky, Chekhov, Lenin, Trotsky and Stalin.

34. Wren, p. 115.

35. Florinsky, II, 639. Alexander's all-important "Unofficial Committee" knew very little about Russia outside the capital. Alexander sought their counsel, fearing the majority of the Russian nobility. In giving them token privileges, he repeated the mistakes of his predecessors: he whetted the nobles' appetite for power. This reached into the Senate (which Alexander battled), which proposed a means of sharing power with the tsar. Alexander's Committee blocked this.

36. Wren, p. 116. In particular, Alexander failed to take notice of an increasingly vocal segment of that group, the intelligentsia.

37. *Ibid.*, p. 117; Florinsky, II, 695.

38. A proposed constitution (by Mikhail Speransky) was "stillborn." In it, the tsar would allow a form of local government, a guarantee of civil rights, a revised law code (to limit the bureaucracy), and a national *duma* (legislature), with limited power and more freedoms for all. It became law later; emancipation, local governments and legal revision came in the 1860s; the *duma* (in modified form) came into existence in 1906. Regarding the serf policy, Vernadsky criticizes Alexander for creating "a new serfdom" that was "almost indistinguishable from full slavery." Vernadsky, p. 268. Interestingly, Alexander in this early period observed that

perhaps a monarchy was not in Russia's best interests: he suggested that a constitutional republic might be best. Had a constitution in which the tsar shared governmental power with the gentry been enacted, it might have placed an obstacle in the way of modernization (emancipation, tax reform, etc.), instead of facilitating it. It would be hard to envisage an unhappy nobility content with sharing power - on the tsar's terms.

39. Florinsky, II, 640-41. One of Alexander's plans for this was the so-called "holy alliance." The idea, inspired by Madame Krdener and others, utilized the Bible as a guide, by which nations would limit their aggression and embrace one another in "brotherly love." Introduced to the tsar as early as 1812, this concept did not become public knowledge until 1814, at the Congress of Vienna. Most nations thought the concept absurd. It should not be confused with the "Quadruple Alliance," a serious effort at maintaining international order which arose from the same conference. One historian notes that Russia's success at that congress was minimal; that it would not achieve an international victory until 1945. Barbara Jelavich, *Russian Foreign Policy, 1814-1914* (Philadelphia, 1964), p. 42.

40. This completed Alexander's acceptance of conservatism. Thereafter, he acted in concert with other European powers to restrict French imperialistic movements and to maintain the *status quo*.

41. Wren, p. 129. Some of the rebellion was the work of students who had returned from western Europe (in accordance with Uvarov's encouragement of the old Petrine policy of sending youth abroad for an education), where they had learned revolutionary methodology.

42. Alexander had died, leaving Constantine and Nicholas in confusion over who would be the next ruler. This, plus alienation, inspired the activities of secret societies, which urged either representative constitutional monarchy (the Northern Society), or an egalitarian democratic republic (the Southern Society). Like the Bolsheviks and the Mensheviks of

the next century, neither Society was willing to compromise; unlike the later scenario, neither group was strong enough to effectively challenge the monarchy. Probably there was no desire in 1825 to end monarchism. The villain, as many still suggest was true of 1917, was not the tsar, but the bureaucracy.

43. Wren, pp. 136-37. Wren concludes that the revolt was significant. Perhaps he overestimates: the main striking force was not the intelligentsia, the army officers. Later they returned to state service. At best, notes Malia, "it was an affair of gentlemen with no participation of the people." Martin Malia, "What is the Intelligentsia?" *The Russian Intelligentsia*, ed. Richard Pipes (New York, 1961), p. 9.

44. Consistent with past *régimes*, to enforce "law and order" Nicholas ordered the creation of his own secret police. "The Third Section" closely resembled the KGB of the USSR. Sidney Monas, "The Political Police: The Dream of a Beautiful Autocracy," *The Transformation of Russian Society: Aspects of Social Change since 1861* (Cambridge, 1961, pp. 165-66).

45. Kochan, p. 149; Wren, p. 139. The *mir*, Wittram notes, can be traced to Novgorod, where it connoted communal responsibility in the legal code, *Russkaya Pravda*. Wittram, *Russia*, p. 25.

46. Florinsky, II, 784-85. One law during Nicholas' reign did abolish serf status for some, making them "free inhabitants dwelling on state land." This pertained, writes Wren, only to state peasants. Actual experimentation with "free peasants" was carried out far from the capital and away from the inquiries of nobles - in Arakcheev's "military colonies." In the end, Nicholas steered a more cautious course, having linked peasant reforms and emancipation to France. He believed that the abolition of serfdom in France in 1789 had not prevented the Revolution, but had helped provoke it. Nicholas sought to prevent this from happening in Russia. Partly, his attitude was tempered by the unstable relationship between the monarchy and the aristocracy: he needed its help. Malia, p. 140.

47. General L. V. Dubbelt, Director of the "Third Section," commented that "here in Russia intellectuals must be treated like apothecaries... they are allowed to dispense their learning only by government prescription." Wittram, *Russia*, p. 83. In line with this, universities in Russia sought the sons of gentry with promises only of "moulding character," in the hope that they would not go abroad to learn "subversive ideas." Wren, pp. 141-42.

48. Ideally, Church and state interests were to go hand in hand.

49. It is important to note that ideas appeared which were neither borrowed from abroad, nor were imitations of foreign theories: they were clearly Russian contributions. An example of this concerns the dispute between the "westernizers" (who insisted on the modernization of Russia by western means) and the "Slavophiles" (who rejected those values and favored native solutions). The intelligentsia, which had elements in both camps, had grown into a kind of managerial *élite*, apart from the rest of society, and was openly class-oriented. Malia, who traces its origins to the 1830s (as separate from the group inspired by Peter the Great), defines intelligentsia as "all men who think independently." It was dominated by the gentry under Nicholas, but shifted to the *raznochintsy* after 1855. Malia, pp. 7-9.

50. Jelavich, p. 911.

51. *Ibid.*

52. Florinsky, II, 881. Alexander sought to prevent a Pugachev-style rebellion. It would have had more support than that earlier challenge to tsarist authority.

53. Michael Karpovich, *Imperial Russia, 1801-1914* (New York, 1932), p. 39. Alexander simply "bolstered" the village commune, which was to exist in order to control peasant land. There was to be no individual own-

ership. Florinsky, II, 893.

54. Malia, in Pipes, p. 16. E.H. Carr has written that rural reforms were designed to represent a revolution from above, in order to prevent the revolution from below that all previous emperors and empresses feared. Because many of the freed peasants flocked into Russian cities to become an integral part of the urban labor market, one may agree with Carr's comment that the rural reforms (and especially emancipation) marked "the first stage of the Russian industrial revolution." E.H. Carr, "The Background of the Russian Revolution," *Revolutions in Modern European History*, ed. Heinz Lubasz (New York, 1966), pp. 112-13. Alfred Rieber re-examined the emancipation and has found the peasant population to be "naive but rebellious children" whom Alexander feared might revolt against the landlords and the crown. He notes the earlier considerations of Alexander I and Nicholas I for rural reforms, but concludes that neither monarch wished to be so progressive as to alienate the landed gentry. Rieber notes that the 1861 edict undermined the entire legal and institutional structure. The new institutions - borrowed in part from western Europe - could only antagonize the powerful minority which influenced the actions of the tsar. Worse, the tsar refused to compensate the nobles for their loss; instead, he issued "redemption certificates," which solved no problems at all. Alfred J. Rieber, "Alexander II: A Revisionist View," *Journal of Modern History* (March 1971), pp. 43-50. See also Nicholas Riasanovsky, *A History of Russia* (New York, 1963), *passim.*

55. Alexander Gerschrenkon, "Problems and Patterns of Russian Economic Development," in Black, p. 45. The land allotments closely resembled the *obrok* and *barschina* (*corvée*). Serf emancipation thus failed to establish a "free peasantry." Very little was done to eliminate earlier abuses. Yet the tranquil nature of the peasant remained. "When a Russian is armed by the government," goes an old saying, "he is made into a brute. We [the peasants] do not use force in our villages because such stands between men. Our way [of peace] brings men together." As told by a peasant in Geoffrey Gorer and John Richman, *The People of Great*

Russia: A Psychological Study (New York, 1949), p. 74.

56. The "new freedoms" were heartily encouraged by the intelligentsia, yet Alexander hoped that in liberating serfs Russia would be rid not only of a moral blight but would also have available a large military reserve that would be loyal to the tsar. He hoped, too, that such reforms would win the lower classes away from the intelligentsia. The reforms were too weak for that. The *zemstva*, as Rieber notes, were just "traditional forms of local government dressed up in new guise": a compromise between political   centralization and socioeconomic decentralization which more resembled 17th century reality than 19th. The *zemstvo* was too large to be truly effective; the *volosty*, or smaller, local units, would have been better for Russia's modernization. It is not true to say (as Wren does) that "no one in Russia any longer approved of bondage." Conservative disapproval of many reforms attests otherwise. Beyond this, the reforms were always very tentative: the tsar retained the right - and exercised it - to give and to void new privileges. Wren, p. 166; Rieber, pp. 51-53.

57. For example, Albert P. Nenarkov, *Russia in the Twentieth Century* (New York, 1968). To be sure, the 1860s marked the beginning of a boom in big industry, with railroad construction and foreign trade bringing large profits to the crown. Florinsky, II, 941.

58. Wren, p. 170. Marc Szeftel has observed that the edict gave Russia "a serious check on the system of absolute government," before which there had been no effective separation of powers. Perhaps he is a bit too optimistic: the tsar's power was by no means restricted. Marc Szeftel, "The Form of Government of the Russian Empire Prior to the Constitutional Reforms of 1905-06," in Curtiss, p. 114.

59. Florinsky, II, 1030. On the other hand, any victory (such as the one over Turkey in 1877) was given great accolades. The triumph over Turkey was "more a war of sentiment than of reason," and like so many of Russia's imperialist adventures was costly in the international arena.

Consequently, as Russia became more aggressive, many European powers came to regard the Eurasian empire with deep suspicion. Wittram, *Russia*, p. 110.

60. The Populists, as they were called, followed no single pattern or leadership. Pisarev, *e. g.,* headed a nihilist order. Whether nihilists, militants or "philosophical anarchists," they had little in common, save the major transformation of Russian society.

61. Wren, p. 175; Florinsky, II, 1030.

62. Florinsky, II, 1087. One effort, to convene a *zemsky sobor* of various groups (a 16th century idea) which would include peasants, met with government ridicule. Consequently, *zemstvo* power was sharply reduced and more authority was recommended for the nobility. *Ibid.,* II, 1091-93.

63. Robert F. Byrnes, "Pobedonostsev on the Instruments of Russian Government," ***Continuity and Change in Russian and Soviet Thought,*** ed. E.J. Simmons (New York, 1955), p. 118.

64. *Ibid.*; Wren, p. 204.

65. Lazar Volin, "The Russian Peasant: From Emancipation to Kolkhoz," in Black, pp. 294-95. The *pogroms,* according to Volin, stemmed from a Pan-Slavic desire to eliminate any force "incompatible with Christian civilization" and Russian history. *Ibid.*

66. Florinsky, II, 1193, 1196, 1213. Witte's efforts also included the recommendation of the creation of peasant committees (1902) to communicate grievances to the government. A 1906 *ukase* gave peasants a share of arable land, thus breaking down the commune's control of the land.

67. Carr has written that the encouragement of the *kulak* ("rich peasant") was Stolypin's idea, and had the consequence of liberating certain peasants, and of "destroying the traditional structure of society and

creating no other." E.H. Carr, in Lubasz, p. 115.

68. Florinsky, II, 1189.

69. The mediocre educational system sparked many protests. The writer Chekhov noted that stagnation in the learning experience had made it "impossible to understand each other." Or, as Florinsky puts it: "the gulf between the educated classes and masses was the basic and fatal weakness of Russia's social structure." *Ibid.,* II, 1256.

70. *Ibid.,* II, 1167.

71. The most notable confrontation was on "Bloody Sunday" (January 1905), a few months before the end of the war. In the preceding October representatives drafted a liberal manifesto which urged various *zemstva* to demand a constitution.

72. Witte's moderate program originally guaranteed the strengthening of popular representation through the creation of a *duma* (which, after 1906, was restricted by the tsar's prerogative to legislate by decree). Florinsky, II, 1179-80.

73. "Industrial workers were still peasants in factory clothes." Carr, in Lubasz, p. 114.

74. Interior Minister Sviatopolk-Mirsky tried to alleviate the harshness of the bureaucracy before 1905, but met strong resistance. *Ibid.,* II, 1169.

75. Interestingly, the inclusion of peasants in the first *duma* stems from an idea expressed years before by Pobedonostsev: so that they would support the tsar's decrees. Partly, the first *duma* discriminated against the proletariat and the intellectuals. Leopold Haimson, "Social Stability in Urban Russia, 1915-17," **Slavic Review** (December 1964), 6-7.

76. Georg von Rauch, **A History of Soviet Russia** (New York, 1967), pp.

22-23.

77. George Kennan says that the first *duma* should have been created in the 1860s, when the radical-revolutionary forces had a better chance at challenging the tsar than did the Cadets. Kennan, in Pipes, p. 9.

78. Rauch, p. 25. The greatest activity came in the first two *dumas*. As strident, Russian liberals who emphasized non-violent change, the Cadets wanted to confiscate the large estates and distribute the land. Essentially, the Bolsheviks - unlike the Cadets - used distribution as a promise to secure peasant support. Distribution *did* follow, but in a thoroughly bureaucratized fashion.

79. As peasants entered industry, labor unrest began to rise. By 1914, the Bolsheviks were winning the support of unions.

80. Rauch, p. 28.

81. Russia's performance in the war was dismal. Low morale was a serious problem, and desertions were commonplace.

82. Rauch, pp. 39-40. The Provisional Government took charge after strikes and riots in the capital produced the March Revolution. Selected by the *duma* and under the initial leadership of Prince Lvov, the new government induced the tsar to abdicate, but pressed for a continuation of the Russian war effort - a serious mistake. Badly divided from the beginning, and lacking any real support from the masses, the Provisional Government lasted until November. Its only "victory" came in July, when it effectively repulsed a Bolshevik demonstration.

83. The present writer had the pleasure of listening to Kerensky reminisce about Russia in a seminar during the fall of 1966. He impressed everyone with his memory of those halcyon days; his opinion of Lenin - even after fifty years - had not mellowed. It was bitter in the extreme.

84. This is in reference to the unsuccessful Kornilov *coup* against the Kerensky Government that August, which resulted in Kerensky's "prestige in liberal circles [having] sunk considerably," and an increase in support for the Bolsheviks. Rauch, p. 54.

85. Florinsky, II, 1388; George Kennan, "The Russian Revolution: Its Nature and Consequences," **Foreign Affairs** (October, 1967), p. 7. Simply put, "the Provisional Government operated in a void," wrote H. L. Roberts, "Lenin and Power," **Responsibility of Power**, ed. Leonard Krieger (New York, 1967), p. 338. From the other side: "the excellent organization of the Bolsheviks and their luck in having a political leader of genius [Lenin]" provided Russia with the winner. Walter Laqueur, **Fate of the Revolution: Interpretations of Soviet History** (New York, 1967), p. 55. Theodore Dan, a Menshevik with a strong dislike for the Leninists, nonetheless regarded the Bolsheviks as the only force that could win. See **The Origins of Bolshevism** (New York, 1964), *passim*; Wren, p. 209. This is a theme which may be found from the time of Peter the Great onward.

86. As it developed, so too, did the chief executive of the state become the proponent of a tight autocracy. This did not disappear after 1917.

87. Trotsky, one of the intellectual fathers of Soviet Russia, fell into disfavor in the 1920s, owing to his disagreements with the Party (*e. g.,* his insistence on the immediacy of world revolution). He came to signify "anti-bolshevism," and had to seek sanctuary abroad. Murdered by Stalinist agents in 1940, he was "rehabilitated" by the USSR in the late 1980s.

88. E. H. Carr, **The October Revolution: Before and After** (New York, 1971), p. 15.

89. One may argue, though weakly, that the tsars based their rule on "ideologies" (*e. g.,* the ultra-conservatism of Nicholas I). Boris Meissner, "Totalitarian Rule and Social Change," draws no parallel, but credits the Party with its "unrestricted autocracy" and its control from above. Zbig-

niew Brzezinski (ed.), *Dilemmas of Change in Soviet Politics* (New York, 1969), p. 74. This blueprint did not go unchallenged. Trotsky's objections have been noted, but not all detractors were "Trotskyites." Exemplary, is the harassment of the non-conforming intellectuals in the purges of the 1930s. The most thorough study of the Party remains Leonard Schapiro, *The Communist Party of the Soviet Union* (New York,1960), and a self-serving counterpoint may be found in B.N. Ponomarev, *et. al., A Short History of the Communist Party of the Soviet Union* (Moscow, 1970). The Party was to be composed of the former proletariat and peasants, and was theoretically to "guide" Russia along its path from Socialism to Communism. Party decisions were to be based on a proper interpretation of Marxist (later Marxist-Leninist) dogma. For a provocative account of this and subsequent events, read I. I. Smirnov, *et. al.,*(ed.), *A Short History of the USSR* (Moscow, 1965), II, *passim.*

90. It was Trotsky who challenged the wisdom of Lenin's and the Party's departure from world revolution. Ponomarev, *et al.,* in a Soviet study of the Party, have portrayed Trotsky as one who "maintained that socialism could not be built in the Soviet Union and had no faith in the strength of the proletariat." They further note that he (correctly?) accused the Soviet economy of "state capitalism, and declared that the Soviet people were building ... capitalism." Ponomarev, p. 194.

91. It appears, though, that the major beneficiaries of the NEP were the *kulaks* and lower-class businessmen and bureaucrats. Most peasants were interested only in improving their living conditions; the proletariat, as always, worked long hours but retained its revolutionary zeal. "Does not the tradition of struggle in the enlarged working class provide continuity with his past?" asks Wittram, *Russia*, p. 157; Bertram Wolfe, *An Ideology in Power: Reflections of the Russian Revolution* (New York, 1969), p. 4; Robert Ferro, "Aspirations of Russian Society," in Pipes, pp. 188-90.

92. Wolfe, p. 4.

93. Wittram, *Russia*, p. 158.

94. Isaac Deutscher, *Stalin: a Political Biography* (New York, 1949), p. 294.

95. *Ibid.,* p. 42. The proletariat was urbanized - what Wittram (p. 158) calls "practical intelligentsia." Stalin's biggest concern was to make sure that *kulaks* and *Nepmen* not be a permanent influence. They represented a challenge to the development of state socialism, and he wanted them erased. To Stalin, the ideal citizen was the *apparatchik*, "an unthinking docile cog" in the Soviet economy. Theodore von Laue, **Why Lenin? Why Stalin?** (Philadelphia, 1964), p. 188. Stalin saw in collectivization possibilities as a Party slogan (emphasizing work for the benefit of the state); thus, to maintain the revolutionary zeal and to prevent *kulaks*, *Nepmen,* and others (including dissident intellectuals) from winning support for their causes. The challenge was real: the Trotskyite rejection of many of Stalin's programs produced a vital counter-movement that helped bring about the purges of the 1930s.

96. Gregory Grossman, "Thirty Years of Soviet Industrialization," *Soviet Survey* (October-December, 1958), p. 18.

97. Throughout all the purges the Russian "man in the street" remained largely unaware that Stalin was the instigator. As Gorer (p. 166) writes of the Russian situation in general, "the Leader, since the medieval period, has always been all-knowing and truthful." In the days of the tsars, most problems were blamed, not on the "little father," but on the bureaucrats. So, too, in Stalin's time did much of the blame fall to that group. Only a few dissidents within the USSR, and observers outside, were aware of the truth. As early as 1922, Lenin wrote "that Georgian [Stalin] is in reality violating the interests of the proletarian class solidarity." Lenin to G.K. Ordzhonikidze, in Roy A. Medvedev, *Let History Judge: Origins and Consequences of Stalinism* (New York, 1972), p. 21. Knowledge of the severity of the purges has prompted Laqueur to condemn Stalin as "being

in line with the cruel tradition" of Russia's tsarist past. Laqueur, p. 98. Deutscher's conclusion is similar: Stalinism was "the amalgam of Marxism with Russia's primordial and savage backwardness." *The Unfinished Revolution: Revolutionary Russia, 1917-67* (London, 1967), p. 34.

98. Ossip K. Flechtheim, *Bolschewismus 1917-67: Von der Weltrevolution zum Sowjetimperium* (Wien, 1967), p. 17.

99. To Lenin, the chief concern of the Revolution of 1917 was "to carry through its creative tasks in conditions of capitalist encirclement." Cited in K. Ivanov, *Leninism and Foreign Policy of the USSR* (Moscow, n.d.), p. 25. Some skeptics have traced the USSR's world revolutionary concepts as far back as the rule of Nicholas I (whose embrace of the "concert system" meant ideals which Russia shared with other nations).

100. Rauch, pp. 191ff.

101. *Ibid.*

102. Gerhard Wettig, "Kontinuität und Wandel der russichen Deutschlandpolitik 1815-1969," in Boris Meissner und Gotthold Rhode (eds.), *Grundfragen sowjetischer Aussenpolitik* (Stuttgart, 1970), pp. 78-79. A Soviet viewpoint of these matters may be found in B. N. Ponomarev, *et al., History of Soviet Foreign Policy, 1917-45* (Moscow, 1969), p. 103.

103. *Ibid.*

104. Ivanov, p. 30

105. *Ibid.*

106. Isaac Deutscher, *The Ironies of History: Essays on Contemporary Communism* (Berkeley, 1966), p. 27. Cited hereafter as *Ironies*. The end of rule by a single dictator was a change that helped Russia's image. Yet Hans Kohn, one of America's most prolific historians, found hardly any

difference between the USSR and tsarist Russia. He found no difference between Party leadership and the autocracy of the pre-1917 period. Soviet historians faulted Kohn for his conclusions and accused him of taking historical facts out of context in order to make the USSR look bad. See especially Y. Karyakin and Y. Plimak, **Hans Kohn Analyses the Russian Mind** (Moscow, 1966). One change, although temporary, concerned the concessions granted by the Party to intellectuals for diatribes against Stalin. Frederick Barghoorn, "Changes in Russia: The Need for Perspective," in Brzezinski, p. 43.

107. Brzezinski, "The Soviet Political System: Transformation or Degeneration?" in Brzezinski, pp. 8,15. The Party's condemnation of Stalin was in conjunction with his development of nationalism, the "personality cult," and the purges. Despite the change, Brzezinski scoffed at Russia's committee rule, as signifying "a *régime* of clerks."

108. Michael Florinsky, "Change and Stability in the Soviet Union," **Current History** (October 1963), p. 205. The USSR defended itself against western charges of anti-Semitism by stating that anyone could leave Russia whenever they wanted. American presidents got political mileage out of that delicate issue. Nixon did it by identifying Brezhnev with Hitler; Carter crowed loudly about "human rights" violations; and Reagan made it an integral part of his "evil empire" speeches.

109. *Ibid.*

110. Deutscher, **Ironies**, p. 33. One must note, however, that only the *organized* Church was discouraged in the USSR. Religion remained an option, but embraced by a smaller part of the population than before. The Soviet attitude about the Church - that it preyed on man's primordial superstitions and fear of the unknown - was based on science.

111. Cited in Werner Philipp, "Wandlungen der Sowjethistoriographie," in Fritz Borinski (ed.), **Marxismus-Leninismus: Geschichte und Gestalt**

(West Berlin, 1961), pp. 72-73.

112. Cited in Wittram, *Russia*, p. 159.

113. Rauch, p. 396.

114. See the excellent essays in Richard Loewenthal und Boris Meissner (eds.), *Sowjetische Innenpolitik: Triebkräfte und Tendenzen* (Stuttgart, 1968).

115. Kh. Momjan, *The Dynamic Twentieth Century* (Moscow, 1968), pp. 240-61.

116. The intelligentsia changed, too. After 1917 it was defined as all who worked for the State with their minds, instead of their hands. Under Soviet rule political ambitions were discouraged, and chief interests were intended to be in machines and technology. Malia, in Pipes, p. 3. From a western viewpoint, the principal handicap was indoctrination, along Marxist-Leninist lines. Deutscher (*Ironies,* p. 50) suggested that as a consequence perhaps some facets of education in Russia spread too fast, while others moved too slow. Kennan (Pipes, p. 7) laughed at Soviet boasts of educational attainment, believing that the tsarist system in 1914 could not have been much behind the West. "One cannot accept," he stated, "the thesis that the old *régime* kept the Russian people in darkness." Malia disagreed. "The brutal utilitarian use of the ideological by the Soviets," he wrote, "[was] no more than a sectarian version of the spirit of the pre-Revolution intelligently carried out to a *nec plus ultra* by the experience of power." Malia, in Pipes, p. 18.

117. One way to get censored materials to the citizenry was via the *samizdat* (privately published, illegal literature) which Deutscher insisted had to be supported "until the nation [recovered] its mind and speech." Deutscher, *Ironies,* p. 100.

118. The present writer addressed the history honor society (*Phi Alpha*

Theta) at San Jose State University on the subject of Zhirinovsky in 1994. One point made was how *deliberately* ignorant we are about him. His memoir (**Last Push to the South**) was available, in English translation, in both Britain and Canada... but not in the United States until midway through the first decade of the new millennium.

Fragile Majesty: Domestic and Foreign Policy in the Habsburg Empire, 1740-1914

This essay dates from the late 1960s, and deals with the most polyglot nation in European history.

Commanding a domain that was steadily growing into a complicated, multinational empire, Austria's Habsburgs early in the eighteenth century found problems at home distressed by a growing involvement in matters dealing with scores of people beyond their borders. Emperor Charles VI, who accepted Turkey's peace terms at Passarowitz, told advisors that retaining former Ottoman holdings after his reign ended was imperative, if his country was to be a major player on the European stage. (1)

Failing to produce a male heir to carry out this task, he suggested a "pragmatic sanction," that would allow his eldest daughter ascend the throne. He hoped that would meet with the approval of diverse elements of the *Oesterreich,* simplify the conduct of foreign affairs, and assure the Habsburgs complete control of the realm. That got popular support from

Austrians, but met with strong opposition elsewhere. Only in 1723, ten years after it was proposed, was the Pragmatic Sanction accepted by the entire country.

Approval was the consequence of much debate in the *diet,* and came about only when Magyars (Hungarian aristocrats) were convinced that acceptance would not restrict Hungarian efforts at autonomy. In extending "house" rule the Sanction became the first fundamental law common to all Habsburg possessions, and marked the first real affirmation of fealty to the *Reich.* (2)

Where the Sanction was important in foreign, as well as domestic policy, may be seen in its reception by other powers. When Austria made a diplomatic agreement with Spain, the governments of Britain, France and Prussia feared that Austria might become imperialistic. Thus, in 1725 they formed a pact (the "Herrenhausen alliance"). Though largely ineffective and short-lived, it had long-range implications: in the next two centuries the signatories would seek to check Habsburg designs, even at the risk of war.

The first real test of the Sanction came when Charles died in 1740. Succeeding him to the throne, was his daughter, Maria Theresa. Ignorant in matters of state policy, Maria encountered the opposition of several European powers. In a conflict which followed - the War of the Austrian

Succession - the contesting powers sought to capitalize on her ignorance to advance their *own* imperialist designs. Friedrich II of Brandenburg-Prussia was particularly interested; he wanted Silesia, with its vast mineral wealth. (3)

The war went poorly for Austria and induced Maria to forgo strictly Austrian forces and seek help from Hungary. As Barbara Jelavich notes, this request inspired other "national" elements, which used the war to initiate a series of demands for a bigger voice in Habsburg affairs. (4)

In 1741 Maria listened to Magyar entreaties for more economic freedom. For their wartime assistance she pledged freedom from excessive taxation. She also employed the talents of Andrei Grassalkovich (Speaker of the Hungarian *diet)* to convince Hungarian aristocrats of the sincerity of her interest in their affairs. Those efforts were successful, and she was able to obtain financial and military assistance from the Nymphenburg Alliance. (5)

That is not to say that she capitulated entirely to the Magyars. There was a long history of mistrust; suspicions did not vanish overnight. Often, in fact, she attempted to reduce Magyar influence. She created a special school (the *Theresanium),* to support her policy of "Germanization" - a **Gesamtstaat,** based in Vienna. (6) She streamlined administrative departments and re-structured the Foreign Office. She created two cadet schools, established a financial office, and as Professor Macartney has noted, even created a War Office. (7)

Alas, the treaty which concluded the War in 1748 was really more of an armistice; eight years later Austro-Prussian friction produced another conflict (the Seven Years War). This imbroglio spawned a noteworthy "diplomatic revolution": France, which earlier had supported Prussia, now joined Austria (thanks largely to the statecraft of *Staatskanzler* Count Kaunitz.) (8) The switch changed little at first, except that Magyars and others took the opportunity to express continuing dissatisfaction with Vienna.

Two years after the end of that war, Josef II of Bavaria began to share his mother's reign. Josef, who Macartney notes had "a terrible genius," was not very influential in foreign affairs. Ruling alone after 1780, he concentrated on domestic affairs, hoping to strengthen Vienna's hold on the multinational realm by extinguishing the various privileges that Maria had bestowed as the *quid pro quo* for cooperation. His most vehement attacks were aimed at the Hungarians, whose *Comitats* he replaced with an "Austrian system" of *Kreise.* (9)

Additionally, he instituted a rigid tax policy, and demanded the conscription of Magyars into the armed services. These, and other stern measures, angered the ordinarily placid Hungarian *diet*, and provoked a hostility toward Austrian policies in all departments. So perplexing and disarming did the situation become, that A.J. P. Taylor speaks of Austria, quite rightly, as "an imperial organization; not a country." (10)

Only indirectly may one speak of Hungarian opposition to Austrian domestic affairs being influenced by Josef's foreign policy. The balance sheet shows a defeat (War of the Bavarian Succession) and a victory (the first Partition of Poland), but these came during his co-rule with Maria. His activities concerning the Ottoman Empire gained him even fewer friends; consequently, his record in foreign policy was abysmal. Hostility from Hungarians only increased, and further efforts at an anti-Hungarian solution (given special impetus in the 1780's by support of the "League of German Princes") only complicated matters.

In some small measure, Hungary's support of the League was notable: it was the first attempt by Magyar nobles to seek outside support. (11) Josef's policy is clear: Austria had to be centralized or risk losing control over all its subjects. Toward that end, he only managed to weaken the state.

Leopold II, who followed Josef in 1790, was an enlightened ruler and a better politician than his predecessor. A master at making concess-ions, he was realistic enough to deal fairly with Magyars. As an offering of friendship he proposed to be crowned their king and to return to Hun-gary its crown jewels. For the realm as a whole he promised religious tol-eration and peasant emancipation. (12) Regardless, the Hungarian *diet* was difficult to please. It seemed that moderation was being practiced in order to bolster Austria, in case there was another war. A war climate *did* exist, though it soon dissipated (due to an eleventh-hour partition of Poland).

Napoleon Bonaparte changed the passive attitude. Because of his policies, Austria lost much of its strength and prestige. This included the formal dissolution of the old Holy Roman Empire. The loss, however, was not ill-received by those groups seeking to express their identity. With Napoleon's defeat (1815) and the ascendancy of Franz I, a repressive and reactionary policy followed - at home *and* abroad - geared to establishing a *status quo ante*. (13)

Napoleon's impact upon the subject peoples of the Austrian empire never had the anticipated disintegrating effect. In fact, his adventures produced a strong surge of *loyalty* to the Habsburgs, and his vague pro-posals to limit Austrian centralism only inspired a virile Francophobia. Unfortunately, Franz was not able to turn the anti-Napoleonic feeling into a permanent pro-Austrian fealty. (14) He was lucky: the Magyars were suspicious of Napoleon's motives for his proposal of Hungarian independence. (15)

In 1809, Franz entrusted the confusing and complicated business of running Austria to Klemens von Metternich, who early on confessed that

"Austria was not ruled, but only administered." (16) Believing that only a balanced foreign policy could produce domestic stability, he urged that the Hungarians be firmly controlled, else Austria would not be able to participate successfully in foreign wars. Napoleon had sought to divide the Habsburg realm by encouraging a Hungarian revolt against Vienna. His mistake was in supporting Slavs; that alienated most Hungarians. (17) Franz may have thought Hungarians incapable of an effective revolt; in any event, in 1809 he announced he would grant no concessions. (18)

His attitude remained steadfast after Napoleon's defeat, and one consequence was the beginning of a liberal movement (soon to be led by Szechenyi) in Hungary. Aimed first at the modernization of its institutions, these practitioners of liberalism worried Vienna, and remained uppermost in its considerations for the rest of the century. (19)

Domestic policy was not the only concern. In the first half of the nineteenth century foreign policy often was equally important. Of particular concern was the growth of Prussia. After instituting the Karlsbad Decrees on the German *Burschenschaften* in 1819 the Habsburg position in *all* the Germanies was weakened. Prussia reaped an early advantage by establishing a customs union *(Zollverein)*. By the 1820's it had expanded in a Prussian attempt to unite the confederated states against Austria.

Richard Charmatz has observed that Metternich attempted to check Prussian designs by bringing Austria into the union. Protests from the Hungarian *diet* - notably in 1825 and 1830 - ended those plans. (20) Thus, one of Metternich's foreign policy objectives was defeated by traditionally antagonistic forces in Hungary, and by newly emerging hostile forces within Austria. It was, as Taylor rightly observes, the beginning of the end of Metternich's power. (21)

Certainly the revolutionary movements of 1830 did not help him or Austria. Not only did Metternich fail to engineer any long-range settlement of Europe's disorders, but Austria itself was no longer effective as the "guarantor of legitimacy." "My whole life's work is destroyed," he grumbled as revolutions spread. As Macartney notes, the events abroad convinced many within the empire that the conservative "system" was the "enemy of true happiness." (22)

Compounding difficulties was the fact that Metternich, who in Taylor's view lacked self-confidence, was concerned that the Habsburgs might not be strong enough to withstand the Russians. (23) They had become interested in the Danube region in recent decades. Importantly, the 1830 revolutions spoke to the ineffectiveness of conservative policies, which encouraged groups within the empire to demand concessions.

Eighteen years later, as Charmatz points out, Andrian von Werburg published a book entitled **Austria and its Future**. Its thesis was that the empire's collapse was "imminent," and that it would come through the efforts of its national groups, not foreign aggression. He notes that the book was "widely read" and may have inspired the 1848 revolutions.(24)

1848 marked the accession to the throne of Franz Josef II. It also signaled the end of Metternich's service to the empire. He had been losing ground steadily since 1830, and his fall marked the end of Austria's domination of European affairs. To Robert Kahn, this was the beginning of the end of the multinational state. (25)

The continental revolutionary wave touched Vienna only after starting in Naples and Paris. Urged on by an economic downturn which had plagued Austria since 1846, and by the more numerous demands of the Hungarian *diet*, many radical groups scored successes. Particularly noteworthy were the efforts of Lajos Kossuth, whose **Pesti Hirlap** clamored for complete autonomy. (26)

For the first time, other nationality groups made strong demands. The Croats, for example, requested autonomy, and the Czechs (at the urging of Palasky) got Vienna's permission to convene a constitutional assembly. Galicia, Dalmatia and Moravia presented similar demands, with varying degrees of success. (27)

To keep control of his subjects the emperor approved what has been called the Stadion Constitution. It promised freedoms for Croats, Hungarians and others. The shallowness of its pledge, however, was evident and did not stem the tide of unrest. Insurrectionists spoke to the insincerity of the decree and accelerated hostilities. (28)

Leniency was a thing of the past. Once order had been restored, Franz

Josef dismissed the notion of a constitution, and consigned to his interior minister, Alexander Bach, a policy of Germanization. (29) "Bach Husars" carried out the repression of Hungarian radicals. (30)

The empire's next major test came in 1854, over a *debacle* in the Crimea. Russia had helped Austria restore internal order in 1848, but was rebuffed by Austria when it asked for assistance in a war against the Turks. Bach reasoned that if Austria got involved, Prussia might cause trouble. He was also concerned about possible French intervention in Austria's Italian territories. Not the least of his worries was Russia's designs on "Austria's" Balkans. (31)

The decision to abstain from that war cost Austria the future support of Russia and credibility *vis-à-vis* the rest of Europe. Five years later, at a moment of acute financial embarrassment, Austria compromised its position by engaging in a conflict with Piedmont-Sardinia.

Austria failed to arouse much support for that war. Not only did the Hungarian *diet* disapprove (Vilagos was still a powerful memory), but Viennese banking houses humiliated the government by denying funds. Finally, in an effort to forestall revolution, Austria withdrew from the ill-considered conflict. The retreat, as Charmatz notes, dramatically laid bare the "internal weaknesses and divisiveness" of the empire. (32) As a result, Bach's ministry fell and was succeeded by Goluchowski, who came in with the new title of Minister of State. (33)

To make up for his disastrous foreign policy, Franz Josef authorized the October Diploma in 1860. It was a new fundamental law for the realm. In Taylor's words, it sought "to revive a federalism which had never existed." (34) Intended to placate the various nationalities, the Diploma offered no real advantages. The Hungarians balked, for they saw in the edict just another attempt to sabotage their efforts for complete autonomy. Simply put, the Diploma allowed for no rights; It reaffirmed the power of the state. (35)

The February Patent of 1861 was Vienna's next effort at coming to an understanding with dissidents. When it also failed, it was clear that some groups - and especially the Hungarians - would never be willing to accept *anything* short of autonomy. Centralization remained Vienna's policy, even at the time of its most disastrous foreign conflagration: defeat by Prussia in 1866.

That war had two important consequences: it reduced the Habsburgs to second place in central Europe, and it necessitated the concession of autonomy to the Hungarians in order to ensure some form of internal order. The *Ausgleich* of 1867 gave the Hungarian ruling class complete control in all governmental matters, save foreign relations, defense and finance. (36) The offer was made *only* to the Hungarians. When Croats reissued *their* demands for autonomy - and for a better relationship with Hungary - Vienna refused. (37)

Defeat at the hands of Prussia forced Austria to look to the Balkans for a workable foreign policy. Although its interests in this region were not new, its present attitude was. Ever aggressive, Austria was compelled to salvage *something* for the sake of pride, while watching out for Russian and German designs. Count Auersperg, "the first cavalier of the *Reich*," as Charmatz calls him, directed the government into a poorly-negotiated (and doubtless reluctant) occupation of the Balkan provinces of Bosnia-Herzegovina.

The Magyars condemned the occupation; rumors soon spread about a possible German-Hungarian "understanding." The Magyars' complaint was an old one: for decades they had opposed the inclusion of Slavs. Noisy demonstrations followed, and it appeared that Austrian foreign policy was being conducted with domestic brinkmanship in mind. (38)

A few months after the Congress of Berlin (1878) resolved this matter, Austria took a big step forward by negotiating a Dual Alliance with Germany. The aim was to defend central Europe against Russian imperialism, demonstrate Vienna's willingness to escape isolationism, and to negate German-Hungarian entreaties. (39) The architect on the Hungarian side was Count Julius Andrássy, who was hit with sharp criticism from Magyars when the terms leaked out. (40)

The alliance came at the beginning of the conservative ministry of Count Taaffe, and during his fourteen years an "iron ring" made such a tangled, bureaucratic imbroglio of imperial administration that it came to be regarded snidely as a policy of *Fortwürsteln* ("muddling through"). (41) At the very least, the alliance gave Austria something it had lacked for many years: the ability to deal with subject nationalities from a position of relative strength. Taylor credits Taaffe with bringing the Czechs back into the fold, and ending a long and bitter dispute with their leading spokesman, Rieger. "This marked a great victory," he writes, "for the unity of constitutional Austria." (42)

Nationalism also grew, and as one group was placated, another felt scorned. Concessions to the Czechs (for education) angered German-speaking groups. Croats pressed immediately for an *Ausgleich* of their own. A coalition of German liberals, Poles and Young Czechs came to-gether to oppose universal suffrage, which they saw as detrimental to their cause.

Neither Taaffe nor the emperor could appease everyone. Resolution short of civil war was impossible. (43) As many expected, Austria's domestic difficulties in the years 1880 to 1893 seriously disaffected its foreign policy. Friction with Russia increased, as each nation stalemated the other in the Balkans and elsewhere with frequent clashes. Awkwardness, the enactment of a wholly unnatural alliance with Italy (1881), and the permanence of a war environment, only fueled the fires of Czech and Slovene opportunists. Karl Renner, the Austrian polemicist, was able to raise the ideological specter with his charge that Austria was a "fossil monarchy" that should be put to rest via a Socialist takeover.

The Young Czechs played a role in the growing discontent. They criticized Austria's impotent foreign policy, arguing that a preoccupation with continental affairs had caused the deterioration of the *Reich*. Still, Franz Josef's position did not change. The promise of small concessions (such as linguistic parity to Poles and Germans) and the hiring of sympathetic ministers (such as Badeni) did not help.

In historical context, Austria's annexation of Bosnia-Herzegovina in 1908 was a colossal blunder. Not only did it bring more Slavs into the empire, it was never very clear whether either signatory - Russia *or* Austria - considered the negotiations final. Russia hoped for Austria's recognition of its claim to the Straits of the Dardanelles. In turn, Austria failed to respect the strict secrecy of the terms. (44) All in all, this *opera bouffe* only served to bring everyone to the verge of war.

The Balkan Wars of 1912-13 provided the "dress rehearsal" for the final disintegration of the monarchy. Fought over familiar ground and for obscure reasons, the Austrians sought to check Russian influence in southeastern Europe. Once again, they were unsuccessful, misguided in their belief that Tsar Nicholas II was willing to grant *carte blanche* to the Serbs. As Austria failed to understand Russian realities, so too, did Count Berchtold fail to dissuade the Serbs from communicating their own nationalism. The long clash, which led to Sarajevo in June 1914, marked "the virtual end of the Habsburg monarchy." (45)

The fact that the death knell of the empire came so late, in part must be due to the absence of unity: there were just too many demands, and too few desires by the Habsburgs to accommodate. Poor leadership merely postponed dissolution. Hungarian demands remained largely un-answered. Despite a decade of peace, Istvan Tisza, scion of an old and respected family, was unable to deal effectively with Hungarian politics, and in particular with the militant activities of the Radic brothers. (46) Nor could much be done to suppress an *Irredenta* movement in Tran-sylvania. Like a similar movement urged on by the Italians against the Habsburgs it only made Austrian administration impossible and produced violence.

From one point of view, the empire's biggest foreign policy blunder after its July 1914 ultimatum to Serbia was the decision not to follow an ally (Italy) into a declaration of neutrality. Militarily unprepared, Austria chose to join Germany in World War I. That the nation was ill-equipped to fight a war underscored its inability to preserve the "Austrian system" against internal rebellion. Its statesmen hoped that a share of a German victory would restore confidence at home. As the contest dragged on, all these presentiments vanished. To its partner, as Taylor has remarked, the view was that the **Kaiserstaat** was "shackled to a corpse." (47)

In its war aims the Austrians tried to combine idealism with practical considerations: the creation of a post-war Polish state, the promise of more liberties and quasi-independence in exchange for everyone rallying "to the defense of the homeland." Little of this made an impression on the nationalities. Their protests continued throughout the war, evolving quickly from requests for autonomy to demands for independence. (48)

Disintegration was accelerated by the death of Franz Josef in 1916. He represented the last chance at unity, and neither his successor (Prince Karl) nor his Minister (Ferdinand Czernin) could prevent the empire from dissolving. A military collapse abroad, an ineffective home policy in coping with socialist revolution, financial bankruptcy, late and sketchy plans for confederation, and Woodrow Wilson's popularly-received call for self-determination, sped up the breakup.

Ultimately, the collapse was the product of the interaction of foreign and domestic policy, all of which now fed the oratory of spokesmen such as Masaryk, Trumbic and Paderewski. As Jelavich concludes, Austria-Hungary was "the first great power in modern times to suffer complete political annihilation." (49)

Notes

1. Barbara Jelavich, *The Habsburg Empire in European Affairs, 1814-1914* (Chicago, 1969), p. 3.

2. Victor S. Mamatey, *Rise of the Habsburg Empire, 1526 to 1815* (New York, 1971), p. 93. For the sake of clarity, "Magyar" does not always connote "Hungarian," as the former was a minority (though quite a powerful one) in the Hungarian part of the domain.

3. To win this "brightest jewel of the crown," Friedrich engineered the Nymphenburg Alliance (with Saxony, Spain, Bavaria and France) in 1741. Though it failed, Friedrich was able to wrest Silesia from the Habsburgs.

4. Jelavich, p.4. This did yet not constitute nationalism. That came later.

5. *Ibid.*

6. A. J.P. Taylor, *The Habsburg Monarchy, 1809-1918* (New York, 1965), p. 15. She obliged the Magyars to swear to respect her "ultimate authority," after acknowledging the Hungarian constitution. Mamatey, p. 105.

7. C. A. Macartney, *The Habsburg Empire: 1790-1918* (New York, 1969), pp. 15-19.

8. *Ibid*. p. 15

9. Taylor, p. 17.

10. *Ibid*. p. 22; Macartney, p. 121. Measures included the retention of the *Robot* (labor service), the Civil Code of 1781, and the Criminal Code of 1787, which made all save the Hungarians equal before the law. Magyars under Maria Theresa had enjoyed the right only to enlist in military service; in non-Austrian provinces conscription was mandatory.

11. Macartney, p. 131. The Hungarians were aroused when Josef sought to remove the Hungarian crown to Vienna. This provoked violent demonstrations and ultimately moved him to change his mind. Meanwhile, his foreign policy was so ineffective that in 1788 he was forced to convoke the old county congregations in Hungary, in order to get enough troops and supplies. In January 1790 the emperor revoked certain "offensive edicts" toward Hungary, and granted it more freedom in the legislature.

12. One is reminded of Maria Theresa's position on religious toleration. Not consenting to a *Los von Rom,* she encouraged any sincere attitude which would buttress the realm against the dictates of Rome. Yet as Habsburg Catholicism grew more and more independent, Jews and Jesuits came to suffer from repression. Thus, an attitude of intolerance, which lasted until Leopold.

13. Mamatey, p. 146.

14. *Ibid.*; Jelavich, pp. 9-12.

15. Arthur J. May, *The Habsburg Monarchy, 1867-1914* (New York, 1968), p. 23.

16. Macartney, p. 155. This was to be helped by an effective state police (*Polizeihofstelle*). It was vigorous in its suppression of political groups and subversive literature.

17. Taylor, p. 33. Hungarian nobles retained their bitterness for countless reasons. Count Berziviczy, for example, continually complained that the nobility "lived much worse than Austrian peasants." Macartney, p.44.

18. Jelavich, p. 25.

19. Macartney, p. 248; May, p. 24. Metternich actually proposed some reforms to "reconcile the forces of opposition." To cancel out Hungarian liberation propaganda, he insisted that Vienna's "grand design" was to

delegate autonomy. He showed how subject minorities would get *diets,* the right to use vernacular, and some administrative control. He hoped this would encourage their fealty to Vienna.

20. Richard Charmatz, **Geschichte der auswärtigen Politik Oesterreichs im 19. Jahrhundert**, Bd. I (Leipzig, 1914), 34-35. Cited hereafter as **Aus. Politik**. This drove a wedge between Metternich and Franz, helped out by Magyar unhappiness over sugar tariffs.

21. Taylor, p. 48.

22. Macartney, pp. 233-34.

23. Taylor, p. 36.

24. Richard Charmatz, **Oesterreichs innere Geschichte von 1848 bis 1907**, Bd. I (Leipzig, 1911-12), 3. Cited hereafter as **Inn. Geschichte**.

25. Macartney, p. 238. Especially after the creation of the *Staatskonferenz*, Count Kolowrat's influence grew, while Metternich's declined.

26. Taylor, p. 50; Jelavich, p. 58. The Hungarian cause was bolstered by news of the "March laws": liberal measures urged at Bratislava to abolish the *Robot* labor system without compensation, to grant economic improvement for peasants, and to allow equal rights for all nationality groups. Charmatz, **Aus. Politik**, II, 19-20.

27. Jelavich, p. 50.

28. Taylor calls those students "the field officers" of the revolution.

29. Outside assistance was requested from the Russians, who felt an ideological obligation to preserve the *status quo.* The Hungarian rebellion was difficult to suppress, and no decision was reached there until August 1849, at Vilagos. Thereafter, states Taylor, the Austrian empire

became for the first and last time, "a fully unitary state." Taylor, p. 85; Charmatz, *Inn. Geschichte*. I, 14.

30. Charmatz, *Inn. Geschichte*, I, 15.

31. *Ibid.*, II, 50. In *Inn. Geschichte*. I, 35, he also notes that Austria was "for the first time isolated, without a substitution having been found to replace the friendship of the tsar." As Taylor correctly observes, "Austria remained thereafter in a state of suspended animation, waiting for extinction." Taylor, p. 91.

32. *Ibid.*

33. *Ibid,* p. 99.

34. *Ibid*, p. 100.

35. May, p. 29.

36. Ibid., p. 36; Charmatz, *Aus. Politik*. II, 62. Jelavich rightly points to the unification of Germany five years later as more important for central Europe than the *Ausgleich*. Jelavich, p. 101. Charmatz had some harsh words for the Austrian minister, Beust: "as he always smiled, so too did he handle all questions - too lightly" [*i. e.,* Austria's policy *vis-à-vis* Hungary was not firm enough]. Charmatz, *Inn. Geschichte*. I, 71.

37. Jelavich, p. 102.

38. Charmatz, *Inn. Geschichte*, I, 84; May, p. 49.

39. Charmatz, *Aus. Politik*, II, 89.

40. May, p. 62. Andrássy had also organized the Three Emperor's League (1873), and at the height of a war scare in 1875 published a note, urging the freedom of Ottoman-held Bosnia-Herzegovina. His encouragement

of Austrian intervention drew much criticism from his countrymen. Few realized that he was a *Realpolitiker,* striving to avoid a war with Russia.

41. Charmatz, *Inn. Geschichte*, II, 13.

42. Taylor, p. 157.

43. *Ibid*, 168. Certainly hampering the situation was the interest - active *and* passive - of foreign powers, such as Russia, which did everything in its power to maximize Austria's plight.

44. Jelavich, p. 150.

45. Taylor, p. 229.

46. Kálman Tisza led the fight in the 1870's and 1880's against Croat "historic interests." The nationalities were regarded as either "historic" or "non-historic," depending on their heritage and development. Leading the historic groups were the Germans, who, though possessing little national consciousness, were dominant. Magyars, who controlled Hungarian affairs, were separatists and had very little in common with other groups. Czechs hoped for a Slavic union, whereas the Poles sought the re-establishment of a Polish kingdom. The Croats' quarrel was with Hungary. Non-historic groups included Slovaks (ruled by Hungary) and Serbs (who were dependent on Croats).

47. Taylor, p. 231.

48. Despite his generally ineffective record, Istvan Tisza helped these protests by saying that a general war could only damage Hungary's privileged position within the realm. His hope for at least a continuation of the *status quo* brings from Taylor the conclusion that he may have been the "only man of resolution and clarity of purpose" in the empire. *Ibid*.

49. Jelavich, p. 176.

"Freedom" in Literature

Of all the subjects that constantly confront and challenge the social scientist, none has had a bigger impact than the one dealing with freedom. This essay touches briefly on that concern.

From late nineteenth century Russia, Fyodor Dostoevsky provided a thought-provoking commentary in **The Brothers Karamazov** about freedom. In a dialogue between a Grand Inquisitor and Christ, one learns that Christ erred by asking the poor to revolt. Why? He misunderstood the peasants. Russia's rural poor were largely conservative, even in the midst of deprivation. They would revolt to achieve their freedom only if they *knew* that their future would be glorious. That is the trap. How is anyone to *know* the future?

Man, as Erich Fromm wrote, is always fleeing *from* freedom. To tell him that he is free does an injustice, for he does not *want* to be free. Dostoevsky, who was imprisoned in Siberia after a failed attempt on the life of the tsar, identified with that idea. He decided that it was better to conform.

In the early twentieth century the Italian poet Gabrielle d'Annunzio canceled out the notion of freedom by insisting on fanatical loyalty and hero worship - *à la* Christ - and together with another poet, Ezra Pound, inspired Italian fascism. Simplicity was the key. Even Karl Marx knew that things were not as bad as he wrote them, so he exaggerated. In *The Communist Manifesto* he simplified matters, so as to win over "the simple-minded masses."

William Golding touched a similar nerve with *Lord of the Flies*. The primitivism (which is chillingly demonstrated in Piggy) betrays a free and open society that fails horribly, and nearly becomes anarchistic. Witness Jack, shouting like a savage, about his dislike for the ruler. Cannibalism arrives shortly thereafter.

Franz Kafka took us in yet another direction. In *The Castle*, one encounters a writer who may have been the first person to see the dangers that lie in the excessive bureaucracy of a powerful state. Was freedom the antidote? In *True Believer*, Eric Hoffer gave us a more modern take on that theme: fanatical leaders emerge because people lead dull, inadequate lives, and seek something extreme, regardless of moral consequences.

Arthur Koestler disturbed millions with *Darkness at Noon*. Written in prison, the novel is an examination of the mind of the revolutionary

(Stalin's Purge trials were in progress). In Koestler's view, revolution had become nothing more than a word and a catchphrase. *What* freedom?

Ultimately, political writers dangle the word "utopia" in front of us. Sir Thomas More gave it usage in 1516, but its meaning was "no place." His perfect world was one of rigid, religious uniformity. Ignatius Donnelly gave us a utopia without Jews (a forerunner of *Mein Kampf*?). In *Walden Two*, B. F. Skinner envisaged a place that gave little thought to human nature. "Man is a plant," and the family was obsolete. His society was made up of planners and managers... no innovation, only stagnancy.

George Orwell brought this theme to its zenith in *1984*. His "proles" do not participate; they have no interest in their political well-being. For increasingly somber analyses like that, we learned a new word: dystopia. Unlike Huxley's *Brave New World*, Orwell's *opus* is drab to the extreme: Freedom? Nonsense. In its place were brainwashing, "Big Brother," and rigid conformism.

It is perhaps not surprising that the best modern interpreters of the human dilemma come from the world of science fiction. Clifford Simak, perhaps the world's best-known pastoral humanist, gave us a prophetic picture of freedom from authority when he penned *City* in 1952. In an epic tale that spans centuries, man seeks sanity, first by leaving the cities for the countryside, and then exiting the planet for the stars. He leaves behind his dogs to steward the earth.

J. R. R Tolkien captured some of that spirit in **Lord of the Rings**. His hobbits were hedonistic, happy, and addicted to beauty and pretty colors. They had "their own scene," resented confusion, ate prodigiously, smoked burning leaves of herbs in pipes of clay, and were isolationists. The battle with evil shows up in the form of Sargon, and requires innocence and a magical ring to save the day. It was not hard to see a parable of Hitler or Mussolini, even though Tolkien said otherwise. And at the end of the adventure? A new power has taken over the hobbits' land. It rules firmly, with the help of a strong police force and a controlled economy. To achieve freedom, the hobbits inadvertently have spawned authoritarianism.

Terry Brooks is one of two recent writers to wonder about the wisdom of freedom. In **The Sword of Shannara**, Shea is intensely conservative and isolationist, whereas his friend Menion is for bringing unity to the land. A mighty wizard, Allanon, intercedes and reminds us of Tolkien's Gandalf. Brooks has gnomes who are yellow and are considered evil (Orientals?). The evil War Lord is spoken of in demonstrably black colors; and the trolls are brutal and slavish (Russians under socialism?) As for the magic: it only works for a half-breed (*à la* Tolkien's halflings).

Also noteworthy is **The Chronicles of Thomas Covenant, Unbeliever**, a staggering and disturbing literary accomplishment from Stephen Donaldson. Written as the Seventies was crumbling, it is a work about the anti-hero as hero... and he's a leper! Like the heroes in Brooks' novels, his magic alone can save the land; like Tolkien, the instrument of salvation or desecration is a ring, that only this half-man can use.

There are others, of course - the works of Asimov, Bradbury, Clarke, and Crichton spring immediately to mind - but this serves as an appetizer. Who knows: you may even get the definitive answer to the question posed by Fromm: *are* we all fleeing from freedom?

Ignoble Service: Franz von Papen and the Rise of Hitler

No collection of historical essays would be complete without at least one dealing with Adolf Hitler. This one seeks to explain *Der Führer* by discussing a man who helped bring him to power. Source notes have been omitted from this version.

While Britain, France, and the United States had reason to celebrate the end of the first World War, Germany did not. Bankrupt, beaten, and emotionally spent, Germany entered the 1920s with little expectation of achieving a "better world." Germany had not only been defeated, it had been humiliated. The treaties of Paris stripped away its army, scuttled its navy, and put troops of the victors on German soil to ensure the peace. German delegates at the Versailles peace talks were forced to agree, in writing, that their country was responsible for causing the War. As a *sui generis,* Germany was obliged to pay the victors more than $32 billion in reparations, and to abandon the monarchy in favor of a democratic government, *à la* Britain, France, and the United States.

The immediate consequences of these massive changes are not hard to imagine. Gross disenchantment and disgust swept through Germany, exacerbating the soul-crippling effects of the economic dislocation that would mar much of Europe in the 1920s. That triggered extreme reaction, and planted the seeds for the Second World War.

One of the key players in Germany's plight during the Weimar Republic (as Germany was now called) was an "Old Guard" aristocrat named Franz von Papen. Students of American history will recognize that name, for he was the military *attaché* largely responsible for Imperial German schemes to "blow up" America in 1915. In the twenties and early thirties he would play a pivotal role in bringing to power the man who sought to avenge Germany's defeat: Adolf Hitler.

꒷꒷꒷꒷꒷꒷꒷

Papen demonstrated both publicly and privately his hope that the democratic government that had been forced upon Germany would be eliminated. From the beginning, he planned to return his nation to a position of power.

At the heart of his criticism was the Weimar Constitution, which was grounded on the principle that "political authority emanates from the people." An arch-conservative who opposed popular rule in any form, he contended that the new Constitution was "diametrically opposed to the teachings and the traditions of the Roman Catholic Church," to which he was dedicated. He also accused the constitution's drafters of favoring Protestant Prussia. In giving that state huge power the architects "made no attempts" to solve the "dualism" that existed between Prussia and the central government. Opposition to the republican form of government - and to its creators (mainly Social Democrats) - was to be Papen's credo during the life of the Weimar Republic.

To put forward his views, he sought out and attended numerous political meetings after 1919. By 1925 he was a frequent guest of the *Herren-klub*, an upper class men's group whose aim, as he recalled years later in in his memoirs, was to bring together in a friendly atmosphere politicians "of every shade of opinion." In the main, the generally conservative tone of the *Herrenklub* was ideal. Soon after its creation in 1924, Papen was exchanging opinions and grievances with General Kurt von Schleicher, Oskar von Hindenburg, and other notables from the military and the world of business.

A gifted and graceful speaker, Papen was able to project his views easily and convincingly, and early on used this asset to work for change. "He carried on politics by social means," writes Theodor Eschenburg, "and apparently wanted not just social goals in the reconstitution of the state," but a complete overhaul. As for political parties, he stood with the far right wing of the Catholic-conservative **Zentrum**, which he joined about 1920. It was a solid base from which he could express his inner-most political aspiration: the restoration of the German monarchy. With the help of friends and associates in his native Westphalia, Papen won election to the Prussian *Landtag* as a **Zentrum** candidate in 1921. For the next decade he put forward his case for the restoration of the monarchy.

Papen's most important weapon was the printed word. In 1923 he purchased forty-seven percent of the Prussian newspaper, **Germania** ("on behalf of the [Centrist] Party"), supposedly because the newspaper had fallen into the hands of "an awkward *frondeur*." Regardless, he used it the same way in which he used the *Herrenklub* (and its publication, **Der Ring**): to convince his countrymen that Germany could be "saved" only by the restoration of an authoritarian government.

    Germania and **Der Ring** served as sounding boards for those views. Through them he leveled his criticism at all political parties, left *and* right. He was not afraid of the recently-formed Communist Party (**Kommunist-ische Partei Deutschlands** - KPD), with which he associated the Bolshevik goal of taking all power from the aristocracy and distributing it among peasants and workers. He was least opposed to the German National People's Party (**Deutschenationale Volkspartei** - DNVP), and was less receptive to the liberal, reform-minded Democratic Party (*Deutsche Demokratische Partei* - DDP).

A special target was the Social Democratic Party (*Sozialdemokratische Partei Deutschlands* - SPD). He believed it to be the party most responsible for promoting and sustaining the Weimar Republic. If its influence could be diminished, Germany would be able to reassert itself as a European power. The SPD's concept of "democracy," he noted, "enslaved the ideals and threw them away with scornful laughter."

Papen was persistent. In 1925 he lent his support to the DNVP in that year's Presidential election, and its candidate, former Field Marshal Paul von Hindenburg. "Such a God-fearing and devout personality as Hindenburg," he said, "would provide the best guarantee" for the re-establishment of the monarchy. By supporting Hindenburg, though, he alienated many in his own party. The *Zentrum* had never regarded Papen very highly, and after Hindenburg's victory their disenchantment only grew.

He recounts that fact in his memoirs, and Eschenburg has noted that after 1925 he was at best "a disaffected member" of the Prussian *Landtag,* and sure of no support from conservative colleagues. The *Zentrum* now referred to him as "a *frondeur,*" and against the spirit of Matthias Erzberger and Joseph Wirth. The left wing of the Party "always considered him the servant of the Right."

As economic problems intensified, President Hindenburg was coaxed into appointing as Chancellor a well-known financial expert and *Zentrum* member, Heinrich Brüning. He believed this would take Germany out of the world-wide Depression. Taking office in March, 1930, Brüning was not successful. His deflationary measures, which reduced the supply of German capital, only worsened the financial situation and resulted in demands from nearly all political parties for his removal.

One of Papen's objections was that Brüning had the support of the SPD, ostensibly in return for a pledge to uphold the Constitution. Speaking in behalf of farmers, he criticized the Chancellor's land reform program. He accused Brüning of breaking up large, "inefficient" estates into smaller ones. On foreign affairs, he was charged with retarding economic progress by accepting British and French demands for full reparations payments. Finally, in Papen's opinion, the Chancellor failed because he did not try hard enough to get the support of Germany's right-leaning parties (specifically, the DNVP, but also the Nazi Party [**Nationalsozialistische Deutsche Arbeiterpartei** - NSDAP], which had grown substantially over the past two years). At a meeting in Dülmen on October 4, 1930, Papen insisted that "there are but Right and Left;" Brüning "must rid himself of parliamentary trimmings" and establish a more authoritarian government. That ended any identification with the centrists.

After two years in office, during which time the German economy continued to crumble, Brüning tendered his resignation. The next move was General Schleicher's. He used his considerable influence with Hindenburg and his circle of friends and advisors to sponsor the candidacy of someone he thought would be acceptable to the president, and one he thought he could control: Papen.

Schleicher met with Papen on May 28, 1932, and had him present himself to Hindenburg as the one person the president could trust. Papen, whose articles in *Der Ring* and *Germania* had urged radical changes in Brüning's policies, later confessed his "surprise" at Schleicher's offer. This is not convincing; in fact, he was honored by the suggestion, and believed that Schleicher was the spokesman for the *Reichswehr* - "the only stable organization remaining in the State," as he put it. He agreed to talk with Hindenburg.

Paramount in Schleicher's thinking was that with Papen as Chancellor, the conservatism of the *Zentrum* Party could be minimized, or even eliminated. He also believed that control of the *Zentrum* would help neutralize the NSDAP. On that Schleicher and Papen were in accord: the monarchy had to be restored; at the very least, the Constitution must be reshaped along less democratic lines. Only to Papen's suggestion that the upper house become more powerful, and working class representation in the *Reichstag* be diminished, did Schleicher disagree.

Two days later (May 30), Papen informed Schleicher that he "had doubts" about seeking the Chancellorship. Schleicher, though, helped dispel those doubts with the promise that NSDAP leader Adolf Hitler had pledged "tacit approval" of a government headed by Papen. Doubtlessly impressed with the thought of extreme right wing support, he decided to ask Hindenburg for the position. Just before meeting Hindenburg, on May 31, he did the prudent thing: he consulted *Zentrum* leader, Monsignor Ludwig Kaas. The meeting was not a happy one. Kaas did not favor Papen's candidacy. He told him that it would not be good for Germany to have another centrist in the government. Kaas asked him to promise not to seek the office. Papen agreed.

Later that same day Papen visited Hindenburg and *accepted* the Chancellorship. "I had tried to make the *Reichspräsident* understand that it would be unwise to entrust me with the Chancellorship," he recalled many years later. "Why the President chose me as Chancellor, I do not know."

Papen quickly formed a cabinet of "national concentration," choosing several nobles and members of the *Herrenklub* - most of whom had no party affiliation. Noteworthy in the formation of this cabinet of *"nationaler Rechten"* (as Eschenburg called it) was the exclusion of Social Democrats. Totally dependent upon the support of the ailing President, the cabinet had little or no popular following.

Almost immediately, Papen showed that he intended to pursue a bolder and more active policy than his predecessor. On June 4, 1932, he got Hindenburg's permission to dissolve the *Reichstag*, a move calculated to get more right wing support. Hoping to get more than "tacit" cooperation with the NSDAP he promised to bring Hitler into line with his views. "In less than two months," he boasted to a colleague shortly after his appointment, "we will have pushed Hitler so far back into a corner that he'll be squeaking."

At the first cabinet session on July 2, Papen enunciated his political views. Economic recovery, he said, was Germany's primary consideration. Toward that end, he proposed a partnership between business and government. He did *not* state that he also planned the elimination of all political parties.

From the beginning, his pro-monarchist, anti-democratic government had sparse support. It was soundly denounced by many parties, including the **Zentrum**. Although he preferred to call his government "an assemblage of all the creative and preservative forces in the State," Papen did *not* have the support of labor, small farmers... or even the business community. He was still a relative unknown, and the main support for his "new State" was Hindenburg. There was even doubt that he had the support of the NSDAP.

The Nazis, to be sure, made it clear that they would not give their support, unless Papen made concessions. One week after taking office, he met with Hitler and was quite firm with the Nazi leader. Hitler's bold, confident manner surprised him, and he rejected most of his demands as "amateurish." He did not wish to alienate Hitler, though, so he agreed to token concessions (such as lifting the two month-old ban on the wearing of S.A. [*Stürmabteilungen*] uniforms). "All that had happened," Papen recollected years later, "was that equal rights for all parties had been restored." It is rather obvious, in the light of subsequent events, that all parties were *not* treated as equals. Papen would treat a party "equally" only if it would help him solidify his position.

Widespread violence followed the lifting of the ban on S.A. uniforms. Over the next two months, Nazi "Storm Troops" clashed periodically with various political groups (and especially the KPD). Papen did not condone the violence. His politics are perhaps best seen regarding the Altona riots of July 17. He used emergency powers (Article 48 of the Constitution) to ban "open-air demonstrations" (which presumably had preceded the riots). He did *not* direct the ban against the NSDAP - which had incited the riots - but the KPD, even though he probably knew the Nazis were responsible. This suggests a strong desire to have Nazi support.

The next step was to hamstring the SPD. Here, Papen chose as his target the government of Prussia, an SPD stronghold since 1929. To do so, he needed the support of the Prussian police - the strongest civilian "peace-keeping" force in Germany. Using the "communist-inspired" riots as a pretext, he tried to remove the Minister-President, Otto Braun, and the Minister of the Interior, Carl Severing. Papen considered that move at least as early as June 6, when he wrote Hans Kerrl, the newly-elected Nazi leader of the Prussian *Landtag*, that he should convene an assembly as soon as possible, and choose a responsible "constitutional" government. By declaring that disorders in Prussia constituted an emergency, he got permission from Hindenburg on July 19 to move against the Braun-Severing government.

On July 20, 1932, Papen asked Severing and Joachlm Klepper (Prussian Finance Minister) to meet with him in Berlin. They did, and he informed them that due to the "threat of communism" he would take emergency measures and suspend the Socialist-backed Prussian government ("for only a short period"). Although this did not come as a surprise, Prussian officials were angry. Severing was especially upset. He said he would yield only to force. Papen acted swiftly and relieved him, Braun and other SPD ministers of their positions.

Then he dissolved the *Landtag*. The only "legal" basis for this action was Article 48: first declaring martial law, and then replacing the SPD functionary, Albert Grzesinski, with Otto Melcher... "a trustworthy civil servant." SPD appeals to the courts fell on deaf ears. Papen overcame protests from south German states, too, and emerged victorious. By the end of July he had convinced many Germans that he and his cabinet stood virtually independent of politics. It was, as Gordon Craig has noted, "an empty victory," for by giving the SPD its worst defeat since the founding of the Republic, Papen had served notice that he intended to establish a dictatorship.

The *Reichstag* elections of July 31 further demonstrated the move to the right: the NSDAP doubled its totals of the previous election and thus emerged as the largest political entity. At the same time, the SPD lost many seats. Believing that the Nazis had reached their zenith with the elections, Papen reopened negotiations with Hitler. On August 6 he met with Schleicher, and expressed surprise when Hitler refused a subordinate position in the government. He would accept only the position of Chancellor, and conduct that job along "non-authoritarian" lines.

An increase in Nazi militancy that summer worried Papen. The murder of a Polish worker (Pietrzuch) in Potempa (Silesia) on August 9, was particularly distressing. He would have to take firm action against the killers - *even if they were Nazis* - if he wanted to maintain order and keep his job. He ordered the arrest of the alleged assailants, and charged them with first-degree murder.

The NSDAP's reaction was predictable: it blamed the murder on the KPD. Unless new elections were called, warned the ***Völkischer Beobächter*** (the Nazi newspaper) Germany soon would be under a military dictatorship. On August 10 Papen told his cabinet that the only way to halt further deterioration was to make *Hitler* chancellor. He did not want this to become common knowledge. He would first try again to bring Hitler into the government in a support capacity. Only if that failed would he be willing to yield his office.

Acting in the hope that he still could mollify Hitler, Papen visited him on August 13. Hitler was cool to the suggestion that he come into the cabinet as Vice-Chancellor. "I soon realized," Papen noted later, "that I was dealing with a very different man from the one I had met two months earlier." Still, he was firm, believing that as long as he had Hindenburg's support, he had little to fear. He suggested that if Hitler was not willing to accept the Vice-Chancellorship, he could stay outside the cabinet and have a colleague take that position. The cabinet, he noted, must be preserved.

In his memoirs, Papen intimates his willingness to "step down" in favor of the Nazi leader, "once the President had got to know him better." He suggested that Hitler should talk to Hindenburg. He did, but without satisfaction. In fact, Hindenburg was *very* cold toward Hitler, and told him he would reject NSDAP demands *in toto.*

Papen now pursued a cautious, middle course. When Goebbel's newspaper, **Der Angriff**, sharply criticized him on August 25, publication was suspended for a week. Papen closed the month with a speech to agrarian interests in Münster three days later. In it, he proposed an enlarged public works program, the extension of the voluntary labor service, and a concession to industry (whose occasional support he had enjoyed), in the form of tax credits. He also promised constitutional and administrative reforms. He then spoke to current political events, saying that the work of strengthening Germany could "be done only by an authoritarian and independent government deeply aware of its duties toward God and nation." It was his duty "to keep partisan influences" from blocking progress toward complete recovery.

In an apparent attempt to divorce himself from the Nazis, he even said that he regarded himself "the servant of the entire people, not that of a class or party." In closing, he told his audience that Nazism "runs counter to all German and Christian ideals of law."

Two days later (August 30), Papen met Hindenburg at Neudeck, ostensibly to discuss constitutional and economic reforms. He repeated his remarks, this time urging the President to dissolve the *Reichstag*. He felt that the Nazis would be weak in the upcoming elections, and this would communicate a vote of confidence in his government.

Once again, he believed the NSDAP had reached its peak. He believed too much. On August 31 the *Reichstag* adjourned. When it reconvened - twelve days later - Papen urged its dissolution. Instead, Herman Göring, whom the membership had elected its President at the end of August, ignored him and gave the floor to a communist, who in turn proposed a vote of no confidence in the government. The vote came as Papen was placing the decree for dissolution on Göring's desk! The *Reichstag* voted against Papen, 512 to 42.

As Karl Dietrich Bracher has commented in his history of the Weimar Republic, Papen's "plan for dictatorship" was shattered when *Reichstag* elections were held on November 6. Although they lost thirty-four seats, the Nazis still constituted the largest party (196). Furthermore, the KPD increased its total by eleven, while the **Zentrum** Party lost seven. Papen had hoped for a Nazi loss; instead, the NSDAP was still a powerhouse.

Although he publicly called the elections a "victory" for his policies, Papen knew he had failed. One week later a large strike among Berlin transport workers was precipitated by *both* the KPD and the NSDAP. He had lost control, and on November 17, he resigned.

At this point, Schleicher showed what *he* wanted. He told Hindenburg that a chancery with him in charge could neutralize the Nazis. Papen did not believe it, but his skepticism was lost on the President. "Our only hope," said Hindenburg, "is to let Schleicher try his luck." On December 2, 1932, Schleicher was named Chancellor.

Thereafter, Papen regarded the new leader as *persona non grata*, believing, among other things, that he had intrigued against him, at least since the preceding May. To discredit his former sponsor, Papen contributed stinging editorials in **Der Ring,** blaming him for all the mistakes and oversights of his *own* administration. "I felt no personal animosity towards Schleicher," Papen pleads unconvincingly in his memoirs [he savaged him in a speech to the *Herrenklub* on December 16]. To this, one associate commented that "Herr von Papen is a 'pompous fellow' [*Wichtigtuer*]. This speech is the swan song of a bad loser."

Papen still tried to enlist Nazi support, but as an outsider. On January 4, 1933, he met with Hitler at the home of the Cologne banker, Kurt von Schroeder. Hitler listened as he suggested that they use their "collective efforts" to replace Schleicher with themselves. Hitler agreed, but insisted that he be in control, with Papen coming in as Vice-Chancellor. Papen refused, even though he must have known it would be the highest office he could achieve: for the NSDAP was only getting more and more powerful.

Another meeting with Hitler followed on January 22, at the home of Joachim von Ribbentrop. Once again, Hitler offered Papen a place in his government. If he would use his influence with Hindenburg to secure Hitler's appointment, the Nazi *Führer* pledged he would *never* adopt radical measures. He even offered Papen control of Prussia. That offer was simply too tempting to refuse, and over the next few days Papen exerted all his influence to win Hindenburg over. The old man finally consented, with the stipulation that Hitler accept Papen as "deputy chancellor." Hitler agreed.

On January 28, 1933, Hindenburg accepted Schleicher's resignation and appointed Hitler Chancellor of the *Reich*. In an emotional celebration Hitler promised to strengthen Germany on the basis of Germany's historic culture and "Christian ethics." The next day the Republic that Papen had despised was dead, and the Nazi era had begun.

Shades of Gray: The Impact of Speculative Fiction since 1945

This essay promotes a theme that few would disagree with today. The authors discussed below are representative of Europe *and* America.

Writers are usually the best communicators of a nation's culture. In their books and essays they measure society, instruct as to its mores, its politics, and its lifestyle. Most do not seek public office, and can be candid and honest in their appraisal of the world around them. A nation without thoughtful writers is one that has not yet achieved civilization.

America has produced a large number of writers. In the first decades of the nineteenth century James Fenimore Cooper and Washington Irving wrote about lost innocence and direction (**Last of the Mohicans, The**

Legend of Sleepy Hollow, Rip Van Winkle). By the 1850s *literati* were writing about issues that otherwise had been ignored. Harriet Beecher Stowe talked about race in ***Uncle Tom's Cabin;*** Nathaniel Hawthorne invented "psychological realism" to explain intolerance in ***The Scarlet Letter***; Herman Melville provided an awareness of the environment in ***Moby Dick***; and Henry David Thoreau admonished people to flee cities and return to their roots in ***Walden Pond***. By century's end, writers were displaying concerns about a frightening technology and the prospects for unlimited war. Edward Bellamy showed us that in ***Looking Backward***, and Mark Twain expressed his fears in ***Mysterious Stranger*** and ***A Connecticut Yankee in King Arthur's Court.***

The twentieth century provided even more examples, especially as the fears about technology came true in the ultimate nightmare, World War I. In the aftermath, a so-called "Lost Generation" moaned about the loss of millions of human beings, and the consequent rise of immorality, insensitivity, and greed. Throughout the 1920s and 1930s readers turned to Sinclair Lewis, F. Scott Fitzgerald, John Dos Passos, Theodore Dreiser, Ernest Hemingway, and John Steinbeck for direction and understanding.

The near ruination of mankind wrought by World War II brought yet another onslaught of intellectual soul searching. But this time there was a difference. The issues of old were still there (racial strife, intolerance, gender inequality, labor unrest, unemployment, oppression), but the latest generation brought something else into the equation: the aberration of science. Writers were frightened as never before, for unlike mankind's other, more familiar problems, this one appeared to have no solution. With the splitting of the atom, and the disappearance from the earth of two Japanese cities in 1945, an old biblical word began to show up in the writing and gain acceptance as prophecy: Armageddon.

As a consequence, mainstream writers all but disappeared. After all, why would a Steinbeck or a Hemingway want to write about science and technology? Their place was taken, not by highbrow *literati*, but by an ever-growing, ever-maturing group of people who wrote speculative fiction. Theirs would be the the voices people would listen to after 1945.

In the beginning, their numbers were small. Isaac Asimov was a noted Boston bio-chemist, who forsook that career for a crack at understanding the world created by the atomic age. His most famous sortie into that arena was **Foundation**, a series of books that had man attempting to get past the hurdles of tyranny and atomic power, as he leapfrogged through the cosmos. Yet another scientist, Aldous Huxley, discussed the wrongful use of science in **Brave New World.** First published in 1932, the book forecast the coming of test tube babies and cloning. Eric Allen Blair, a British civil servant, is best known by the *nom de plume* George Orwell. He riveted the post-War world, first with **Animal Farm**, and then **1984**.

Both books were so gloomy, with their predictions of man-manipulated techno-terror, that they inspired a new word in our lexicon: dystopia.

The Cold War was the immediate villain (and literary salvation for countless new writers). Just as the generation before had made its living off the recklessness of the Twenties and Thirties, this one grappled with an ideological conflict that few understood. Exponential leaps in science were taking place: relativity, atomic energy, and fissionable materials. Arthur C. Clarke was a trained scientist, whose cautionary tale, *"The Star"* (1947), had both hope *and* doom in it (as did another of his stories, which predicted computer chips).

In the late 1940s and early 1950s, with A-bombs followed by H-bombs, an apocalypse of our own making seemed inevitable. "Day-after" stories appeared, and by the end of the century those stories numbered in the hundreds. Perhaps none was better-written and more poignant than George R. Stewart's **Earth Abides** (1949). Three years later, Clarke borrowed a page from nineteenth century doomsdayers, and took Darwin into a probable future. The result was **Childhood's End**, one of the best-received science fiction novels of all time. Ten years later he continued the quest for extraterrestrial intelligence with **2001: A Space Odyssey**. Several years after that he brought the story down to 2010.

At the same time, our questionable evolution was the subject of at least two other treatments. Ray Bradbury, the "poet laureate" of science fiction, wondered if fascination with technology would be our undoing. In his short story, *"The Pedestrian"* (1953), conformism meant staying home at night to watch television. Violators were chillingly punished. He also produced two distinct classics: **The Martian Chronicles** and **Fahrenheit 451.** The first was an old-fashioned space opera that urged us to leave the earth for greener pastures. The second was a dystopian nightmare: in the near future firemen in a totalitarian state did not extinguish fires, they started them. Their special target: books.

The other prominent writer of this new *literati* was Wisconsin-born Clifford D. Simak. He shared many of Bradbury's concerns, and until his death in 1988 many of his short stories and novels had us wondering about the impact of technology. His efforts, deliberately nostalgic in tone, portrayed an evolution beyond technology that did not always lead to unhappy conclusions. Perhaps the finest stylist of all twentieth century speculative fiction writers, Simak was a pastoral humanist who won every award his craft had to offer. One of his works was **City,** a long tale of man's exit from the cities to the countryside,subsequent to his departure for the stars. The planet's inheritors are dogs, whom man has given, with the guidance of some very humanistic robots, the power of speech.

The Fifties witnessed a profound change in the way science fiction was written. No longer was it exclusively the domain of "bug-eyed monsters" and extraterrestrial contraptions that violated every maxim of physics with monotonous regularity. In its place - probably *because* of the realities that were being forced upon us - was a sensitivity and intelligent inquiry that would be polished and perfected. Simak wrote *Time and Again*, in which his characters struggled with the question of civil rights... for androids. That question attracted Philip K. Dick. His story, *Do Androids Dream Electric Dreams?* later encouraged Hollywood to make *Blade Runner.* In *Ring Around the* Sun (1951) Simak concluded that there were better places in the universe for man to live (parallel worlds - an oft-used plot device), were he to keep spoiling the earth with his greed and stupidity.

In the last hours of innocence that was the early 1960s, Simak once again took pen in hand to craft *Time is the Simplest Thing*. In that one, the next step in evolution involved a mastery of parapsychology. In *Way Station* (1964), an award-winning masterpiece, he gave us a lonely, civilized man, his work in behalf of a cosmic brotherhood, and the struggles that confronted him when he had to make a choice: be an outlander, or stay a native of Earth. The following year he reprised the idea with *All Flesh is Grass*. Somewhat more lighthearted, it presented the reader with the author's long-standing philosophy: we are not the only ones in the cosmos who are "human"... and maybe *others* are more human than we.

The mid-Sixties saw the shattering of that innocence, with political assassinations, racial unrest, and the beginning of an unpopular war... plus Cold War jitters, with the USSR and mainland China in everyone's thoughts. One change had to do with social behavior: an energetic and vocal minority created a "Counterculture." It was big into drugs, loud music, protests, and the questioning of authority. Several hard-edged writers emerged (like Robert Heinlein and Harlan Ellison), whose mind-numbing commentaries seemed throwbacks to Orwell and Huxley.

Little-known Frank Herbert was part of this wave, and **Dune**, which was published in 1965, told of a galactic struggle, with drugs (spice), the paranormal, and Zen-like exchanges re-shaping the cosmos. Its primarily youthful readers made it a cult classic. It may even have prodded Simak to write **A Choice of Gods** (1972), with humanistic robots once again helping people make the right decisions about the future. This time, all Mankind (save for a few whites and some American Indians) vanishes, allowing those still here to forge a better world... without machines. The idea, though not original (in 1951 Philip Wylie had posed a similar quandary in **The Disappearance**), granted the inheritors of the earth near immortality. The book today is considered one of Simak's best.

The truth seekers continued their inquiries into the 1970s and beyond. A newcomer, Michael Crichton, combined his concerns about the nuclear issue with his skepticism of scientists in general. He first did that with *The Andromeda Strain*, and followed that with *Westworld* and *Futureworld*. He wondered what would happen if we lost control of our machines. In the 1980s and 1990s he reiterated that skepticism, first with *Sphere* (about finding a UFO at the bottom of the ocean) and *Jurassic Park*, in which creations in yet another theme park got to do things *their* way.

There have been concerns about population: too many of us; too few opportunities for everyone; too few possible solutions (most of them unpleasant). In that arena, Simak gave us *Our Children's Children*, where our descendants emerge in our own time, because in the future they are being exterminated by aliens. Their stay is a short one, but all the questions are raised: what to *do* with so many people? In *Mastodonia* (1978) he used that theme again. This time, a friendly alien introduces a way to travel in time, and the protagonist is compelled to use that knowledge to send "our unwanted masses" deep into earth's pre-historic past, so they could make a new start.

In the last half century the strains and stresses wrought by what Alvin Toffler called "Future Shock" have even blurred the difference between science fiction and fantasy. Before, fantasies were largely simplistic morality tales, like *Alice in Wonderland* and *The Wizard of Oz*. Newer generations turned fantasy into large-scale chronicles of modern civilization, with vastly complex genealogies that in many cases resemble histories.

The architect of this was J.R.R. Tolkien, an English professor of medieval languages. During the dark days of the 1930s and 1940s he devised a classic struggle of good vs. evil. By the 1960s, *The Hobbit* (and more importantly, *The Lord of the Rings*) had become immensely popular. Readers could see in those stories the Cold War and the Counterculture: all the realities of *their* time.

A plethora of fantasies followed, most notable of which is Stephen Donaldson's majestic six-volume opus, *The Chronicles of Thomas Covenant, Unbeliever.* It followed a most unlikely character - a writer who had become a leper - into a parallel world that he refused to accept, even though it magically gave him the appearance of health. No less than Clifford Simak called it the best fantasy since *Lord of the Rings*.

Terry Brooks also took the fantasy route, first with *The Sword of Shannara* (and many sequels), and a parallel world of magic that became the *Landover* series. Other writers - like D. B. Kier - were similarly moved. *Jody* follows the travails of an unappreciated youngster from nineteenth century Ohio into a parallel world in which, for the first time, he is compelled to make choices about life. Another of Kier's works, *Ravenscroft*, is an epic fantasy that takes an impressionable young man in search of knowledge - with consequences far beyond his wildest imagining. A sequel, *The Door to the Shadows*, depicts the impact of those heroics twenty-five years later. Finally, J. K. Rowling gives us magic, escape from reality, and kids as heroes in a number of books about another unappreciated youngster named **Harry Potter**.

These are just some of the more important writers in the speculative fiction genre who have emerged since World War II. In most ways, they have replaced the traditional writer as the well-spring of information, wisdom, and entertainment. They sell more books, and influence more people, than all the *literati* of the nineteenth century and the "Lost Generation" combined. Nothing on the horizon gives any indication that that trend will soon change.

Western Civilization and the Movies: An Interpretation

Like the essay on American history, this one has been in classrooms since the late 1970s.

Pre-History

The least explored area in western civilization is the one that deals with its roots. The prehistoric past has been explained mostly via wildly implausible or impossible films that, as a rule, were created for juvenile, undemanding audiences. *One Million B.C.* was a 1967 film with Raquel Welch. It was little more than cheesecake. "Beatles" drummer Ringo Starr put together *Caveman* in 1984. In that one, he and his fellow Neanderthalers violated anthropological maxims with monotonous regularity. For more sophisticated audiences, one can watch 1993's *Jurassic Park*, a Steven Spielberg film that, even though it savaged Michael Crichton's brilliant novel and made it politically correct, was an electrifying attempt to bring dinosaurs into the world of the here and now. Not so enjoyable was his 1997 trashing of the sequel, *The Lost World*. A third film, which was released in 2000, ran into no such problems: there was no third book to abuse.

For purists, a Canadian film company broke new ground in 1982 with *Quest for Fire*, the closest thing to a true window on the prehistoric past we are likely to get. It had no dialogue in the conventional sense. Instead, *Quest* was a visual experience that asked the viewer to believe that he was witnessing that significant step forward from *homo erectus* to *homo sapiens*: the conquest of fire and the first real utilization of weapons. Not since the first few minutes of *2001: A Space Odyssey*, have audiences been treated to such a realistic scrutiny of our ancestors. Sadly, improved special effects do *not* guarantee a winner in any genre. For proof of that, watch *10,000 B.C.* (2008)... if you dare. It's dreadful.

The Ancient World

Egypt

Considering the extraordinary longevity of Egyptian civilization, it is not surprising that audiences have been inundated with many versions of the Land of the Pharaohs. That is not to say that quality has always been evident: witness Hollywood's countless attempts to breathe life into mummies, in the wake of Howard Carter's discovery of King Tut's tomb in the early 1920s. Certainly, the horror-as-history motif gave Lon Chaney, Bela Lugosi, Boris Karloff, Peter Cushing, Christopher Lee, and others a way to make a very lucrative living, but told us little about the secrets of the pyramids, the complex nature of Ramses II, or why Egypt rose and fell.

Of course, making money rarely has anything to do with enlightenment: so enjoy 1999's special effects extravaganza, *The Mummy,* and the sequel, *The Mummy Returns*. And *The Egyptian*? That was a 1954 effort that displayed the delicate charms of Jean Simmons, but did little to explain the internecine power plays that plagued much of Egypt's early history. Still, it was better than 1947's *Caesar and Cleopatra*, the first big-budget look at the Rome-Egypt axis, with Vivien Leigh in her first substantial film role since *Gone With the Wind.* Her version of "the Queen of the Nile" disappointed viewers everywhere.

The biggest letdown came in 1963, when Richard Burton and Elizabeth Taylor pooled their modest talents to make *Cleopatra*. Done at a time when people had an almost desperate longing for the past, *Cleopatra* set a record for losing money that was not surpassed until *Heaven's Gate* came along in the 1980s. The shock was colossal, for the public and the critics gave the film high marks... and then stayed home. Ultimately, *Cleopatra* suffered from too little coherent dialogue, too much mindless action, a flood of confusion, and four hours of unremitting boredom.

Incredibly, a remake in 2000 was just as bad. It's a wonder that Egyptology was not dealt a death blow.

Greece and the Aegean

As we wander through the Mediterranean, it is easy to fall into something of a "black hole." Much of the early history of that region is woefully shrouded in myth. Documentation is sparse and frequently unreliable. The result is a vast co-mingling of fact and fable. This has not deterred the motion picture establishment, especially during the 1950s and early 1960s, when the "norm" was a world filled with one dimensional heroes.

Helen of Troy (a joint Italian-American production) was a 1956 low-budget love story concerning the efforts of Agamemnon to rescue the famous *femme fatale* (Rosanna Podesta) during the Trojan War. Since historians really know very little about that conflict (even whether it took place at all), it's a safe bet that the film's historicity would be questioned. Still, it was a modest success, and inspired another Italian company to grind out the first of the *Hercules* sagas (1959) with muscle man Steve Reeves. Five sequels and many box office dollars later, Hollywood cashed in with its own yawner, *Jason and the Argonauts* (1963), which retold the story of the fabulous Golden Fleece. Equally forgettable was *Clash of the Titans.* Called "trash of the titans" by bemused critics, it was a huge embarrassment for Laurence Olivier. A computer-generated remake in 2010 fared no better, making the point that Hollywood should leave that subject to comic books.

As well, avoid Ted Turner's *Odyssey* (1997), which also was aimed at a juvenile audience. Proof that the Trojan War has not been completely forgotten is found in *Troy* (2004), with Brad Pitt bulking up to bury Homer's classic tale. Stupid, insipid, and just plain dull (at one point Peter O'Toole can be seen, probably wondering what had happened to his fine career) it demonstrates that a cast of thousands and a cost of millions cannot guarantee success.

The battle of Thermopylae was explained in *300* (2007). Politically correct and filled with massive errors of fact and distortion, it spilled over with enough blood-letting to satisfy even the most sanguine viewer. It was a comic book treatment that combined the best (and the worst) features of *Gladiator* and *Braveheart*.

To date, the only worthwhile rendering of ancient Greece can be found in *Alexander the Great* (1956). It died ingloriously at the box office. A revitalization of that story staggered into view in 2004, and thoroughly embarrassed Anthony Hopkins and Christopher Plummer. As for Socrates, Plato, Aristotle, and the others who made Greek civilization the model for our heritage? Their cinematic undraping is yet to be seen.

Rome

Interestingly, the moguls of movie America have had better luck with the Rise and Fall of the Roman Republic and Empire. Perhaps that is because much of our modern society seems more Roman than Greek; perhaps it's because the Romans were, like us, a war-like people; perhaps it's because....Whatever the reasons, Rome has sold well on all levels. (1)

Thanks in part to William Shakespeare, the pivotal ruler of the first century B.C. has been a film maker's favorite for many generations. The 1953 version of *Julius Caesar* - cashing in on that decade's backwards-hopping - presented young Marlon Brando just one year before his stellar performance in *On the Waterfront*. It also enchanted us with the deliciously nefarious James Mason. Their fine performances made it easy to forget (or ignore) the failed attempt of Charlton Heston to remake it in 1970. (2)

Unquestionably, one of Hollywood's finest attempts at historical translation came in 1961, with the release of *Spartacus*. Based on an actual slave rebellion in the first century B.C., it wove a credible story, provided ample action scenes, and sported the fine talents of Kirk Douglas, Jean Simmons, Laurence Olivier, Charles Laughton, and Peter Ustinov (who won an Oscar). The slaves were depicted as heroes, while the aristocracy and the military came across as the villains. It was a "statement film" by members of Hollywood's liberal-left community ... and almost prophetic, considering what was to come in the real world of the 1960s.

It is something of an irony that **Spartacus** made an impact because of the enormous success of **Ben-Hur**, the MGM extravaganza that appeared in movie houses two years earlier. First made as a silent film in the 1920s, **Ben-Hur** was "a tale of the Christ," set in the first century A.D. It was populated with many of Hollywood's most conservative actors and was entertaining and uplifting, replete with a moving musical score. Despite their very different approaches to the period, **Spartacus** and **Ben-Hur** deserve the honors that have been heaped upon them as film classics. (3) Hollywood remade **Spartacus** in 2009... making it even *more* politically correct than the original. It bombed.

Gratefully, Hollywood has not always taken itself seriously. See, for example, *A Funny Thing Happened on the Way to the Forum* (1966), that spoofed Rome deliciously. It was a transition film, sandwiched between the earlier costume dramas, and the grimmer, more honest essays that were to follow. It was also redemptive: the first movie for Zero Mostel and Jack Gilford since the dark days of the early 1950s, when they (together with screenwriter Dalton Trumbo) were blacklisted for holding political views that ran counter to Movie America's version of reality. It was also the last movie for Buster Keaton, whose daughter, Diane, was just starting her career.

Judeo-Christianity

Charlton Heston made a career of playing larger-than-life characters, and nowhere was this more clearly displayed than in *The Ten Commandments*, 1954's sluggish and almost interminably long adaptation of the Bible-as-history. He played Moses in a way that evoked rhapsody in all True Believers. Likewise, *Quo Vadis* (1952), *The Robe* (1954), *The Silver Chalice* (1955), and *Solomon and Sheba* (1960) played to audiences of little sophistication. (4) That trend continued well into the Sixties. In *The Bible,* a 1967 box office dullard, Michael Park's character tried to heal anyone who moved; it went nowhere. The same was true of *The King of Kings*, which made only the smallest impression before disappearing onto the late show.

The spoof-merchants eventually made their own contributions: one maverick company cashed in on the resurgence of rock music in 1973, when it presented The Lord as a high-stepper in *Jesus Christ, Superstar*. That won Him converts among the young, and eternal damnation among traditionalists. It could not have been made even ten years earlier, but with the recent ravages of misdirected wars, the deterioration of traditional mores, and corruption in high places, *J.C.* was a film whose time had come.

Ultimately, humor taken to extremes becomes parody, and in 1981

Monty Python's Handmade Films, Inc., played the entire Christian period for laughs in the wholly irreverent, *Life of Brian.* It aped a then-popular and controversial Michael Moorcock novel, *Behold the Man*.

Few really dared to delve deeply into the maybe real, maybe mythic, Christ. In 1981 a fundamentalist group bankrolled *Jesus of Nazareth*, an eight-hour torture that only the Truly Devout could love, and in 1988 there was *The Last Temptation of Christ*, based on the bombastic 1950 novel of Greek Socialist-atheist, Nikos Kazantzakis.

Temptation unleashed a maelstrom of protest from fundamentalist groups and evangelists the world over, for its less than reverential look at Christ. The outpouring of hate was, in fact, quite shocking, especially when it was revealed that most of the protesters had not even *seen* the movie! That tied in beautifully with the Weighty Eighties, and when that film appeared on video, the despoilers took another tack: harassing video shops into not acquiring it (or, at the very least, keeping it below counter, like some hard-core pornography).

In 2004 conservative actor-activist Mel Gibson bankrolled *The Passion of Christ*, which critics predicted would fail. It didn't. In an age of "culture wars," *Passion* was a huge success. Painstakingly accurate, it was graphic in its depiction of the violence visited upon Christ. It was ignored or vilified by liberals and the left (in much the same way that *Temptation* was targeted by the right), but it struck a responsive chord in those who believed that the new millennium was experiencing a move away from traditional moral values. Finally, in 2006, viewers could see how Hollywood portrayed Jesus' bloodline, in the controversial liberal vehicle, **The Da Vinci Code.** A sequel of sorts, **Angels and Demons**, continued the assault in 2009.

The Middle Ages

The Medieval period (roughly 450-1400 A.D.) presents some puzzlement. Mention that time at a party, for instance, and see how quickly a deathly quiet strangles all conversation. Suggest to someone that they actually read a *book* on that period (like Froissart's **Chronicles**, or Chaucer's **Canterbury Tales**), and you'll probably clear the room. But say the words to movie moguls, and broad smiles will appear: the Middle Ages translates into box office gold.

The problem is one of perception. To most people, the Medieval period was "the Dark Ages," a time filled with plagues, famines, holy wars, and a long procession of corrupt popes, anti-popes, heretics, and so forth. It was also one of the most romantic times in history. It was the Age of Chivalry; it was the time of Arthur.

In the Hollywoodization of that theme we've seen numerous interpretations. First and foremost has been that involving the mythic hero of Sherwood Forest: Robin Hood. A multitude of heroic-looking actors have made their fortunes playing that legendary rogue: from Errol Flynn to Walt Disney's Richard Todd, to Kevin Costner (whose *Prince of Thieves* [1992] was called "Prince of Dweebs"), to Russell Crowe. There has even been a Robin Hood-as-old-man version (1976's *Robin and Marian*, with Sean Connery and Audrey Hepburn); and a first-rate 1980s British television series (with Michael Praed, and Sean Connery's son, Jason). (5)

Likewise, there have been many interpretations of Arthur. Bing Crosby gave us a comedic version of *A Connecticut Yankee in King Arthur's Court*, a 1949 revision of "reality" that charmed audiences, but would have infuriated its creator. Seventy years before, Mark Twain wrote the story as a pungent satire on western society. In the book, an uneducated man of his time goes back to Camelot and severely disrupts the moral and socioeconomic fabric by introducing nineteenth century technology. (6) In the film version, the traveler (Crosby) merely used that technology to insure that "Good" would triumph over "Evil."

Fifteen years later Walt Disney performed similar surgery on T. H. White's *The Once and Future King.* The result was the animated feature, *The Sword and the Stone*, which retold only the first part of the beloved classic, and not the somber, melancholy second part, which dealt with Arthur as a lonely old man.

The Arthur legend has even been put to music: in 1967 Vanessa Redgrave teamed up with Richard Harris (a veteran of British historical epics) to make *Camelot*. At least their credible performances spared us the ordeal of the original Broadway play (and Robert Goulet's ear-shattering singing).

To date, the most exotic (and erotic) rendering of Arthur is **Excalibur** (1981). It faithfully followed Mallory's classic novel, **Le Morte d' Arthur**, and compensated for two popular (but historically inconsequential) love ballads: **Ivanhoe** (1952) and **Prince Valiant** (1954). The former over-utilized the small talents of Elizabeth Taylor, while the latter wasted the skills of James Mason. A 1997 Hallmark made-for-television treatment, **Merlin**, told the story from the wizard's point of view (Sam Neill). A charming, family-oriented movie, it was helped by state-of-the-art special effects. Finally, for an entertaining antidote, watch **Monty Python and the Holy Grail**, a 1975 romp to irreverence that slaughtered all sacred cows.

Still, not all English history in the Middle Ages has been enveloped in myth. See **Becket** (1964), a brilliant and engaging account of the grim religio-political struggle between Thomas à Becket and his king, Henry II, in the century after William the Conqueror. It approximated history in a way that is rare for Hollywood. It was an important step forward in the career of Peter O'Toole (fresh from his success in 1962's **Lawrence of Arabia**). It also helped co-star Richard Burton salvage some of the dignity he lost the year before in his association with **Cleopatra**.

As a rule, sequels of highly-successful films are disasters, but a happy exception to that was **The Lion in Winter** (1968). In that one, O'Toole carried the saga of Henry II forward into the monarch's old age. He was assisted by Katharine Hepburn, as his exiled queen, Eleanor of Acquitane, who left her cloister to spend one last Christmas with her husband. The result was an enormously powerful film, which, like Becket, said much about the times in which it was made. Becket was shot in a quieter, less complex time. Five years later there had been a tremendous, world-wide mood change: Vietnam had become an embarrassment, the USSR had invaded Czechoslovakia, an Arab Israeli conflict was producing increased pessimism in the Middle East, and the world was reeling from numerous political assassinations.

The Lion in Winter was grimmer and much more somber than the first film, but it may have been a better teach: it was a realistic look at a failed king, and was seen - and understood - by a generation that was getting used to failure in high places.

Of course, Hollywood could not leave a classic alone. Witness the remake in 2003: just one of that generation's efforts at replication that made no sense.

Contrast that with **El Cid**, a 1962 Technicolor spectacular that told the story of Spain's struggle with Islam. As a true-to-life rendering, it failed every test (especially in its treatment of Christians as heroes and Muslims as villains). It was a predictable love story, pitching sultry Sophia Loren against Charlton Heston. In the end, it excited no one.

Similarly, our fascination with the Vikings compels us to distort history in the name of profit... or ignore it altogether. Historically, Scandinavia is a dreary and violent place, with Thor and Odin giving Christianity a run for its money. Hollywood has found that to be a good vehicle for adventure yarns. Toward that end, we have been inundated with a lot of Norse "westerns," most notably *The Vikings*, a 1958 release with Kirk Douglas, and *The Long Ships*, a 1964 fantasy with Richard Widmark flexing his muscles while telling the story of the conflict between Christian and Muslim cultures. It also permitted Sidney Poitier to disarm film audiences with a whisper. Much more incisive was *The Thirteenth Warrior*, a 1999 Michael Crichton book-into-movie with Antonio Balderas as a Muslim diplomat turned reluctantly into a warrior, assisting Vikings against evil.

Then there is that "other" Middle Ages: an often indefinable stretch of time when hordes of conquerors spilled out of China and Russia, all searching for treasure and territory in the West. This has been easy fare for Hollywood and the prepubescent audiences that it has attracted.

Typical of films of this type (which seem to dominate the late show) are *Attila*, an inept "study" of the leader of the Huns (with Anthony Quinn stumbling through his lines); *Barabbas*, a 1963 mind-numbing bomb (again, with Quinn); *The Mongols*, also 1963, this time with Jack Palance and sexpot Anita Ekberg laying waste to the Orient; and *Ghengis Khan*, a 1965 disaster that asked patrons to accept Stephen Boyd as a blue-eyed Oriental. James Mason managed to misplace his talents in this atrocity. Nowhere in the recounting of his long and illustrious career is this listed as a memorable film. (7)

Perhaps the best of these "barbarian epics" sprang from the pen of Robert Howard. Nearly eighty years ago he wrote about a warrior from the East. His character became so popular that the books were churned out, one after another. He then sought the assistance of L. Sprague de Camp, whose first training had been in history. Hollywood brought their collective efforts to the screen in 1981 with **Conan the Barbarian**. It was a "safe" vehicle for audiences of the 1980s, for the worldwide mood had become more conservative. Backwards-looking, nostalgia-oriented souls were ready for a hyper-macho hero (with assistance from a young Oliver Stone) who defined Good and Evil in very simplistic terms. To no one's surprise, **Conan** was a hit. What *did* surprise most people was the fact that it was such a *good* film.

Alas, the predictable sequel - **Conan the Destroyer** (1984) - was a disaster: it even won an award for "Worst Picture of the Year." Essentially, it suffered the fate of many sequels (in a decade that seemed to produce nothing but sequels of hit films). It lacked much of the original cast, including James Earl Jones (of **Star Wars** fame), Max von Sydow, and the original director. The finished product was therefore aimed at a much less sophisticated audience. Its muscular and charismatic star, Arnold Schwarzenegger, learned from this, and made subsequent action films with an eye to quality control.

Save for the treatment of the English, the overwhelming preponderance of films that have tried to "explain" the Middle Ages have been top-heavy with violence and very sparing on content and character development. To date, no noteworthy films have appeared in English about the evolution of the Papacy. Nor is there anything on the Black Death of the fourteenth century. As well, there is nothing meaningful about medieval life in France, Germany, or Holland.

Early Modern Europe

As we turn the corner into the Renaissance, we see the hand of William Shakespeare crafting the plays of the Elizabethan Age that chronicled the rebirth of the classical tradition and the first steps toward modernity.

Many films have captured the efforts of "the Bard," beginning with *Hamlet*, that shadowy psychodrama about the Prince of Denmark. Four excellent screen versions exist: one with Sir Laurence Olivier (1949); the highly-acclaimed 1966 Soviet production; Nicol Williamson's 1970 effort; and (surprisingly) 1990's entry, with Mel Gibson. They depict the torment of the High Middle Ages, with a longing for better, happier days.

Othello carried that hope forward and boasts two notable screen adaptations: a 1956 *tour de force,* with Orson Welles, and one with Olivier, ten years later. Tragicomedy, coupled with ill-starred romance, is treated in two regrettably mediocre treatments of ***Romeo and Juliet.***

The first one embarrassed Laurence Harvey (1955); the second tortured audiences by making them watch Olivia Hussey (1969).

As a chrono-biographer, Shakespeare has been luckier: see **Henry V**, a dire commentary of the life of the English king of the 1400s, done admirably by Olivier, and remade in 1989 with Paul Scofield and Kenneth Branagh. Olivier also deserves *kudos* for bringing to life a later monarch, **Richard III**, in 1956.

The task of interpreting the most controversial of English kings, however, has been left to others, and the best look at Henry VIII and his Age was achieved in **A Man for All Seasons** (1966). Despite an overly-reverential tone, it quite rightly has been hailed as one of Hollywood's finest historical renderings.

It was a look at Henry through the eyes of Sir Thomas More, scholar-cleric who popularized the notion of utopia. **Seasons** was the high-water mark of a decade whose fascination with historical drama has not since been equaled or surpassed. Robert Shaw was a good choice for Henry, Leo McKern rang true as the mischievous Cromwell, and Paul Scofield gave the performance of a lifetime as More. Truly, it was a feast for the mind and the soul. (8)

Unfortunately, **Anne of the Thousand Days** (1970) was not successful. Timing may have been the culprit: 1970 was a year of intensified warfare and serious social and economic distress (as exemplified by the Kent State shootings in May and the nationwide student riots that followed).

So Movie America hungered for simpler heroes (like **Patton**). There are no heroes in **Anne;** only victims. (9)

Interest in that Age became strongly evident in the late 1990s. **Ever After**, for instance, pretended to be the "true" story of Cinderella. Yes, there was a Prince Henry, who became king and married his Lady...but not the way Hollywood told it. Why did the filmmakers put Leonardo da Vinci in the script? Granted, he had the best lines - but considering the fact that he died in 1519 and Henry became king in 1547, played fast and loose with historical accuracy.

Two other Nineties films also took liberties. A comedy, **Shakespeare in Love**, had but a smidgen of history, yet was named Best Picture of the year (1998). That same year **Elizabeth** was released, a feminist film that gave the Virgin Queen more control and more power than she really had. It even jettisoned her Prime Minister years before his time, and changed the persona and the fortunes of her lover.

Regardless, our attempts to understand England Henry go on, often in a less morbid vein. Mark Twain's classic, **The Prince and the Pauper**, has had three major interpretations since the Sixties, including an early 70s romp with Oliver Reed and George C. Scott. They're all half looks: many of Twain's social criticisms are absent, replaced instead with whimsy.

The "cradle of British civilization" has also drawn Hollywood's interest. Witness **Mary, Queen of Scots** (1972). That one starred versatile Vanessa Redgrave. It more than adequately made up for **Rob Roy**, a 1954 Disney mangling of the story of rebellious Scots. The 1995 Liam Neeson remake was more palatable, as was **Braveheart**, an over-the-top "freedom flick" by Mel Gibson, portraying fourteenth century patriot, William Wallace, in a much better light than history records, and Patrick McGoohan as King Edward I ("Longshanks"), in a much worse light than he deserved.

A century before Henry, France had Joan of Arc, the tragic heroine of the Hundred Years War. Broadway has gotten a lot of mileage out of her heroism, but film treatments have been few (Ingrid Bergman playing her too romantically in 1949, and a forgettable cast playing her far too politically correct in 1998). Likewise, Martin Luther (whom Thomas More branded a heretic) has been interpreted only twice (1953 and 1974). Oliver Cromwell, who helped transform England into a constitutional monarchy by trying to destroy it, has been explained only once (1971).

As for France, movie audiences have preferred the swordplay and chase scenes that involved D'Artagnon and company, over the much more important "Sun King," Louis XIV. Hollywood has produced many treatments of Alexandre Dumas' **The Three Musketeers**, the most entertaining of which was in 1974. That one brought together Michael York, Oliver Reed, Frank Findlay, Richard Chamberlain, and Charlton Heston, and so delighted fans that a series of sequels was necessary. (10)

As for the seminal figure of the period? The best treatment has come, oddly enough, via television. In 1972 an Italian company produced a four and a half hour mini-series on **Leonardo da Vinci**, that blended narrative and forceful dramatization. Michelangelo was examined (poorly) in *The Agony and the Ecstasy* (1965, with Charlton Heston), and both Michelangelo and Leonardo were highlighted in a horrid 1990 American television mini-series, *Season of Giants*. As for the Dutch humanist Erasmus? His turn is yet to come.

Finally, the Russians awoke from their long slumber and have evoked an interest bordering on awe. Soviet film maker Sergei Eisenstein captured the barbaric but heroic Slavic spirit of Russia in *Alexander Nevsky* (1938). He also did the controversial *Ivan the Terrible* (1945 and 1958). (11) Another, more sympathetic, Soviet treatment appeared in 1960. In 1986 an American mini-series told the story of the first "westernizer." *Peter the Great* was aired just as *glasnost* was beginning, and despite dozens of historical inaccuracies (and having Maximillian Schell play the 6 feet, 8 inch tall Peter), it was better than nothing. (12)

The Eighteenth Century

Except for a touching 1984 production of Wolfgang Mozart (*Amadeus*, that featured F. Murray Abraham as Mozart's tormentor and rival, Salieri), the eighteenth century belongs to England and France. In the case of Britannia, the contemporary novels of Henry Fielding lend themselves to an understanding of that bustling and rebellious time.

Tom Jones, the colorful spectacular that was based on Fielding's 1749 novel, was a bawdy *exposé* of England at its most licentious. (13) It was well-received in 1963, as one of several films that poked harmless fun at the English. Another was *The Amorous Adventures of Moll Flanders*, a good vehicle for Albert Finney, a decade before he played Hercule Poirot in *Murder on the Orient Express*.

The Fielding novel, *Joseph Andrews*, had to wait until 1978 - a time when the more "respectable" side of the middle class was being assailed by almost every kind of satire and commentary. It was Menckenish, for it railed unrelentingly against the affectations of vanity and hypocrisy that came to typify the "me" generation.

Also of note is Daniel Defoe's 1719 classic, *Robinson Crusoe,* a look at the machinations of a stranded castaway on a desert island who is selfish and imperialistic. It's also a commentary about racial subservience: Friday, the rescued cannibal, is treated not as a friend, but a slave.

The first cinematic attempt (1953) was watered down, and starred Dan O'Herlihy (1953). One can hardly imagine sophisticated viewers of later decades flocking to see it. In 2000 Tom Hanks told the story in a politically correct way (*Castaway*). (14)

French happenings in that volatile century have been adequately expressed. The satirical philosophies of Voltaire were brought to life by Jean-Pierre Cassel, in the French production of *Candide* (1963). But it was a film about an almost forgotten prelude to the French Revolution, that has produced the largest response: *Barry Lyndon*.

Made in 1975 - at a time when war as an instrument of national policy was in decline - *Barry Lyndon* was a loose interpretation of William Makepeace Thackeray's 1844 best-seller about a freebooter's travails in the Seven Years Wars (1756-63). A number of critics dismissed it as "a rather overblown historical pageant," but, despite its slow pace and extreme length, the theme of the protagonist (Ryan O'Neal) as a victim of alienation was clearly stated. A large segment of the public apparently was unimpressed: *Barry Lyndon* did poorly at the box office. Perhaps it was just bad timing that sealed its doom: the Vietnam War ended the year of its release. Americans were tired of between-the-lines analogies about war.

Surprisingly, there have been no major films in English on the French Revolution. Perhaps the staggering complexities of that major historical turning point have scared off potential filmmakers. As it is, the only notable investigations of that event include *Marat/Sade*, a stunning adaptation (with Glenda Jackson) of the 1960s Broadway play, that presented a re-enactment by the inmates of an insane asylum of the assassination of Jean-Paul Marat. In *De Sade* (1969) Keir Dullea turned in a fine performance just a year after *2001: A Space Odyssey*. *Danton* was a critical (but not a commercial) hit. A lengthy, provocative, and subdued film (in French), it appeared in the early 1980s and centered on the opposing activities of Georges Danton and Maximilien Robespierre. Timing dictated that there was more sympathy for the popular Danton, as opposed to the more radical Robespierre. That ignited heated dialogue in France and colored much of their bicentennial celebration of the French Revolution. Finally - and strictly for laughs - was 1970's *Start the Revolution Without Me*, with spoof-master Gene Wilder, just before making the enormously successful *Blazing Saddles* and *Young Frankenstein* for Mel Brooks.

For a long time historians and the viewing public fared no better with the Age of Napoleon (1795-1815). King Vidor's overlong and poorly crafted re-telling of Tolstoy's *War and Peace* (1956) gave audiences only brief glimpses of *L'enfant terrible*, and the remake did no better. Rod Steiger played the Imperator perhaps too casually in *Waterloo* (1971), and Ian Holm's treatment (*Time Bandits*) was just for laughs.

As the third millennium began, there was a glimmer of hope. An *A&E* mini-series, *Horatio Hornblower* captured the drama of Britain's endeavors to thwart Napoleon on the high seas. It told the tale, in larger compass, than Gregory Peck did forty years earlier. It may have inspired Hollywood to make *Master and Commander* (2003), a big-budget sea saga that featured Russell Crowe (in his first film since *Gladiator*). Not as thorough as *Hornblower*, it nonetheless excited audiences.

Mostly noted because it was the first full-length Technicolor film, *Becky Sharpe* (1935) - based on Thackeray's *Vanity Fair* - projected a look at society that "obscured the potential for systematic social criticism," in one writer's view, in favor of the conception of the world as "fundamentally individualistic." For Depression-weary people, that was as much of Thackeray as they were willing to tolerate. In any case, the film was mildly prophetic: at one point a camera shows the specter of Napoleon falling over the land... a not-so-subtle hint that another specter was falling over the land in 1935: that of Adolf Hitler.

Then there was Jane Austen's 1813 masterpiece, **Pride and Prejudice**, a pungent commentary on the British gentry class. The film version (1940) deliberately obfuscated much of Austen's criticism, for the war in Europe made it necessary not to alienate any potential ally. The film was a small success (as was a made-for-TV miniseries in 1995). There doubtless will be others in the years to come. (15)

The Nineteenth Century

Most treatments of the nineteenth century have shown the inside (and the underside) of European society. Just as we have thanked Shakespeare for properly assaying the mood of western civilization in the sixteenth century, so, too, are we indebted to Charles Dickens for his insights into the nineteenth.

David Copperfield is one example. That was Dickens' favorite book, and *cine* historians agree that the 1935 interpretation (starring Freddie

Bartholomew and W. C. Fields) is the most faithful adaptation. (16) It was an important film, largely because it encouraged Depression-battered audiences to identify with positive, future-oriented characters. **Great Expectations**, Dickens' 1860 masterpiece, was a 1946 directorial *coup* for David Lean, starting a career of epics that would take him to **Lawrence of Arabia** and **Doctor Zhivago.**

Oliver!, presented in 1968, was the musical incarnation of the more somber **Oliver Twist**. Still, it closely followed the Broadway play, and was the last of the "traditional" musicals to enjoy any measure of success at the box office. A new generation of moviegoers would prefer offerings like the rock opera, **Tommy** (1975).

Of course, Dickens' magic has especially touched us in his most famous and popular story: **A Christmas Carol**. Written in 1843, the first film version was in 1938, with Reginald Owen as cantankerous old Ebeneezer Scrooge. A rival was the 1951 release, with Alistair Sim. It was neither a critical nor a box office success. The Korean War was going badly, and there were other horrors: Cold War tensions between Moscow and the United States; anguish over the West having recently "lost" China; and the fact that McCarthyism was at full boil. All of that made the Christmas season of 1951 a dreary one. So film critics advised people to stay away, for the movie was "too grim for the kiddies, too dull for adults." (17)

Time has been kinder to Dickens' yuletide classic. With its humanistic message (which once inspired a Pope and Leo Tolstoy to declare it one of the giants of world literature), it remains a favorite at Christmas.

Fascination with the 1800s is not limited to the works of Dickens. In 1939, for example, William Wyler brought Emily Brontë's 1847 novel, **Wuthering Heights**, to the silver screen. This "dark and stormy night" romance drama (which drew upon the talents of Laurence Olivier and David Niven) was followed by sister Charlotte's **Jane Eyre**, in 1944. It was a watered-down look at Brontë's time. One would have to stretch credulity quite a bit to picture young Elizabeth Taylor advocating Brontë's call for feminism!

The dark side of the nineteenth century has been shown equally well in horrific fantasy. One book, written in the "wet, ungenial summer" of 1816 by Mary Shelley was the result of several factors: she had lost a baby the year before, had endured the suicide of a half sister, and was consoling her husband, upon the suicide of his first wife. The daughter of feminist Mary Wollstonecraft and radical philosopher William Godwin thus was in the appropriate state of mind to write **Frankenstein**. For the next thirty years it was the most popular novel in the English-speaking world. (18)

Hollywood has made the book and its principal characters well-known in any language. The trek began in 1931, when Boris Karloff played "the monster." For the most part, that kind of presentation has appealed to many generations: a tale of immutable horror, with Good and Evil served up in easy to understand stereotypes. Ideologues and religious fanatics alike have identified with it: for the Left, **Frankenstein** represents the onus of enslavement; for fundamentalists, it reads as punishment for anyone who dares to play God (and especially after 1847, when Charles Darwin's controversial theories on evolution were made public). To most audiences - whether it is 1931, when the Depression was uppermost in everyone's mind, or 1975 (**Young Frankenstein**), when the world was reeling under the weight of the war in Vietnam, the oil crisis, and the exacerbation of Cold War tensions - Mary Shelley's story has meant escape from reality.

A year after **Frankenstein's** cinematic debut, Hollywood added **Dr. Jekyll and Mr. Hyde** to its flotilla of fright features. The 1932 release presented Frederic March in his most famous role. It took liberties with Robert Louis Stevenson's 1886 novel, but was very popular. The social commentary that was so pronounced (as it was in Shelley's opus) was omitted, to make it easier for people of the Thirties to relax for a couple of hours.

Bram Stoker's 1897 thriller, **Dracula**, has also been a gold mine. Starting with a silent treatment, **Nosferatu**, in 1920, it has been done too many times to count (there's even been a spoof: **Old Dracula**, with David Niven, in 1975). Recent incarnations include one with Julie Christie; Klaus Kinski (**Nosferatu, the Vampyre**), both 1979; and Gary Oldman, in Francis Ford Coppola's compelling essay, in 1992. It followed the novel more closely than any of the others. (19)

The latter part of the 1800s was filled with "Russian realism." ***Anna Karenina*** was made into a motion picture in 1949, and told the story of life in Old Russia. So, too, did ***The Brothers Karamazov*** (1958), the Dostoevsky novel that served as a springboard for Yul Brynner. Perhaps most moving of all has been ***Fiddler on the Roof***, the 1972 adaptation of the long-running Broadway play. It introduced the world to Topol as Tevya, who detailed the plight of the Jews in western Russia just before the turn of the century. Haunting, informative, and interwoven with beautiful music, ***Fiddler*** was a foreboding that many traditions were about to be sacrificed to a new century that would reshape the world.

Much of the nineteenth century's soul-searching involved escapism. Stevenson showed this with ***Treasure Island***. Of all the versions, only Walt Disney's (1950) captured its magic by withholding the novel's somber ending. It also gave us Robert Newton, as the ultimate Long John Silver.

Stevenson was a progressive, whose concern for social reform was genuine. The same was true of another writer from that time, who was a historian, philosopher, scientist, and novelist. Perhaps more than anyone else in his lifetime, H. G. Wells saw things the way they were, and set out to change them.

Consider his 1895 novel, ***The Time Machine***. As first portrayed (1960) by Hollywood, the Traveler (with Rod Taylor as Wells) so hated his own era that he went forward in time, in search of a utopia that was without prejudice or war. Instead, a visit to the twentieth century was bitterly disappointing: there was only more greed and violence. So he traveled far into the future, only to be let down again. There he encountered an effete group (the Eloi), who were little more than vegetables. They existed to satisfy subterranean cannibals called Morlocks.

Here we go to the heart of Wells' "message." In the book, the Eloi were referred to as "communists" (Wells himself was a Fabian Socialist): intelligent, refined creatures, who had succumbed after a centuries-old catastrophe to a less urbane branch of humanity - the descendants of the industrial, capitalistic classes. Wells' book, then, was a condemnation of Social Darwinism, with its point that a victory of the strongest did not necessarily mean the best. One witnesses devolution on a grand scale, with its characters representing easily identifiable abstractions of the oppressor and the oppressed.

It is interesting to note that the Traveler believed that the future could be saved by the careful cultivation of technology. In the 1960 film version - made at a time when traditional western values were being called into question - the Traveler returns to his own time briefly, and arms himself with three books to help the Eloi. "Which three books do you suppose he took?" asks his friend, David (played by Alan Young). Which three books, indeed.... (20)

Ever since, time-tripping has been a favorite plot device of writers, and has meant box office magic for the motion picture industry. In 1979's

Time After Time, Malcolm McDowell (as Wells) traveled to modern-day San Francisco to ferret out Jack the Ripper (played by David Warner). He also found his "true love" (Mary Steenburgen, whom McDowell actually married). This was a clever (and profitable) use of the time machine concept. So, too, was *Time Bandits* (1982), a hilarious romp from Monty Python's irreverent troupe, that had a little boy and a band of mischievous dwarfs racing through the centuries in their attempt to find The Most Wonderful Thing (and to escape the clutches of The Supreme Being, played deliciously by Sir Ralph Richardson, in his last role). David Warner got into that one, too, as The Evil One.

In every major culture one will find satire, whose true intent might not be recognized until years after it appears. In England, during the eighteenth century, that was true of Jonathan Swift's *Gulliver's Travels*. A hundred years later one finds it in Lewis Carroll's *Through the Looking Glass*.

The adventures of Alice sprang from the mind of a shy and emotionally backwards mathematics professor, and represented both an escape from his personal problems, and the pulpit for his indictment of England. Essentially, Carroll attacked the excesses and the prejudices of his time. He was very caustic toward Queen Victoria (the Queen of Hearts), so it is ironic that the most-beloved motion picture presentation of his stories came from Walt Disney. *Alice in Wonderland* (1952) is a family-oriented fantasy with hidden meanings buried beneath the antics of the Mad

Hatter, the March Hare, and company. (21)

Hans Christian Andersen also debuted in 1952. It was a stilted and clumsy family feature that had Danny Kaye singing and dancing his way through "wonderful, wonderful Copenhagen." Nearly two decades later, Edvard Grieg's musical career was made the subject of *Song of Norway.*

Celebrations of "things French" have been standard Hollywood fare for a long time. This may best be exemplified by *Gigi*, a 1958 interpretation of Collette's feminist stories, which took movie audiences to the "Gay Parree" of the 1890s. Stellar performances by Leslie Caron, Maurice Chevalier, Louis Jourdan, and Hermione Gingold pleased millions. Despite its massive unreality, *Gigi* was fun - and *very* much a film of the "happy days" Fifties. Its success opened the door for a turn-of-the-century farce called *Can Can*. Made in 1960 with Frank Sinatra and Shirley MacLaine, it was lambasted by Soviet premier Nikita Khrushchev as "typical of decadent bourgeois society" when he visited the West.

The Age of Imperialism

There was also concern about global politics. In fact, the nineteenth century was the most active time, imperialistically-speaking, since the days when Rome ruled the world. At the heart of that was England.

On that subject, Hollywood has *really* cashed in. There was *Khartoum*

(1966), with Charlton Heston playing Charles "Chinese" Gordon, a Bible-quoting general ordered by the British government to bring order to the Sudan in the 1880s. There he clashed with the Mahdi, a Muslim prophet (an over-the-top performance by Laurence Olivier). Gordon lost his life, but the Mahdi lost his following. One can find all kinds of "messages," including one that Occidentals should stay out of the Muslim world.

That message was thinly veiled in *Zulu*, an overlong 1964 production that introduced Michael Caine. It, plus a "prequel," *Zulu Dawn* (1988), told of British stuffiness and stupidity in their clumsy attempt to control "darkest Africa." Oddly enough, the severest indictment of British imperialism in print - Josef Conrad's *Heart of Darkness* (1902) - was not made into a movie until 1979... and as a condemnation of America's presence in Vietnam (*Apocalypse Now*).

A long romantic fascination with India partly explains why England was so reluctant to give up its hold on that subcontinent. In 1954 Hollywood thrust Tyrone Power into the dilemma of choosing loyalty to the Crown, or accepting the verities of Indian life and destiny (*King of the Khyber Rifles*). India-born Rudyard Kipling fueled the fires of expansionism with his 1888 story, *The Man Who Would Be King*. John Huston brought that gem to the silver screen in 1975. (22)

On the other hand, *Passage to India*, David Lean's 1984 spectacle that tried to humanize the Brits, was a weak rebuttal to David Attenborough's magnificent *Gandhi*. That 1982 feast for the soul scrupulously followed the Mahatma's journey from South Africa in the 1890s to his death at the hands of a Hindu fanatic in 1948. Referential and graceful, *Gandhi* was one of the best bio-films ever made, rivaling *A Man for All Seasons*, and landing for Ben Kingsley (like Paul Scofield) the role of a lifetime.

China has had poorer luck. *55 Days at Peking* (1963) is one of a few attempts to shed light on western interests in the Orient. It was a ghastly retelling of the siege of foreign troops in the northern capital during the summer of 1900. History calls it the Boxer Rebellion; Hollywood turned it into a clumsy love story, with Gregory Peck and Ava Gardner.

For those who think that Hollywood has "matured" in the intervening years, stay away from *The Last Emperor* (1988). It was far too long, had a muddled story and was shackled by spiritless acting. It appears that Peter O'Toole was pressed into service (as Henry Pu-yi's mentor) to lend some stature. The ploy failed.

World War I

In the mid-1960s the motion picture industry showed a powerful longing for the early twentieth century. In particular, it focused on 1910. Why? As Barbara Tuchman noted in her Pulitzer-Prize-winning book, *The Guns of August* (1960), that year saw the death of the last of "the old school" of British kings (Edward VII). It marked the passage of Halley's comet; the fall of the Manchu Dynasty; and the death of Mark Twain. It was also the last year of peace for the *ancién régime:* in 1911 a serious crisis would threaten the major powers over Morocco. Tensions would escalate all over Europe, and three years later the major war that everyone had been dreading for fifty years would break out, precisely as Otto von Bismarck had predicted: because of "some damned thing in the Balkans."

Selected, then, as the "last year of normality," Hollywood has flooded the market with three very different and enduring films: Disney's **Mary Poppins**, which catapulted Julie Andrews to stardom; George Bernard Shaw's **My Fair Lady**, with Audrey Hepburn instead of Julie Andrews; and **Those Magnificent Men in their Flying Machines**, a hilarious romp whose real stars were the vintage aircraft. All three were light and airy; all were about England; all did very well at the box office. (23).

The reality, of course, was impossible to ignore: war *was* coming. One gets an inkling of that in **Titanic**, the dramatization of a world that was shattered when the doomed ship was ripped apart by an iceberg in the North Atlantic in April 1912. Three cine interpretations of that tragedy exist: 1953, with Clifton Webb; 1958, as **A Night to Remember**, based loosely on historian Walter Lord's book; and James Cameron's 200 million dollar blockbuster in 1997 (the poorest of the three, yet the one which inexplicably won the award for Best Picture). When war came, in 1914, there would be other doomed ships, but they would be gutted by marauding submarines, not icebergs.

The first World War marked the twilight of European imperialism, and Hollywood has recounted that tale with zeal. *The African Queen* (1952) was a low-budget effort to show the evil intentions of Germans in Southeast Africa in 1914 and the pro-British sympathies of a Canadian (Humphrey Bogart) and an English spinster (Katharine Hepburn). Though at times spotty, and with a storyline that is somewhat contrived, *Queen* has had audience appeal for nearly sixty years. Historians consider it one of the finest motion pictures ever made. (24)

Certainly another war film, made in 1962, belongs in that famous picture category: *Lawrence of Arabia*. That David Lean masterpiece brought together an outstanding cast (Peter O'Toole, Omar Sharif, Claude Rains, Alec Guinness, Anthony Quinn, and Anthony Quayle), to explain T. E. Lawrence, an eccentric, classics-trained British officer, who used his skills with Arab languages and customs to unite the Arabs against the Turks in 1917-18. (25)

On the other hand, historical amnesia makes us forget the unromantic hell that was Verdun, the Somme, and Gallipoli, and instead encourages us to admire the soldiers in their ceremonial uniforms and to respect their chivalry. For that reason, we need more films like *The Blue Max* (1966). It debunked heroics by showing that the "clean" side of war (as exemplified by history's first aerial fighting) was just as dirty as the war in the trenches. War was ugly, and warped even the best-intentioned soldiers (in this case, Bruno Stachel, an up-from-the-ranks officer, played by George Peppard).

Another entry was *Zeppelin*, a 1971 mish-mosh that commanded us to regard Michael York as a British spy trying to get as much information as possible about German dirigibles. An unconvincing plot left us with the opportunity to see a lot of pretty scenery from the air.

The grimmest part of that long-ago war took place in Russia. Wracked by more cumulative disaster than the rest of the Powers combined, Russia still has not recovered from the almost unimaginable bloodshed and disruption that took place between 1914 and 1917, and in the cataclysmic Revolution and Civil War that followed.

From strictly a box office point of view, the most successful offering of that tumultuous time has been David Lean's *Doctor Zhivago* (1965). Omar Sharif, Rod Steiger, Julie Christie, and Alec Guinness impressed audiences with their acting, and Lean caught majestically the color and the pageantry of Russia. The finished product, though, drew howls of indignation from the Soviets, and even some westerners, for although Lean closely followed the text of Boris Pasternak's 1958 Nobel Prize-winning novel, there were many Cold War-related distortions. (26) An early twenty-first century remake did not help.

Sadly, real East-West relations were not much better in the 1970s, when another company made *Nicholas and Alexandra*. Based on Robert Massie's best-selling book, it was an inept look at the last tsar and his ill-fated family. Also lamentable was **Anastasia** (1957), in which Yul Brynner and Ingrid Bergman tried to keep alive the foolish story that Nicholas' eldest daughter had somehow survived the family's massacre in 1918. An animated version, made in 1998, was even more ludicrous, owing to the fact that in 1992 incontrovertible proof, via DNA samples, showed that Anastasia did not get out of Russia alive.

As for "the mad monk" of Russia: there have been cinematic treatments as far back as the 1930s (John Barrymore). Horror film actor Christopher Lee made a particularly odious movie about him in 1966, but it was left to the Soviets to provide an honest treatment. **Rasputin** (1975) was informative (with English subtitles), but was not shown in Russia until the late 1980s (on Leonid Brezhnev's orders). It has become a minor classic. And if you want a visually and psychologically stunning look at Russia (and specifically the Hermitage), see **Russian Ark** (2004). It was done in *one* take, and rivets its viewers from start to finish.

There are only two other films of the period that merit our consideration. One is the fine Russian-language version of Mikhail Sholokov's **And Quiet Flows the Don** (1960); the other is the American production of **Reds** (1981). The latter was a 187-minute history lesson that followed an American journalist's commentary on the Russian Revolution and Civil War. Somewhat loose with the facts, it nonetheless received kudos from most critics and the Soviet press. At the box office, however, it did not do well. Viewers who were raised on generations of red-baiting tended to ignore it.

The Inter-war Period

It's interesting to note that the award for best motion picture in 1981 went not to **Reds**, but **Chariots of Fire**, a superb (if hyper-reverential) bio-drama of two athletes who "ran for the gold" at the 1924 Olympic Games in Paris. Funnily enough, that is just about the *only* noteworthy movie about Europe in the 1920s. Hollywood has found little there in which to invest its energies and money. Instead, it has devoted much of its time to the more turbulent and chaotic Thirties.

Indicative of that interest is **Cabaret** (1972), a look at Berlin prior to the ascendancy of Hitler. Drawn from the **I Am a Camera** stories of Christopher Isherwood, **Cabaret's** dark, Daliesque tones show us starkly and hauntingly what was to come. Translated perfectly from Broadway, it gave us a wonderful musical score and Joel Grey's best-ever role (as the unwholesome and nefarious Emcee).

Curiously, we still have no definitive analysis of that period's major villain. **Mein Kampf**, released in 1961, was a documentary; **Hitler** (1962) burdened us with an unconvincing Richard Basehart; and 1973's **Hitler: The Last Ten Days** cast Alec Guinness rather awkwardly in the role of *Der Führer*. (27)

The Spanish Civil War has inflamed more than a modicum of contro-versy (especially in the United States), but this has rarely shown up in the movies. Certainly **Behold a Pale Horse** (1964), with Gregory Peck, has left few lasting impressions. Graham Greene's **Monsignor Quixote** (1985) told the story of a small-town priest (Alec Guinness) and a communist (Leo McKern), reminiscing about the war while driving across modern-day Spain.

Ship of Fools, on the other hand, was a poignant tale about the years just before the Second World War. Filmed in 1965 (why was that such a banner year for movies about history?), this treatment of Katherine Anne Porter's celebrated novel damned both Europe *and* America - while per-mitting a superior cast (Oskar Werner, Simone Signoret, Jose Ferrer, and Vivien Leigh) to tell the ill-starred story of the **S.S. St. Louis**. It left people with a chilling question, posed to the film's narrator (played by the dwarf actor, Michael Dunne): "what are they [the Nazis] going to do: kill us all!" The disbeliever was a Jew.

A less serious (but still haunting) variation on that theme was **The Sound of Music** (1965), the Julie Andrews-Christopher Plummer musical that is a family favorite about Salzburg "in the last golden days" before World War II. It can be compared favorably with the original version of **Goodbye, Mr. Chips**, the perfect 1939 film about historical change and the evolution of a British schoolmaster, played lovingly by Oscar winner, Robert Donat.

World War II

The Forties, of course, was the War Decade (Hot *and* Cold), and it has had a full complement of interpretations. To start with, there is ***To Be or Not to Be*** (1942), a comical farce about a Shakespearean troupe performing in occupied Poland. The film was roasted by critics as mocking, unpatriotic, insensitive ... and worse. With the passage of time, it has gained approval, thanks, in no small part, to second looks at the performances of Carole Lombard (her last movie) and Jack Benny. A Mel Brooks version, which assaulted everyone's senses in 1984, must rank as one of the worst movies of all-time.

And then there was that *other* low-budget movie of 1942: ***Casablanca***. They made it up as they went along, with no one knowing until the last day how it was going to end. Its release coincided with the Casablanca Conference, thereby cinching its saleability. (28)

The rest of the story on the War is, as it should be, grisly telling. See ***Catch-22*** (1970), which borrowed from Joseph Heller's novel. Alan Arkin, Jon Voight, and Art Garfunkel showed the horror, as well as the hypocrisy, of war. (29) ***Slaughterhouse-Five*** (1972) did the same thing. It was a commentary from Kurt Vonnegut about the alienation of the film's protagonist, Billy Pilgrim, and his escape to another planet (Tralfalmadore). Along the way there is caustic criticism of the American fire-bombing of

Dresden (which Vonnegut witnessed). These films are also seen as indirect indictments of the then-raging Vietnam War.

Though it is hard to find (except on the late show), *The Diary of Anne Frank* (1959) deserves a look, especially for those who doubt the validity of the Holocaust. As well, one should see *Judgment at Nuremberg.* That 1962 entry presented Maximillian Schell, Spencer Tracy and Burt Lancaster in a liberal interpretation of the "crime of the century."

Then there's Steven Spielberg: *Schindler's List* (1993). Made when "cultural sensitivity" was everywhere, this politically correct look at the Holocaust made quite an impact (and got Spielberg an Oscar). But not without controversy: some Blacks booed it; the historicity of the Holocaust was debated; and Spielberg ("a Jewish Walt Disney") added to the fires by complaining that he had been victimized by anti-Semitism as a teenager in the 1960s!

Finally, a 2002 film about the siege of Stalingrad needs to be mentioned. *Enemy at the Gates* relates the real-life tale of a Soviet sniper, defending his city in the dark days of 1942. Ed Harris is chilling in the role of a sniper. The film is an honest look at the horrors of war.

Since the War

Since the end of World War II western civilization has largely been the story of Russia and the United States, and can best be dealt with elsewhere. (30) Still, a few films, not exclusively about the superpowers, deserve our attention.

The first is **Zorba, the Greek**, another 1965 box office hit that saw life in the Mediterranean through the eyes of a Greek Everyman (Anthony Quinn). One should also see **Z**, a 1970 political thriller (in French), with Yves Montand and Irene Pappas recounting the story of a major crisis in France's recent history.

Finally, there are three important dystopian essays: **The Lord of the Flies** (1963), which showed us what boys stranded on an island would do to pass the time; **Fahrenheit 451** (1967), which told us, via Oskar Werner, what firemen of the future would do; and **1984**, George Orwell's depressing look at what we *all* would be doing, if we did not resolve our seemingly insurmountable differences (there have been two versions: 1960, with Michael Redgrave, and 1984, with John Hurt).

Notes

1. Even the despoilers of Rome have fared pretty well: witness **Hannibal**, based loosely on the exploits of the Carthaginian general of the second century B.C. It excited young audiences everywhere in 1960, and especially those who lionized Victor Mature, one of that generation's "macho men."

2. Sir John Gielgud appeared in both versions ... but in different roles!

3. In the 1959 remake, the original scriptwriter was liberal Gore Vidal, whose homosexuality worked its way into the dialogue of Juda (Charlton Heston) and Massala (Stephen Boyd). Heston never caught on. More interesting was 2000's *Gladiator*. Despite some glaring errors (like the non-existence of Maximus and the finale [Commodus' death]), it was a good, intelligent film, and deserved the praise given to director Ridley Scott, and actors Russell Crowe and Joaquin Phoenix. Other interpretations of Rome have not been so grand. *Caligula* was a 1980 "blue movie" (released in "R" and "X" versions) that wasted the talents of Malcolm McDowell, Peter O'Toole, and John Gielgud.

4. Paul Newman so hated his performance, that he took out a full-page newspaper ad, apologizing to the public.

5. By the mid-1980s Connery had distanced himself from his James Bond persona, and was getting serious, high quality acting jobs. One was *The Name of the Rose*, a medieval who-done-it.

6. One is reminded of Washington Irving's, *The Legend of Sleepy Hollow*, an 1820s satire on pre-Revolutionary America. Walt Disney chose to ignore the polemics and made his 1950 short subject purely for family entertainment. Ichabod Crane, who was Irving's protagonist, was much like Twain's. Both film roles were done by Bing Crosby.

7. It was an ill-starred film from the beginning. One major scene, with thousands of Mongols swarming down on their adversary, had to be re-shot because the cameras captured on film the trail of a passing jet!

8. Hollywood remade the film in 1990, with Charlton Heston in the lead role. It bombed.

9. *Lady Jane*, from the late 1980s, was yet another casualty.

10. There was a "sequel" in 1975 (*The Four Musketeers*). In fact, it was just excess footage from the 1974 release. Next was *The Fifth Musketeer*

(1979). It lacked charm and died at the box office. In 1991 cable television pitched **Return of the Musketeers**, showing much of the original cast in old age. A less polished version of the tale was released by Disney in 1993.

11. The first part of the film was released just as World War II was ending, and had Stalin's approval. The second part did not: he saw it as critical of his *régime.* It was not released to the public until five years after his death.

12. Catherine the Great (1762-96) has not fared so well. Douglas Fairbanks tried to tell her story (1934), and failed, and in 1991 Ted Turner released a bit of fluff called **Young Catherine**, with Maximillian Schell as Frederick the Great. There was no call for an encore performance.

13. In the 1980s it was learned that **Tom Jones** was made on film stock that is slowly deteriorating. Those who own a video version (made from the original print) may wind up with a copy that will outlast the original.

14. In 1961 Disney gave us its interpretation with **Swiss Family Robinson**, which followed the Pollyanna-like adventures of Dorothy McGuire and some well-scrubbed kiddies, through an island paradise that could just as easily have been located in Disneyland.

15. Greer Garson, who played the lead, almost did not get the part... for she was considered "too beautiful." Over the "dull ears of the scriptwriters" she got the part, and became a "hot" property.

16. Despite protests from literary "authorities" that **Copperfield** was really no more than a trial balloon for another book.

17. In 1970 Albert Finney presented **Scrooge**; in 1984 George C. Scott offered his interpretation ; and in 1989 Bill Murray spoofed it wildly with **Scrooged**.

18. This brings to mind Margaret Mitchell's recuperation from a broken ankle in 1926, whereupon she took her husband's advice and wrote a book about the Old South. The result was *Gone With the Wind.*

19. There really was a Dracula. He was a Rumanian nobleman named Vlad, nicknamed "the Impaler," for the way that he dispatched 10,000 Turks who had invaded his lands.

20. Hollywood liked the idea so much that it produced a remake in 1983. It was, by any standard, an abomination.

21. The Disney version was a box office dud, one of a rare few in Uncle Walt's heyday. It was considered "too frightening" for youngsters.

22. Huston had wanted to make that film for nearly thirty years. He had once considered Clark Gable and Humphrey Bogart for the leads. In the end, the roles went to Sean Connery and Michael Caine. It was worth it.

23. There was a sequel of sorts, called *Those Daring Young Men in their Jaunty Jalopies* (1969). Some of the cast of the first film participated. They advanced the calendar to the late 1920s and used cars, instead of planes.

24. Like *Casablanca*, a decade earlier, this Bogart film was a "sleeper," surprising everyone with its success. Its producer, Sam Spiegel, allowed himself credit as the thinly-disguised "Sam P. Eagle."

25. The running time of the 1963 film was 200 minutes. In 1990 a "fully restored" version was released, with an additional 20 minutes.

26. It was not shown in the Soviet Union until 1990, just before the end of communism. It was remade in 2002, and was a predictable waste of time and money.

27. On the same day that Ronald Reagan was sworn in as President,

ABC's prime-time movie was *Ten Days*. To many in the audience not in sympathy with the politics of the new chief executive, the selection seemed more prophetic than coincidental.

28. And yes: Bergman and Bogart were not the first choices: they were third, behind Tallulah Bankhead and George Raft, and Ann Sheridan and ... Ronald Reagan.

29. *Catch-22* was intended as a commentary on the Korean War.

30. See my essay, *American History and the Movies: An Interpretation.*